Return to an Address of the Honourable the
House of Commons dated 15th February 2000 for the

Report of the Tribunal of Inquiry into the abuse of children in care in the former county council areas of Gwynedd and Clwyd since 1974

l ____ re

ll

Ordered by The House of Commons to be printed
15th February 2000

HC 201
SUMMARY (English only)

LONDON: THE STATIONERY OFFICE

£21

TRIBUNAL OF INQUIRY INTO CHILD ABUSE IN NORTH WALES

The Rt Hon Paul Murphy MP
Secretary of State for Wales
Gwydyr House
Whitehall
London
SW1A 2ER

30 September 1999

Dear Secretary of State

On 20 June 1996 it was resolved by both Houses of Parliament that it was expedient that a Tribunal be established for inquiring into the abuse of children in care in the former county council areas of Gwynedd and Clwyd since 1974.

On 30 August 1996 your predecessor, the Rt Hon William Hague MP, appointed us, by a Warrant of Appointment, to be a Tribunal for the purpose of this Inquiry and declared that the Tribunals of Inquiry (Evidence) Act 1921 should apply to the Tribunal, which was constituted as a Tribunal within the meaning of section 1 of that Act.

We have carried out the Inquiry and now have the honour to submit our report.

We acknowledge and express our gratitude to the many persons who have helped us in this very wide-ranging investigation in Appendix 1 to the report. Here, however, we wish to mention particularly Sir Ronald Hadfield QPM, DL, who was appointed by your predecessor as an assessor to the Tribunal to advise us in respect of police matters and whose assistance has been invaluable.

Sir Ronald Waterhouse

Margaret Clough

Morris le Fleming

Members of the Tribunal

Sir Ronald Waterhouse
Morris le Fleming
Margaret Clough

Assessor to the Tribunal in respect of police matters:
Sir Ronald Hadfield, QPM, DL

Clerk to the Tribunal: Fiona Walkingshaw

Terms of reference of the Tribunal of Inquiry

(a) to inquire into the abuse of children in care in the former county council areas of Gwynedd and Clwyd since 1974;

(b) to examine whether the agencies and authorities responsible for such care, through the placement of the children or through the regulation or management of the facilities, could have prevented the abuse or detected its occurrence at an earlier stage;

(c) to examine the response of the relevant authorities and agencies to allegations and complaints of abuse made either by children in care, children formerly in care or any other persons, excluding scrutiny of decisions whether to prosecute named individuals;

(d) in the light of this examination, to consider whether the relevant caring and investigative agencies discharged their functions appropriately and, in the case of the caring agencies, whether they are doing so now; and to report its findings and to make recommendations to the Secretary of State for Wales.

Outline of the Report

APPENDICES

Appendix 1:   Acknowledgements

Appendix 2:   The Tribunal and its staff

Appendix 3:   Representation

Appendix 4:   Note by the Chairman of the Tribunal on its procedures

Appendix 5:   Report of the Witness Support Team

Appendix 6:   Main statutory regulation from 1974 until the Children Act came into force on 14 October 1991

Appendix 7:   Statutes and Statutory Instruments cited in the report

Appendix 8:   List of main relevant publications

Appendix 9:   Welsh Office and other departmental Circulars cited in the report

Appendix 10:   Anatomy of a weekend

Appendix 11:   Statement of Sir Ronald Hadfield, assessor to the Tribunal in respect of police matters

GLOSSARY OF ABBREVIATIONS

Please note:

— The Appendices and the Glossary of Abbreviations are not reproduced in this Summary.

Table of Contents of the Summary of the Report

Page

Please note:

— Complainants and some others are identified in this Summary by a capital letter instead of by name. The identification by letter is consistent within individual chapters but has no application outside that chapter unless expressly stated.

— The following abbreviations have been used throughout this Summary:

ACPC	Area Child Protection Committee
CPS	Crown Prosecution Service
CQSW	Certificate of Qualification in Social Work
CRCCYP	Certificate in the Residential Care of Children and Young People
CRPC	Children's Regional Planning Committee for Wales
CSS	Certificate in Social Services
DHSS	Department of Health and Social Security
DoH	Department of Health
ESN(S)	Educationally Sub-normal (severe)
HMCI(Wales)	Her Majesty's Chief Inspector of Schools (Wales)
HMI	Her Majesty's Inspector of Schools
LEA	Local Education Authority
OHMCI(Wales)	Office of Her Majesty's Chief Inspector of Schools (Wales)
PILO	Placement Information and Liaison Officer
RCCO	Residential and Child Care Officer
RDCO	Residential and Day Care Officer
SEN	Special Educational Needs
SRCCO	Senior Residential Child Care Officer
SSD	Social Services Department
SSIW	Social Services Inspectorate for Wales
SWSO	Social Work Service Officer
SWSW	Social Work Service for Wales
WOED	Welsh Office Education Department

INTRODUCTION (Chapters 1 to 6)

The appointment of the Tribunal and its proceedings (Chapter 1)

1.01 On 20 June 1996 the setting up of this Tribunal, with the powers conferred by the Tribunals of Inquiry (Evidence) Act 1921, was approved by resolutions of both Houses of Parliament.

1.02 The Tribunal heard the evidence of 575 witnesses, of whom 264 gave oral evidence, between 3 February 1997 and 12 March 1998. In all we sat on 207 days, including 4 preliminary hearings, other days when we heard opening statements and final submissions and a two day concluding seminar held on 6 and 7 May 1998 to consider potential recommendations.

1.03 Preliminary work involved scrutiny of 9,500 unsorted children's files and some 3,500 statements to the police as well as other records of both former County Councils and about 85 children's homes. For the purposes of our hearings 12,000 documents were scanned into the Tribunal's database, including documents extracted from a large number of files submitted by the Welsh Office.

1.04 The Tribunal made the following statement for the assistance of the press and media:

> "The Tribunal wishes to indicate that it will regard the following as prima facie evidence of a contempt of court:
>
> publication of any material in a written publication (as defined in section 6(1) of the 1992 Act[1]) available to the public (whether on paper or in electronic form), or in a television or radio programme for reception in England and Wales, which is likely to identify any living person as a person by whom or against whom an allegation of physical or sexual abuse has been or is likely to be made in proceedings before the Tribunal, with the exception of those who have been convicted of criminal offences of physical or sexual abuse of children in care."

We said also that this was a general intimation but that it was open to the Tribunal to give a different ruling in relation to any specific witness.

1.05 Our main reason for issuing this notice was that we considered that there was a substantial risk that the course of justice in our proceedings would be seriously prejudiced or impeded in the event of such publication because witnesses might be deterred from testifying fully to the Tribunal.

---

[1] Sexual Offences (Amendment) Act 1992.

The general background to the Inquiry (Chapter 2)

2.01 It had been known for several years that serious sexual and physical abuse had taken place in homes managed by the former Clwyd County Council in the 1970s and 1980s. A major police investigation had been begun in 1991, resulting in 8 prosecutions and 6 convictions of former care workers, but speculation that the actual abuse had been on a greater scale had persisted in North Wales.

2.02 A focal point of disquiet in 1996 was the non-publication (on advice) of the report by John Jillings[2] on his investigation into the management of Clwyd Social Services Department from 1974 onwards, with particular reference to what had gone wrong with child care, which had been commissioned by Clwyd County Council in January 1994. There was concern also that a report in May 1996 by Adrianne Jones CBE[3] and her examination team, commissioned by the Secretary of State for Wales, had disclosed serious shortcomings in child care procedures and practice in Clwyd and Gwynedd.

2.03 There had also been persistent complaints from 1986 onwards by Alison Taylor, who had been the Officer-in-Charge of one of Gwynedd's children's homes until that year, of alleged child abuse in the homes, particularly by (Joseph) Nefyn Dodd, and about Dodd's roles in management. An investigation by the police of Taylor's early complaints had been carried out between 1986 and 1988 but no criminal proceedings had ensued and there was dissatisfaction with the outcome, fanned by a number of newspaper articles and television programmes, particularly in the latter months of 1991.

2.04 One of the persons to whom adverse reference was made in some newspaper articles and broadcasts was a former superintendent of the North Wales Police, Gordon Anglesea, who brought libel actions in respect of them against the publisher of the *Independent on Sunday*, The Observer Limited, HTV Limited and the publisher of *Private Eye*. The consolidated action reached trial in November 1994 and resulted in an award of a total of £375,000 and costs to Anglesea against the 4 defendants on 7 December 1994.

2.05 In the period under review by this Tribunal, namely, April 1974 to April 1996, no less than 15 persons[4] were convicted of relevant offences in Clwyd, of whom 12 were or had been employed in children's homes. In Gwynedd, only 2 persons, a foster parent and his son, were convicted of such offences. The most serious offenders were **Malcolm Ian Scrugham** (1993, 10 years' imprisonment), **Reginald Gareth Cooke** (known as Gary Cooke) (1980, 5 years; 1987, 7 years), **(Arthur) Graham Stephens** (1980, 3 years), **Stephen Roderick Norris** (1990, $3\frac{1}{2}$ years; 1993, 7 years), **Peter Norman Howarth** (1994, 10 years, but he died in prison on 24 April 1997) and **John Ernest Allen** (1995, 6 years).

---

[2] A former Director of Social Services for Derbyshire County Council.

[3] A former Director of Social Services for Birmingham City Council.

[4] See paras 2.07 and 2.35 of our report for the details of these convictions, except that of Scrugham, who was not part of the main investigation but whose convictions are set out in para 42.09 of the report.

2.06 Against this background there were repeated calls for a public inquiry. On 7 September 1992 the Parliamentary Secretary to the Welsh Office, Gwilym R Jones MP, announced that such an inquiry would take place when the North Wales Police had completed their enquiries but he did not specify the form that the public inquiry would take. The main part of the police investigation was completed in 1993 but important prosecutions followed in the succeeding years and are continuing.

The legislative and administrative background in 1974 (Chapter 3)

3.01 The Social Services Departments of the new Clwyd and Gwynedd County Councils were in a state of turmoil when they took over responsibility for the former 5 county areas on 1 April 1974, following upon:

(1) the recommendations of the Seebohm Committee on Local Authority and Allied Personal Social Services (1968), as implemented in the Local Authorities Social Services Act 1970;

(2) the proposals set out in the Government's White Paper, "Children in Trouble" (1968), as enacted in the Children and Young Persons Act 1969; and

(3) the reorganisation of local government and administrative areas throughout North Wales pursuant to the Local Government Act 1972.

3.02 The Seebohm Committee's proposals involved radical changes in the administration of social services, including social services for children. A new local government department, the social services department, was to be formed, taking over responsibility for a wide range of services, including children's services previously provided by children's departments under a children's officer and responsible to the Home Office. In Wales, responsibility for children's services moved from the Home Office to the Welsh Office on 1 January 1971 (responsibility for other social services in Wales had passed from the DHSS to the Welsh Office in March 1969).

3.03 Major changes proposed by "Children in Trouble" and implemented in the Children and Young Persons Act 1969 were the abolition of both approved schools and remand homes. The White Paper outlined a proposed integrated system of community homes embracing existing local authority children's homes and hostels, remand homes, reception and remand centres, approved schools and some voluntary children's homes that regularly accommodated children in care. Local authorities were to participate in joint (regional) planning committees to draw up comprehensive plans for developing the full range of residential homes.

3.04 Detailed provisions putting into effect these proposals were contained in the Act of 1969. However, responsibility for approved schools and remand homes was not transferred to the Secretary of State for Wales until 1973. In the interim period from 1 January 1971 it was the Secretary of State for Social Services who bore the responsibility of overseeing the integration of approved schools and remand homes into the system of community homes throughout England and Wales.

3.05 The Children's Regional Planning Committee for Wales was set up under section 35 of the Act of 1969; it met for the first time on 24 June 1970 and continued in existence until early in 1984. Its first Plan (the 1971 Plan) came into operation on 1 April 1973 and it was revised in 1979. But the Government announced in 1979 "its intention to remove the statutory basis for Children's Regional Planning as part of a policy of placing greater responsibility for local matters on local authorities and of increasing their freedom of action"[5]; and this was given effect to in section 4 of the Health and Social Services and Social Security Adjudications Act 1983.

3.06 Under the Local Government Act 1972 the number of Welsh Counties was reduced from 13 to 8. In North Wales Gwynedd replaced the previous county administrative areas of Anglesey, Caernarvon, Merioneth (less a former rural district) and a small part of Denbigh, whilst Clwyd replaced Flintshire, most of Denbigh and the former rural district of Merioneth.

3.07 This reorganisation, following closely upon the establishment of the new social services departments, led to much disruption of newly established working teams, working practices and administrative systems.

Residential care provision for children in Clwyd, 1974 to 1996 (Chapter 4)

4.01 On 1 April 1974 Clwyd County Council had 542 children in care of whom 451 were the subject of care orders. The number of children in residential care was 203 and 212 children were in foster care.

4.02 At that time there were 17 local authority community homes in Clwyd, of which 10 were in the Wrexham area. The largest was Bryn Estyn in Wrexham, a former approved school, with accommodation for 49 boys (shown as 61 boys in the 1979 Regional Plan) in the intermediate and senior age ranges.

4.03 We received no complaint about 6 of these community homes and only one complaint each in respect of 2 other homes, both complaints dating back to periods prior to 29 April 1974. The other 9 homes are dealt with in detail in our report.

4.04 There were 2 other community homes in Clwyd on 1 April 1974. One was a controlled home, which closed in 1978, and we have not received any complaint in respect of it. The other was an assisted community home, Tanllwyfan at Colwyn Bay, run by the Boys and Girls Welfare Society, and we give a detailed account of it.

4.05 We received complaints about 2 other non-private residential establishments in Clwyd and they are dealt with in the report. The first, Gwynfa Residential Unit, a clinic for children at Colwyn Bay, was operated by a National Health Service Trust; the unit was transferred to Cedar Court in the same town in

---

[5] Department of the Environment: Central Government Controls over Local Authorities, September 1979, Cmnd 7634, HMSO.

March 1997. The second, Ysgol Talfryn, at Brynford, near Holywell, is a local authority school for pupils with emotional and behavioural disorders, which opened in April 1978.

4.06 The Tribunal received complaints also about private children's homes or residential schools in Clwyd run by 3 organisations, which are dealt with in Part IV of the report. These organisations were the Bryn Alyn Community, Care Concern International Limited and Clwyd Hall for Child Welfare.

4.07 By 1985, half way through the period under review, the number of local authority community homes in Clwyd had been reduced to 8 of which 4 were in the Wrexham area. Bryn Estyn closed in September 1984. Tanllwyfan also had closed but Gwynfa and Ysgol Talfryn continued. Of the private establishments, only those of the Bryn Alyn Community remained open in Clwyd. Care Concern's activities in North Wales were focussed on 2 establishments in Gwynedd and Clwyd Hall School had closed in 1984.

4.08 The overall residential care provision in Clwyd was much the same 11 years later in 1996, in the limited sense that there were still 8 local authority community homes, but the number of residential places had been reduced to about 24. The identity of most of the homes had changed and none of the new homes accommodated more than 4 children. We did not receive any complaints in respect of the new homes. Complaints about Ysgol Talfryn related to periods up to 1990 but there was only one complaint about events at Gwynfa after 1985. There were no new relevant private residential establishments in Clwyd outside the Bryn Alyn Community but complaints about the latter related to periods into the 1990s.

4.09 By 1996, according to Adrianne Jones' evidence, only 4 per cent of Clwyd's looked after children were in residential care. The latest figures that we have show that the number of children being looked after on 31 March 1995 was 244.

Residential care provision for children in Gwynedd, 1974 to 1996 (Chapter 5)

5.01 The number of children in care in Gwynedd on 1 April 1974 was 290, of whom 189 were the subject of care orders. Of the children in care, 80 were in residential care and 122 in foster care.

5.02 At that time there were 6 local authority homes in Gwynedd, 2 in the former Anglesey, 3 in the former Caernarvonshire and one at Barmouth. We have received relevant complaints about only 2 of these homes, namely, 5 Queen's Park Close, Holyhead (hereafter referred to as "Queens Park"), and Tŷ'r Felin, Maesgeirchen, Bangor, which are dealt with in detail in the report. The 4 others all closed by 1979. There was a complaint in respect of one of them only and it related to events prior to 31 December 1968.

5.03 The 1971 Regional Plan referred to 2 registered voluntary homes in Gwynedd, although neither was described as controlled or assisted. One of them was Benarth at Llanfairfechan in respect of which there were no complaints. The other, Cartref Bontnewydd, is the subject of Chapter 37 of the report. It became a local authority community home eventually in 1988 but we are not aware of any complaints about it prior to then.

5.04 There were no private residential establishments in Gwynedd in April 1974 about which we have received any complaints.

5.05 By April 1985 the number of children in care in Gwynedd, 280, was approximately the same as in April 1974, but the number in residential care had declined to 23; and there were 5 local authority community homes. The 3 new homes were Y Gwyngyll at Llanfair PG, Pant yr Eithin at Harlech and Tŷ Newydd at Llandegai, near Bangor. We are aware of only one minor complaint of slapping at Pant yr Eithin made by a complainant who does not blame the person who administered it. The other 2 new homes are dealt with in Chapters 34 and 35 of the report.

5.06 Care Concern International Limited operated 2 schools in Gwynedd between October 1975 and April 1989. The first was Cartref Melys in the Sychnant Pass near Conway, a residential special school for up to 20 emotionally disturbed children aged 11 to 17 years (subsequently SEN children), which closed in or about July 1986; and we have not received any evidence from a complainant about this school. The second was Hengwrt Hall School at Rhydymain, between Dolgellau and Bala, which was also a residential special school from August 1976 until April 1989. Its history during that period, and subsequently as Aran Hall School from November 1991, is recounted in Chapter 38.

5.07 Hett owned and operated 3 private residential establishments in Gwynedd, which were the subject of close scrutiny by HMIs and the SWSW (later SSIW) between 1974 and 1991. They were Ynys Fechan Hall at Arthog, Dôl Rhyd School at Dolgellau and Hengwrt House at Llanelltyd. The complex history of these establishments is set out in Chapter 39.

5.08 We have not received any complaint in respect of the Bryn Melyn (Farm) Community, which was established at Llandderfel, near Bala, by Brendan McNutt in 1986 and which has attracted public attention from time to time. It began as a private children's home for young people aged 15 to 18 years and was later registered under the Children Act 1989 for up to 10 children. It now has a number of units, across North Wales accommodating one child at a time, which are open to children from inside and outside the United Kingdom.

5.09 By 31 July 1995 (the latest date for which we have figures), the number of children looked after in Gwynedd had fallen to 157, of whom 18 were in residential care. There were then 3 surviving local authority community homes, namely, Cartref Bontnewydd (7 places), Queens Park (5 places), and Tŷ'r Felin (9 places) but the latter closed in the autumn of 1995 and was demolished in March 1997.

The Tribunal's approach to the evidence (Chapter 6)

6.01 The nature and scope of the Tribunal's inquiry has given rise to a number of special, but not unique, evidential problems. These include the long lapse of time since most of the alleged abuse occurred, the few complaints that were made before the major police investigation began in 1991 and the very limited documentary evidence relating to specific incidents. The difficulties have been similar for complainants and alleged abusers: supporting evidence either way has been difficult to trace and patchy at best.

6.02 Having regard to these difficulties and the scale of the alleged abuse we do not consider that it would be either practicable or appropriate for us to attempt to reach firm conclusions on each specific allegation that has been made to us. We interpret the first sub-paragraph of our terms of reference as a requirement that we should hear the available evidence of the alleged abuse and reach such conclusions as we properly can as to its scale and when and where it occurred as a necessary preliminary to examining the other matters specified in the terms of reference and to formulating relevant recommendations.

6.03 The proceedings before the Tribunal have been civil proceedings in which grave allegations against individuals have been made. We have applied to those allegations, therefore, the standard of proof enunciated by Lord Nicholls of Birkenhead in his speech in *In re H (minors)* (1996) AC 563, 586 D to G, with which the majority of the House of Lords agreed.

6.04 The nature and volume of evidence from former children in care has been such as to enable us to reach firm conclusions about the pattern of behaviour of the more prominent alleged abusers and we state them in our report. In reaching those conclusions we have had fully in mind the many criticisms levelled against the complainants both generally and individually. Despite these substantial criticisms and other allied attacks upon their credibility, we have been impressed generally by the sincerity of the overwhelming majority of the complainants that we have heard. No one who has sat through their evidence and listened to their evidence impartially can have failed to have been impressed by what they have said and their stated motivation in giving evidence. What has been most striking is the similarity in the accounts of conditions in particular homes given by former children in care from widely separate areas of the country between whom there was no contact in the home or afterwards.

6.05 Responding to Counsel's submissions, we accept the gravity of a finding of sexual abuse. There are few such findings in our report except those that we make in respect of persons already convicted of sexual offences against children in care. The reasons for this are that the allegations against other specific individuals have, in general, been very few in number, have not been corroborated and are so distant in time that, in our view, no one could safely conclude that the abuse had occurred without the risk of grave injustice to the alleged perpetrator. In respect of those individuals already convicted of relevant offences, however, our approach has been that, in the absence of a successful appeal, the convictions are evidence that the offences were committed and that it has not been within our jurisdiction to question the correctness of those convictions, unless (possibly) fresh evidence were to be tendered going to the root of the convictions.

6.06 In the event no such fresh evidence has been submitted and there has been no successful appeal against any of the convictions. We have, however, heard evidence from additional witnesses not named in specific charges before the courts and witnesses in support of charges ordered to remain on the Court's file and have assessed this evidence in reaching our conclusions about the scale of abuse that occurred.

6.07 Conversely, we have not deemed it appropriate to question the correctness of verdicts of juries in respect of those persons who have been acquitted of all or some of the charges laid against them, in the absence of compelling fresh evidence against them. A similar approach has been adopted in respect of the allegations against Gordon Anglesea, having regard to the way in which the central issue in his consolidated libel action was formulated for the jury by the trial judge.

6.08 In writing our report we have decided that it is in the general public interest to preserve the anonymity of all the complainants and we are satisfied that the impact of their evidence will not be significantly diminished by that decision.

6.09 We have exercised a restrictive discretion in naming alleged abusers in the report. Assurances were given to a substantial number of persons in this broad category that they would not be named as abusers because of the comparative triviality of the allegations against them or the very limited number of minor allegations made against them over a long period. In some other cases no assurance has been given but we do not consider that the evidence has justified naming the alleged abuser.

6.10 In our judgment, however, we would be failing in our duty if we did not identify in our report:

(a) those persons who have already been the subject of relevant court proceedings;

(b) individuals against whom a significant number of complaints have been made, with our assessment of them;

(c) other persons who have figured prominently in the evidence, whether or not they have been the subject of substantial complaints;

(d) a limited number of persons who should be identified in public in order to deal with current rumours; and

(e) persons who have not been the subject of allegations of abuse but who were in positions of responsibility and whose acts and omissions are relevant to our full terms of reference, including council officials and police officers, but who have not had the benefit of any anonymity ruling by the Tribunal.

Such identification is, in our view, essential to enable us to report coherently and fully upon the evidence that we have heard and as a basis for our recommendations.

6.11 We have been unable to report at all upon some allegations because they are, or were at the time of our hearings, the subject of continuing police investigations or criminal proceedings. A summary of the latest developments in relation to these is given in paragraphs 50.19 to 50.25 of this Summary.

6.12 The findings of fact and expressions of view in the report are those of the full Tribunal.

ALLEGED ABUSE OF CHILDREN IN CARE IN LOCAL AUTHORITY HOMES IN CLWYD BETWEEN 1974 AND 1996
(Chapters 7 to 17)

In this part of the report we discuss 9 local authority community homes in Clwyd. Allegations of sexual and physical abuse at Bryn Estyn were principal causes of the Inquiry and we devote 5 chapters to this community home, including a chapter on the allegations against Gordon Anglesea. There were grave allegations also of sexual abuse at Cartrefle, which are dealt with in Chapter 15. Complaints about the other 7 community homes were at a lower level. Cherry Hill (Chapter 16) is discussed only because of inaction by the local authority in the aftermath of the disclosures at Cartrefle but the other homes all provide illustrations of abuse that was occurring and serious shortcomings in the quality of care that was provided.

Bryn Estyn, 1974 to 1984 (Chapter 7)

7.01 Bryn Estyn Hall, on the outskirts of Wrexham, is an Elizabethan style manor house that was built as a private home in 1904. It became an approved school in 1942 and then, from 1 October 1973, a community home with education until it closed in September 1984.

7.02 The first Headmaster of the approved school was James Bennett, who remained there until 1967. In his time the regime was criticised as rigid, authoritative and punitive for both staff and boys.

7.03 **Granville (Matt) Arnold** became Headmaster on 1 May 1973 (before responsibility for Bryn Estyn passed to Denbighshire County Council on 1 October 1973) and continued as Principal of the community home until July 1984. Arnold was nearly 44 years old when he was appointed and had already held senior teaching positions in approved schools for 13 years, the last as Headmaster of Axwell Park School in County Durham. He died on 9 June 1994.

7.04 Clwyd County Council took over responsibility for Bryn Estyn on 1 April 1974 and appointed a Management Committee in 1975 with responsibility for Bryn Estyn and 2 other Wrexham community homes (Bersham Hall and Little Acton).

7.05 When Arnold arrived there were about 30 resident boys but the number rose to over 60 in the following 2 years. In the second half of the 1970s the number of residents gradually declined so that the average by the end of the decade was about 40. Fewer than half of the boys at Bryn Estyn were placed by Clwyd: many of the residents were from South Wales and some from neighbouring English and Welsh counties. Lengths of stay varied considerably: between June 1979 and May 1980 there were 75 admissions and 91 discharges. Overall, it is estimated that between 500 and 600 boys were residents at the home between 1974 and 1984 but this may be an underestimate.

7.06 In 1975 the staff establishment at Bryn Estyn was 44, led by the Principal, a Deputy Principal and an Assistant Principal. There were 8 teachers and 18 houseparents, including 7 senior houseparents, and 2 nightcare officers. The Deputy Principal and Head of Education from 1969 to 1976 was Brynley Goldswain. He was succeeded by **Peter Howarth**, who had been Assistant Principal from November 1973. However, Howarth did not become Head of Education. Instead, a second Deputy Principal (Education), **Maurice Matthews**, was appointed with effect from 1 June 1977. Both Howarth and Matthews remained in post until shortly before Bryn Estyn closed.

7.07 The organisation of Bryn Estyn changed from time to time. Early on during the period under review there was a working boys' unit called Cedar House but it became a unit for immature boys in April 1977. Then, in or about September 1978, the latter unit was transferred to a 12 bed purpose built house, which was named Clwyd House.

7.08 Various methods of organising the boys who lived in the main building were tried. There was no "house" system at first but such a system was put into operation by the late 1970s: an attempt at 4 houses failed and they were succeeded by 2 houses, based on age, until reducing numbers obviated the need for them.

7.09 Bryn Estyn was provided with an 8 bed secure unit, which was ready for opening in November 1979, but it was never approved for use as a secure unit by the Welsh Office. It appears to have been used intermittently to restrict or restrain recalcitrant residents, particularly glue sniffers, for short periods with, at best, dubious legal authority.

7.10 The teaching staff had a formidable and largely thankless task, bearing in mind the continuous flow of pupils in and out of their classes. A substantial proportion of residents were in need of remedial education and many of the students with brighter potential were quite severely disturbed. The shortcomings in the provision of education are dealt with in Chapter 11 of the report.

7.11 Considerable emphasis was placed on outdoor activities, in which some members of staff played an active role. These activities were much more successful in the 1970s than later, when the future of the home became uncertain and numbers declined.

7.12 Arnold's periodic reports to the Management Committee presented an optimistic picture until the closure of the home loomed. He did report from time to time, however, underlying disciplinary and other difficulties at Bryn Estyn. Glue sniffing and drinking were recurring causes of concern; the rate of absconding was persistently high; and Arnold reported on occasions anxieties about the vulnerability of staff, threats of violence to them and internal damage within the campus by younger residents. As early as October 1976 and on several subsequent occasions he drew attentions to a growing group of "hard core homeless" within the home, who had lost hope for themselves and seemed unable to re-create any thoughts for their future or plans towards adulthood. He said that it was from this group that sheer self-destruction emerged, infecting others.

The allegations of sexual abuse at Bryn Estyn (Chapter 8)

8.01 About 70 former residents of Bryn Estyn between 1974 and 1984 complained to the police and/or the Tribunal that they had been victims of sexual abuse by a member of staff whilst living there. The overwhelming majority of these complaints were against **Peter Norman Howarth**, the Deputy Principal, and **Stephen Roderick Norris**, the senior housemaster in charge of Clwyd House from its opening in or about September 1978.

8.02 Of the total of 48 complainants of sexual abuse at Bryn Estyn who gave evidence to the Tribunal, 26 alleged sexual offences by Howarth and 13 alleged such offences by Norris but 5 of them alleged offences by both of them.

8.03 A total of 14 other members of the Bryn Estyn staff were the subject of allegations of sexual abuse but all but 3 of them were named by one individual only.

8.04 **Howarth**, a bachelor, was about 42 years old when he was appointed Assistant Principal of Bryn Estyn in November 1973 and he had been a housemaster in special and approved schools for 16 years. He had obtained a Certificate in the Residential Care of Children in 1965 at Ruskin College, Oxford, where he met Arnold, who was a visiting tutor. Arnold subsequently invited him to apply successively for posts at Axwell Park, where he became Third Officer-in-Charge in 1971, and then Bryn Estyn.

8.05 The allegations of sexual abuse by Howarth span the whole of his period at Bryn Estyn to July 1984. They were centred mainly on the flat that he occupied there on the first floor of the main building. It was Howarth's practice to invite boys, usually 5 or 6 from the main building at a time, to the flat in the evening for drinks (including some alcohol) and light food: they would watch television and play cards or board games. Invitations to these sessions were by a "flat list" compiled by Howarth or made up on his instructions and boys who went to the flat were required to wear pyjamas without underpants. Attendance was part of the agreed programme of activities available to boys in the evening. The sessions would begin at about 8.30 pm and end at 11 pm to 11.30 pm.

8.06 Howarth had begun the flat list system when he was at Axwell Park and Arnold knew of it, both then and at Bryn Estyn.

8.07 Howarth was tried in July 1994 in Chester Crown Court on 3 counts of buggery and 9 of indecent assault. These offences were alleged to have been committed between 1 January 1974 and 11 May 1984 and they involved 9 boy residents. Howarth denied all the charges and persisted in his denials until he died in prison in April 1997, before he was due to give evidence to the Tribunal. He was convicted on 8 July 1994 of one offence of buggery and 7 indecent assaults, for which he was sentenced to 10 years' imprisonment. He was acquitted of the other charges.

8.08 One of the charges against Howarth was a joint charge against him and Paul Wilson[1] of indecent assault upon a boy but both were acquitted of this charge.

---

[1] See para 10.04 et seq of this Summary.

8.09 There was no appeal by Howarth against his convictions, although we were told that he was considering an application for leave to appeal out of time. The Tribunal heard compelling evidence in support of the charges of which he was convicted and of similar offences committed by him against other residents. Some of the evidence was of less than satisfactory quality but we are satisfied both that the convictions were correct and that they were merely representative of a pattern of conduct by Howarth throughout the time that he lived at Bryn Estyn.

8.10 We are satisfied that all the senior members of staff and most of the junior staff were aware of the flat list procedure. Many were aware of Howarth's favourites being called "bum boys" and many thought it highly unwise of Howarth to place himself in such a vulnerable position, open to allegations of sexual misconduct. But only 2 former members of staff admitted that they suspected Howarth of sexual impropriety and none said that they ever actually knew that it was occurring.

8.11 In our view Arnold must be criticised strongly for permitting the flat practice to continue. He must have been aware of the obvious criticisms to which we refer and, quite apart from the sexual implications of the flat list, its impact on the conduct of the community home was such that he clearly ought to have intervened. Nevertheless, Howarth instructed his Counsel and solicitors that he had the full support of Arnold.

8.12 A small number of the former Bryn Estyn staff still refuse to believe that Howarth was guilty of any sexual misconduct, despite the weight of the evidence against him. Their view was expressed by the Chairman and the Secretary of the Bryn Estyn Staff Support Group but we are unable to sympathise with it and regard it as ostrich-like.

8.13 We have not heard any acceptable evidence of contemporary complaints by any of Howarth's victims to members of the staff at Bryn Estyn but the latter must, in our view, share a degree of blame for the failure to stop his activities.

8.14 The consequences of the abuse by Howarth on his victims were immeasurable and remain so. Their lives were grossly poisoned by a leading authority figure in whom they should have been able to place their trust. They felt soiled, guilty and embarrassed and were led to question their own sexual orientation. Most of them have experienced difficulties in their sexual relationships and their relationships with children ever since and many have continued to rebel against authority. Even more seriously, their self-respect and ability to look forward to the future has been shattered.

8.15 **Stephen Norris'** sexual offences were similar in kind to those of Howarth, although his method of operation was different. He was 38 years old when he became a joint houseparent, with his wife Margaret, at Cedar House on 1 March 1974. He had had varied employment until 1970 when he had become a houseparent at Greystone Heath Approved School, near Warrington, for which he took a pre-qualifying course in residential work. Margaret Norris was not implicated in any of her husband's offences and we have not received any complaint about her.

8.16 Norris obtained the CRCCYP qualification in December 1976 and was appointed as a senior houseparent at Bryn Estyn a year later, after interview by a panel. He was appointed head of Clwyd House without further interview and he remained there until it was amalgamated with the rest of the home in November 1983. Norris was then in limbo at Bryn Estyn until his transfer to Cartrefle on 8 July 1984.

8.17 Norris pleaded guilty on 11 November 1993 at Knutsford Crown Court to 3 offences of buggery, an attempted buggery and 3 indecent assaults, involving 6 former Bryn Estyn boys. There were 10 other counts in the Bryn Estyn indictment against him, to which he pleaded not guilty. They alleged buggery (2), indecent assault (7) and assault occasioning actual bodily harm; and the charges involved 9 boys, 3 of whom were named in counts to which he pleaded guilty. By this time Norris had already served $3\frac{1}{2}$ years' imprisonment imposed in October 1990 for sexual offences committed at Cartrefle after his Bryn Estyn offences[2]. For the latter he received 7 years' imprisonment and the Court ordered that the 10 counts that he denied should remain on the Court file.

8.18 All the charges against Norris related to the period when he was head of Clwyd House. We heard evidence from 9 of the victims named in the Bryn Estyn indictment and from 3 other former residents of Bryn Estyn who alleged that they had been sexually abused by him. That evidence showed that he was a coarse man of poor general education, who should never have been placed in charge of a unit providing for the needs of immature and disturbed young boys. At least 8 of them and some members of staff spoke of his obsession with sexual matters and his practice of making inappropriate sexual comments about, for example, the size of boys' genitalia and their sexual capacity. Norris would be present in the shower block precincts when boys were taking a shower; he would observe them, comment upon them and often wash their private parts on the pretext that the state of their foreskins made this necessary. Subsequently, graver forms of assault would occur there and elsewhere, in bedrooms at Clwyd House and at Norris' smallholding at Afonwen, to which he would invite residents of Clwyd House.

8.19 In his evidence to the Tribunal, Norris' admissions did not go beyond what was implicit in his pleas of guilty in the Crown Court. He denied threatening any child but said that he had required a "101 per cent assurance" from a child that he would not tell anyone. One boy victim would not know that any other was being abused. Norris disliked Howarth, with whom he had as little as possible to do: he was "totally and utterly" unaware that Howarth was sexually abusing children, although he knew of the flat list, on which Clwyd House children were rarely included.

8.20 We conclude that Norris' sexual abuse of residents of Clwyd House went well beyond his own admissions and we have no reason to doubt the veracity of most of the witnesses who alleged abuse by him.

---

[2] Ibid, paras 15.02 to 15.11.

8.21 We have not received any evidence of contemporary complaints by victims or witnesses of Norris' sexual abuse whilst he was at Bryn Estyn and there is no basis for a finding that other members of the staff there knew about it at the time. Although some of the latter were less than frank in their evidence about their attitude to Norris when he was their colleague, we are satisfied that many of them disliked him because of the coarseness of his thoughts and conversation and regarded him as unsuitable for his post at Clwyd House.

8.22 Like Howarth, Norris bears an overwhelming responsibility for disfiguring the lives of so many children in his care in pursuit of his own sexual gratification.

8.23 The limited sexual complaints against 14 other members of the Bryn Estyn staff do not add significantly to the general picture.

8.24 The only members of staff named by more than one complainant were David Gwyn Birch, Paul Bicker Wilson and Frederick Rutter.

8.25 There were 2 complainants against Birch but he was acquitted on 12 January 1995 of 2 charges based on those complaints.

8.26 Similarly, Wilson was acquitted on 8 July 1994 of 3 charges of indecent assault involving 2 boys, one of which charges was laid jointly against Wilson and Howarth. We heard the evidence of both these boys but no additional evidence justifying a different conclusion from that of the jury has been produced.

8.27 We considered the evidence of 5 other complainants against Wilson but the prosecution charges were based on the strongest evidence available. Two of these other complainants spoke of physical rather then sexual assaults; 2 others described acts intended to humiliate them rather than with a sexual motive; and the fifth, who made his complaint in 1978, could not be traced and had been uncertain in later statements to the police about important detail.

8.28 Rutter is currently serving 12 years' imprisonment, imposed on 30 July 1991[3] for offences of rape and indecent assault committed between 1988 and 1990. He was employed at Bryn Estyn as a temporary RCCO between July 1982 and November 1983, when he was in his middle 30s, but we are aware of only 2 complaints against him of minor indecent assaults in relation to his period at Bryn Estyn. The evidence of both complainants was unreliable for reasons that we indicate in paragraph 8.42 of the report and we are not persuaded that Rutter was guilty of any sexual abuse at Bryn Estyn.

8.29 The individual allegations against 10 other members of the staff are not to be dismissed out of hand. A small number were complaints of heterosexual abuse and 2 involved a known and a probable homosexual acting independently of each other. However, the alleged isolated incidents were not the subject of complaint at the time and we have not found any contemporaneous documentation or other corroboration to support them.

8.30 There has been a small amount of evidence of sexual abuse by resident boys upon each other but the complaints about it that have reached us have been remarkably few; and, in most of them, the alleged perpetrator has not been

---

[3] Ibid, paras 26.01 to 26.10.

identified. We would not be justified, therefore, in finding that the scale of inter-resident sexual abuse at Bryn Estyn was greater than in other residential establishments in which pubescent boys are segregated.

8.31 The picture that we have given of a community home in which 2 of the most senior members of staff were habitually engaged in sexual abuse of many of the young residents without detection is truly appalling. Unhappily, however, it is not the complete picture because we heard other evidence suggesting that there was a pervasive culture at Bryn Estyn of immature and unhealthy attitudes to sexuality, which were very unhelpful to teenage boys whose developing sexuality needed handling with sensitivity.

The case of Gordon Anglesea (Chapter 9)

9.01 The issues in relation to **Gordon Anglesea's** alleged sexual misconduct at Bryn Estyn were considered by a jury in November and December 1994[4], when the jury found in Anglesea's favour by a majority of 10 to 2. The trial of the consolidated libel action occupied about a fortnight before a very experienced judge with all the parties represented by eminent counsel; and there has not been any appeal from the jury's decision.

9.02 The allegations against Anglesea have been repeated to the Tribunal and we have investigated them as fully as possible as explained in detail in Chapter 9 of the Tribunal's report.

9.03 We are unable to find that the allegations of sexual abuse made against Anglesea have been proved to our satisfaction or that the trial jury in the libel action would have been likely to have reached a different conclusion if they had heard the fuller evidence placed before us.

9.04 We have been left with a feeling of considerable disquiet about Anglesea's repeated denials of any recollection of Peter Howarth and the way in which his evidence of his own presence at Bryn Estyn has emerged. We agree with the trial judge in the libel action (the Honourable Mr Justice Drake), however, that such disquiet or even disbelief of this part of Anglesea's evidence would not justify a finding that he had committed sexual abuse in the absence of reliable positive proof.

9.05 The case against Anglesea was investigated very thoroughly by the North Wales Police, who recommended to the CPS in February 1993 that he should be prosecuted on the basis of the evidence available to them. Anglesea's membership of the freemasons had no influence on the investigation or its outcome and no other relevant senior police officer from the Chief Constable downwards is or was a freemason.

[4] Ibid, para 2.04.

The allegations of physical abuse at Bryn Estyn (Chapter 10)

10.01 Complaints to the police and/or the Tribunal of physical abuse were made against one or more members of the staff at Bryn Estyn by 113 former residents who had been there between 1974 and 1984 (about 38 per cent of them alleged sexual abuse as well). Of the 113, however, 17 referred only to unidentified assailants.

10.02 We heard the evidence of 64 of these complainants; 35 gave oral evidence and the statements of the other 29 were read to us. We received, therefore, a very representative account of the scale of the alleged abuse by identified abusers.

10.03 Only 6 former residents complained of physical abuse by **Howarth**, mainly of a comparatively minor nature; and the number alleging such abuse by **Norris** was 4.

10.04 The principal target of complaint by an overwhelming margin was **Paul Bicker Wilson,** against whom 53 former residents are known to have made complaints of physical abuse. Complaints against most other members of the staff were very thinly spread. In all about 30 of the staff were named but it is necessary and appropriate to refer to only a small number by name.

10.05 Wilson went to Bryn Estyn as a temporary RCCO on 27 May 1974 at the age of 34 years and was promoted to senior RCCO from 1 July 1974, after interview. He remained at Bryn Estyn until it closed in September 1984 and was then transferred to Chevet Hey as a supernumerary RCCO[5].

10.06 We heard the evidence of 39 complainants of physical abuse by Wilson, spanning almost the whole period of his employment at Bryn Estyn; and 26 of them gave oral evidence to us. All of them gave evidence that they had been physically assaulted by Wilson and many said that they had witnessed assaults by him on others. Seven members of staff admitted in evidence that they regarded Wilson as a violent bully and 2 of them described assaults by him that they had seen. Other witnesses described incidents of random cruelty by Wilson, such as kicking a boy's crutches away from him; capsizing canoes and holding boys under water; deliberately exposing rock climbers to risk by dropping the rope or leaving a fearful climber dangling on a rope; and removing the steering wheel of a minibus whilst driving it in order to terrify the occupants.

10.07 Wilson pleaded guilty on 28 November 1994 at Knutsford Crown Court to 3 offences of assault occasioning actual bodily harm and one of common assault committed between July 1980 and March 1984 on boys at Bryn Estyn. A not guilty verdict was entered in respect of another charge of common assault in 1984 because the complainant had hanged himself on 6 January 1994. One other count of assault and 2 alleging cruelty to a child, involving 3 other Bryn Estyn boys, were ordered to lie on the Court file. Wilson was sentenced to a total of 15 months' imprisonment suspended for 2 years. The sentencing judge decided to suspend the sentences because of the time that had elapsed since they were committed and the good character that Wilson had established in the

---

[5] Ibid, paras 14.11 to 14.14.

intervening years, in which he had done much work on a voluntary basis for youngsters.

10.08 There was no discernible pattern to Wilson's assaults. In paragraphs 10.09 to 10.27 of the report we give details of serious assaults on 7 boys identified as A to D, G, J and M, in one of which C's nose was broken by a punch to the face from Wilson. A, B and C were the complainants in respect of 3 of the counts to which Wilson pleaded guilty in November 1994. As far as we have been able to ascertain, contemporary complaints of assaults by Wilson were recorded in 6 cases.

10.09 In his evidence to the Tribunal Wilson denied that he had been a bully: he had been a disciplinarian. He admitted that he had lost his temper at times but denied that he had ever gone beyond "a clip or a slap" in anger. In general, the allegations against him were totally untrue and the most that he had done was to thump or punch a boy on the arm sufficiently to cause a bruise. He had been unaware of Clwyd County Council's prohibition of corporal punishment in the Council's community homes[6].

10.10 We have no doubt that Wilson was rightly convicted of the offences to which he pleaded guilty in November 1994 and that they represented only a very small sample of a long catalogue of similar offences that he committed during his period of 10 years at Bryn Estyn. It is both dismaying and astonishing that he was allowed to survive as an RCCO for so long and then to move on to similar employment in another community home.

10.11 Wilson's history illustrates the absence of any realistic complaints or whistleblowing procedures. There was also a lamentable failure on the part of the Clwyd SSD to carry out any adequate investigation of the few complaints that did get beyond the walls of Bryn Estyn. Monitoring and supervision of Wilson and consideration of the complaints about him ought to have demonstrated starkly his unfitness for the work that he was given. A substantial share of the blame for the failure to act must be borne by Arnold and Howarth, who appear to have protected Wilson and also gave the firm impression to other members of the staff that they were ready to shield him for reasons that will never now be known.

10.12 For very many residents Wilson caused or contributed to substantial distress and unhappiness that have lingered, in some cases, for as long as 2 decades.

10.13 Between paragraphs 10.40 and 10.156 of the report we consider the allegations of physical abuse made against 13 other named members of the Bryn Estyn staff, beginning with David Birch.

10.14 **David Gwyn Birch**[7] was the only one of these to be charged with offences against boys at Bryn Estyn. The indictment against him included 4 counts alleging assaults occasioning actual bodily harm and 2 alleging cruelty to a child. Following his acquittal on 12 January 1995 of 2 counts alleging sexual offences, which were tried separately, the prosecution decided not to offer any

---

[6] Ibid, para 30.02.
[7] Ibid, para 8.25.

evidence in support of the other 6 counts and the Court entered verdicts of not guilty in respect of each of them.

10.15 In all, 17 former residents of Bryn Estyn, including the 4 named in the 6 non-sexual charges in the indictment, complained of physical assaults by Birch during the period of 5 years when he worked as an RCCO at Bryn Estyn. We received evidence from 13 of these complainants, 7 of whom gave oral evidence to the Tribunal.

10.16 Birch was taken on as a temporary houseparent at Bryn Estyn on 21 May 1979 at the age of 21 years. His contact with Bryn Estyn was through the nearby Wrexham RFC and he had no relevant training or experience, except (perhaps) that he had taken a two year course in physical education before working as a labourer. However, he became an established RCCO with effect from 1 August 1979, following a formal interview, and he remained on the staff at Bryn Estyn until June 1984, when he was transferred briefly to Park House and then, on 1 November 1984, to Chevet Hey.

10.17 Our conclusion is that Birch was at fault from time to time in using physical force to boys when he should not have done and, on other occasions, in using excessive force when some physical action by way of restraint was permissible. It would be wrong, however, to be very harsh in one's strictures upon him personally, having regard to his age, inexperience and lack of training and the climate of violence in which he was working. It is noteworthy that there were only 5 complainants who alleged physical abuse by him in the following 5 years when he was at Chevet Hey, although there were other criticisms of him then.

10.18 In the event, Birch has suffered substantially as a result of his employment at Bryn Estyn. There was a long wait before his trial. Since then, he has felt unable to work with children and there was some adverse publicity about him prior to the setting up of this Tribunal.

10.19 It would be inappropriate to particularise in this Summary the varied allegations against all the other members of the staff named in the report. We refer particularly to 3 members of the teaching staff and 3 members of the night staff.

10.20 The evidence about one of the teachers, **John Ilton**, compelled us to conclude that, despite his excellent general character, he was unsuitable for the demanding work of teaching mainly disturbed and recalcitrant pupils. We heard persuasive evidence that it was his practice to throw blackboard dusters and other objects at boys who misbehaved and 8 witnesses gave oral evidence describing serious other assaults by him. He was said to have a "low fuse" and there were occasions when he lost all control of himself so that he, rather than the provoker, had to be restrained.

10.21 There were substantial complaints also about the Deputy Principal, **Maurice Matthews**, and another teacher, **David Cheesbrough**. The former admitted in his oral evidence to the Tribunal that there were 3 occasions when he struck or grabbed boys: in 2 of the incidents he lost his temper and the incidents were reported. We do not think it would be right to characterise Matthews as an abuser of children on the basis of these 3 proved incidents but the fact that he felt able to use unjustified force when holding a very senior position is a serious reflection on the general climate of the home.

10.22 **David Cheesbrough** was another teacher with a "low fuse". After 2 years on the care staff, starting when he was 22 years old, he transferred to the teaching staff from 4 January 1978 until Bryn Estyn closed. He was a member of the "rugby set" amongst the staff at Bryn Estyn and a number of residents spoke well of him but we heard evidence that he used manifestly excessive force on occasions. He was young, large, fit and strong and we have no doubt that he was heavy handed from time to time. Cheesbrough was not guilty of deliberate or habitual abuse of residents, in our judgment, but he was prone to lose his temper, whereupon his reactions to misbehaviour tended to be excessive. These failings could and should have been eradicated by firm and sensible leadership; and we are not aware of any similar complaints against him after he left Bryn Estyn.

10.23 A substantial number of former residents (15) complained of the activities of one or other members of the night staff at Bryn Estyn , who seemed to be a law unto themselves. One of the 3 named, **Stan Fletcher**, who was there from 1974 to 1984, died in December 1992. A recurring allegation made against him and **Tom Davies** was that they would hit boys in bed with the large torch that each of the night care staff carried and there were more serious allegations of assault. The third member of the night staff, **John Cunningham**, was accused, in particular, of 2 serious assaults, one of which (on 30 April 1984) led belatedly to his prolonged suspension from March 1992 to December 1995.

10.24 We have no doubt that the night care staff had to face difficult problems from time to time but we are satisfied that each of them did use inappropriate and excessive force to some residents. However, Davies was himself the victim of what he described as a "vicious" assault in June 1984 and Cunningham was subjected to an excessive period of suspension, which ended with a relegation under the disciplinary code on the footing that he had committed an act of gross misconduct and had given conflicting accounts of the relevant incident.

10.25 Six former residents of Bryn Estyn alleged that they had been physically ill-treated by **(Joseph) Nefyn Dodd**, who is a major figure in Parts VII and X of the Tribunal's report. He was a housemaster and then senior housemaster at Bryn Estyn from August 1974 to October 1977, interrupted in 1975 by a year's course for the CRCCYP. Some witnesses spoke well of him there but we are satisfied that he did on occasions administer physical punishment with punches and slaps. There was evidence also of his intimidating manner, which was to become more prominent at Tŷ'r Felin.

10.26 As we have said earlier[8], **Frederick Rutter** was at Bryn Estyn from July 1982 to November 1983 as a temporary RCCO. He was suspended on full pay from 12 January to 8 February 1983 by Geoffrey Wyatt, pending investigation of an allegation by a 14 years old resident that Rutter had punched him on 5 January 1983. The police, who investigated it, decided that no further action should be taken "mainly due to the direct conflict of evidence". There was no separate investigation by the SSD and the complainant was transferred to Neath Farm

---

[8] Ibid, para 8.28.

School shortly after making his complaint. However, the latter told the police in January 1992 that he had no complaints about the way he was treated by any of the staff at Bryn Estyn and he has not come forward as a complainant to the Tribunal.

10.27 Two witnesses did give oral evidence to the Tribunal of physical abuse by Rutter but there are serious difficulties about the credibility of both these witnesses. There was limited other evidence of a more general kind that Rutter would clip or punch boys on the head but we do not consider that the evidence before us has been sufficiently clear and specific to justify an adverse finding against him in relation to his conduct at Bryn Estyn.

10.28 To sum up, although we have been restrained in our criticisms of inexperienced and untrained individual members of staff, the overall picture of physical abuse at Bryn Estyn is bleak. Paul Wilson was obviously a rogue elephant on the staff but it would be quite wrong to heap all the blame upon him. Our general finding is that there was an excessive use of force in day-to-day contact between staff and residents as well as in disciplining residents. Bullying by peers was also commonplace and was accepted by the staff, at least to an inappropriate extent, as part of a means of control, based on recognition of successive "top dogs". Thus, violence was endemic in the system and it persisted, whether or not it was inherited initially from the approved school regime.

10.29 The broad picture is that there was a regrettable and alarming lack of effective leadership by **Arnold** throughout. Similarly, there was grave fault on the part of **Howarth** because he accepted responsibility for the day to day running of the home throughout the 10 year period that we have reviewed, except during a period of months when he was disabled. **Matthews** also bore substantial responsibility from 1977 and must shoulder part of the blame. In the absence of clear directions and guidance, and without meaningful discussion of disciplinary and allied issues at staff meetings, members of the care and teaching staff were left to make up their own rules to an impermissible extent. A policy of drift appears to have been adopted, accompanied by increasing disillusion as numbers declined, and Arnold's reports to the Management Committee gave only occasional hints of the unsolved problems that he faced.

Other aspects of the Bryn Estyn regime (Chapter 11)

11.01 In this chapter we deal with the cult of silence or cover up at Bryn Estyn, the use of the secure unit, educational aspects of the regime, the recruitment and training of staff and the quality of care generally.

11.02 Many residents of Bryn Estyn no doubt understood that they could complain, for example, to a parent or their field social worker or an approachable member of the staff but the perceived disincentives for doing so were numerous and substantial and none of the residents whom we heard thought that anything positive to their benefit would result from a complaint.

11.03 Despite this, some complaints were made and we give numerous examples in the report of how they were discouraged and, in effect, suppressed[9]. Much of the responsibility for this rested upon **Arnold**, who (in our judgment) adopted thoroughly discreditable means of avoiding "official" complaints, including condoning the practice of making neutral, uninformative entries in log books when injuries occurred and, on one occasion, providing false information to a hospital casualty department about how an injury had been sustained. Moreover, he chose to delegate to others the task of investigation when he must or should have known that the effect upon a child complainant was likely to be intimidating.

11.04 Permission for the secure unit at Bryn Estyn to be opened, subject to 2 conditions, was given by the Welsh Office in a letter to the Chief Executive of Clwyd dated 26 September 1979 but it appears that a further approval, once the conditions had been met, was required before the secure unit could be operated as such; and that further approval was never given. Arnold, however, thought that the unit was in operation, at least for some months because he reported to the Management Committee on 16 May 1980 that the unit was being used "on a very limited level".

11.05 We heard conflicting evidence about the actual use of this unit from about November 1979 onwards. It is probably conceded that it was used to detain for short periods, measured in hours, some persistent absconders and glue sniffers who were out of control but 7 complainants alleged that they had been locked in a room in the secure unit, one for as long as 12 days on bread and water only.

11.06 We think that this last claim is probably exaggerated but we accept that residents were on a few occasions locked in a room of the secure unit and, regrettably, that a small number were physically chastised there.

11.07 The legal position in relation to the required approval by the Secretary of State was unnecessarily confused and it was eventually withdrawn by a letter dated 1 July 1983 on the grounds that the secure unit was not in use and that there were no plans to bring it into use in the foreseeable future.

11.08 It is striking that the Management Committee appear to have failed throughout to consider the proper use of the secure unit or the Committee's own powers and duties in relation to it and no guidance appears to have been sought by or given to Arnold in respect of it.

11.09 We know of only one resident who expressed any satisfaction with the teaching arrangements and he dealt only with Gwen Hurst. All the other complainants who were asked about the matter were severely critical.

11.10 Our conclusion is that a significant number of children who needed remedial education received substantial help from Gwen Hurst and Justin Soper but that very many others, particularly those who were emotionally disturbed at the time, received virtually no educational benefit from their stay at Bryn Estyn. It seems that only one boy resident was allowed to attend a local school because of his potential.

---

[9] See Chapter 10 and the first section of Chapter 11.

11.11 The Parliamentary Under Secretary of State for Wales, the Rt Hon Barry Jones MP, visited Bryn Estyn on 9 January 1976 and commented that full advantage was not being taken of the educational provision at the home. He asked for a joint visit by an HMI and an SWSO to be arranged urgently but, despite such visits in March 1976, March 1977 and June 1978 and a further visit by the Minister in February 1979, very little positive action ensued. A working party, set up by Clwyd County Council to consider support by the Education Department, made a series of recommendations in or about June 1978 but few, if any, of them were implemented. As late as April 1982, Arnold was expressing concern that assistance and advice which the Education Department had promised[10] had not materialised.

11.12 There was no curriculum before 1978. The WJEC's syllabus was adopted then, at Welsh Office insistence. Between 1978 and 1984, 37 residents took CSE examinations in one or more subjects. The grades obtained were usually 4 or 5 but 3 boys obtained Grade 1 in art and design and one of them staged an exhibition of his work.

11.13 The problem of recruitment of suitable residential care staff was never discussed by the Management Committee in any depth throughout its existence and recruiting at Bryn Estyn appears to have been largely haphazard.

11.14 Most of the care staff named in Chapter 10 of the report were taken on when they had no training in residential care work and no experience of it. Four of them had undergone teacher training but only one of them underwent further relevant training whilst at Bryn Estyn. The picture in relation to teaching staff was broadly similar, although they all possessed general teaching qualifications. In addition to their difficult teaching and assessment duties, teachers were expected to perform the duties of care staff for at least 15 additional hours each week but none of them had received any training in residential care work.

11.15 There was a degree of hostility between the teaching and care staff and the absence of joint staff meetings further militated against exchanges of information. Even when seminars for the staff were arranged during the winter of 1979/1980 to discuss topics relevant to community homes with education on the premises, the 2 categories of staff were divided into separate groups for the purpose.

11.16 Finally in this chapter of the report, we express grave concern at the lack of individual care for children at Bryn Estyn between 1974 and 1984.

11.17 Arnold started with high principles, but the subsequent practice at Bryn Estyn failed, disastrously for many, to implement those principles and aspirations. He began with the intention that every resident should have a "key worker" to advise and console him but it seems likely that he abandoned the idea in favour of a "house" organisation which did not provide the kind of relationship that he had had in mind originally.

[10] cf in this connection Welsh Office Circular 194/73 dated 31 August 1973.

11.18 There was also a glaring lack of close personal relationships between residents and field social workers. This was felt particularly by residents from outside Clwyd but the overwhelming majority of residents complained of lack of contact with, and inability to confide in, their assigned social worker; and this problem was aggravated by frequent changes of social worker.

11.19 The only planning mechanism was the statutory review and there was little evidence of long term planning. Many children and young people endured frequent changes of placement and we criticise specifically 2 aspects of the placement system at Bryn Estyn, namely, (a) the practice of transferring summarily to another (often remote) establishment any resident who made a complaint and (b) unnecessarily long detention of children at Bryn Estyn, of which Arnold complained to the Management Committee[11], because of the reluctance of social workers to permit them to return to the community.

11.20 We conclude with the comment that the Children and Young Persons Act 1969 demanded a significant change in thinking and approach, involving treatment rather than punishment, but Bryn Estyn continued to be regarded as a place catering essentially for aggressive and disturbed boys, with a strong criminal element, and the approved school culture continued untouched to a large extent. The result was that there was a harsh institutional regime in which, for many, there was a heavy atmosphere of fear; and little consideration was given to the needs of individual boys, including the most vulnerable, and the problems that had given rise to their admission to care.

Little Acton Assessment Centre, 1974 to 1980 (Chapter 12)

12.01 This purpose built community home for 15 boys and girls was handed over by the builders to Clwyd County Council on 1 April 1974 but it survived as a community home for only 6 years until its closure in May 1980. It was the second of the 3 homes for which the Management Committee referred to in the preceding chapters was responsible.

12.02 The site in Box Lane, Wrexham, housed the assessment centre, a residential nursery and a hostel building with a day nursery on the ground floor. The assessment centre had 3 separate units within the same building: one was designed as a semi-secure unit and the other 2 as open units. Each unit was a self-contained flat, to accommodate 5 children and one sleeping-in member of staff; and residential accommodation was provided in 4 flats for the senior staff.

12.03 Difficulty in recruiting appropriate senior staff was experienced from the outset and the first 4 years were particularly troubled. A report commissioned by Clwyd SSD in 1978 was highly critical of the Officer-in-Charge, **Peter Bird**, and his deputy, **Carl Evans**. Disciplinary proceedings against both men followed.

12.04 **Bird** was informed of 19 matters of complaint that were to be discussed with him and he subsequently admitted 8 of the allegations on the understanding that the 11 others would be dismissed. He received a written warning dated 3

---

[11] See para 7.12 of this Summary.

October 1978 and was transferred 6 days later to work as a craft instructor at an Adult Training Centre.

12.05 **Evans**, who had succeeded the first Deputy Officer-in-Charge, Huw Meurig Jones, on 1 May 1976, following the latter's resignation, was suspended from 13 January 1978 and left on 8 October 1978. The investigating team's report on Evans was a damning indictment of his performance and conduct, although the team did not interview him. Disciplinary proceedings against him were based on 17 allegations, of which 4 were admitted by Evans, including one of making unauthorised fieldwork visits to an adolescent girl in care and another of supporting her application for housing without notifying the Officer-in-Charge of his involvement. Evans too received a written warning and he was then seconded to other work for 6 months before being appointed Deputy Superintendent of an assessment centre in Islington.

12.06 The 1978 investigation had been into the conduct, administration and management of the assessment centre with particular regard to disciplinary measures taken earlier against 2 other senior members of the staff. One of these was the matron, who had been absent for about 9 months before her resignation on 9 December 1977, a week after pleading guilty to offences of dishonesty committed at the home.

12.07 More relevantly, **Leslie Wilson**, a housefather at Little Acton from 1 August 1974 and then a senior housefather from 19 April 1976, had pleaded guilty on 22 December 1977, in the Crown Court at Chester, to offences of indecent assault, gross indecency and attempted buggery, for which he had been sentenced to 15 months' imprisonment.

12.08 The victim of Wilson's offences was a boy resident at Bryn Estyn, who had previously undergone assessment for 4 months at Little Acton. Wilson's visits to the boy at Bryn Estyn had been reported by Arnold to Bird as a matter for concern and the boy was later found in Wilson's flat at Little Acton, after absconding from Bryn Estyn. Wilson confessed to 2 members of the staff that he had slept with the boy and the facts were reported to Geoffrey Wyatt, who referred the matter to the police. Wilson was suspended without pay from 14 July 1977 and dismissed by Clwyd County Council on 28 February 1978.

12.09 We estimate that there were about 275 admissions to Little Acton whilst Bird was Officer-in-Charge but we are aware of only 15 residents who have made complaints of abuse by members of the staff during that period and 4 of them were unable or unwilling to identify the member of staff concerned. The complaints by the other 11 former residents, from 9 of whom we received evidence, involved only 7 members of the staff.

12.10 In the report we deal specifically with the evidence of complainants who made allegations against Bird, Meurig Jones and Evans.

12.11 The allegations against **Bird**, by a male who was 10 years old at the time and by 2 girls, then 14 years old, were of physical assaults, including slapping across the face, throwing into a bath (for smoking) and lifting by the hair. The former boy resident said also that he spent a lot of time in the "lock-up" because he kept running away. Bird denied these allegations and said that the semi-secure unit was only used for disciplinary purposes on 3 or 4 occasions. Nevertheless, we are satisfied that the allegations have not been invented and that Bird did use violence of the kind described on occasions. He believed in a strict regime and neither he nor the staff under him had any clear understanding that corporal punishment was prohibited or of the proper boundaries of physical restraint.

12.12 There were complaints about the conduct of **Huw Meurig Jones** by 3 witnesses. One former boy resident alleged that Meurig Jones had made sexual advances to him on 2 occasions and another said that he was a pure "faggot", who used to walk around the units blowing kisses and nipping backsides. The third witness alleged that he had assaulted her physically, punching her heavily in the stomach. Whilst it is not possible for us to reach firm conclusions about these individual allegations, which were all denied by Meurig Jones, it is perturbing that allegations of sexual impropriety were made against him also by former Bryn Estyn residents and others in later phases of his life. As we explain in paragraph 12.34 of our report, it would be impossible, in our judgment, for the public, with knowledge of the facts, to have the degree of confidence in his judgment and probity that is essential for employment in social work involving the care of children.

12.13 Fellow members of the staff alleged that the behaviour of **Evans** towards adolescent girl residents at Little Acton was inappropriate: it was said that he spent long periods of time alone with some of them, claiming to be counselling them, and that there was excessive physical contact between him and them.

12.14 One girl, R, with whom he had spent the whole of a Christmas party in 1977, subsequently alleged that he had raped her. It was this allegation that caused his suspension initially, although it was withdrawn and then reinstated before investigation by the police. R repeated the allegation in a written statement to the Tribunal but was unwilling to give oral evidence about it and 2 letters found in her room at the time of her complaint suggest that she was then infatuated with Evans.

12.15 There is no proper basis, therefore, on which we could accept that R's allegation has been proved. Nevertheless, we record our view that Evans was very unsuitable for the responsibilities that he undertook as Deputy Officer-in-Charge: his conduct in relation to other staff and discipline generally, coupled with his behaviour towards resident adolescent girls, demonstrated that he was temperamentally unfitted for the work. He showed an alarming lack of judgment. In these circumstances we do not consider that he is a suitable person to be employed in the residential care of children.

12.16 We did not receive any evidence of physical or sexual abuse at Little Acton in the last 2 years of its existence, when **Michael Barnes** was the Officer-in-Charge, having been asked to take over in an acting position initially from 21 April 1978.

12.17 On the evidence before us Little Acton failed in its primary role as an assessment centre. The assessment process was carried out by largely untrained staff, who were insufficiently involved with the children to take full advantage of getting to know them. The centre suffered also from lack of consultation with professionals with special skills, such as educational psychologists and psychiatrists. In the later stages its description was changed to Reception and Assessment Centre and admissions on a reception basis dominated. Its assessment function was ultimately taken over, for boys by Bryn Estyn and for girls by Bersham Hall.

12.18 The balance of the evidence before us points to the conclusion that the teaching staff were dedicated in the work that they did with little support, no opportunities for special training and very limited facilities.

12.19 It is regrettable that a purpose built institution with an important primary function should have remained in use so briefly and unsuccessfully.

Bersham Hall, 1974 to 1993 (Chapter 13)

13.01 Bersham Hall was a family residence before it was acquired by Denbighshire County Council to provide an observation and assessment centre for up to 12 boys. It is a large red brick house set in an acre of land in a small village near Wrexham and it opened as a community home in August 1972. From 1975 until 1984 it was under the aegis of the Management Committee for 3 Wrexham homes set up by Clwyd County Council.

13.02 The function of Bersham Hall changed in 1980 and it closed for a short time. It re-opened as an assessment and reception centre for up to 21 boys and girls, taking over many of the functions of Little Acton, but it seems that the assessment process was limited to girls. A cottage in the grounds began to be used then as an independent training facility for children of school leaving age.

13.03 Education was provided on the premises until 1990, by which time the majority of residents had been provided with school places locally. The teaching staff were employed by Clwyd SSD until 1987, when they were transferred to the Education Authority.

13.04 The community home closed in September 1993 but it was re-opened the following year as a registered private children's home called Prospects, which continues in being.

13.05 In the first period of its existence under Clwyd County Council, from 1974 to 1980, Bersham Hall was plagued by frequent changes of staff. There were 9 senior officers in that period and chronic staff shortages at lower levels. Moreover, little had been done initially to adapt the premises and extensive building work had to be carried out from March 1976 onwards. Most of this work was finished by January 1978 but the extended educational unit was not opened until 3 months later. There was 18 months delay also in completing the secure unit, which was approved by the Secretary of State by a letter dated 26 September 1979 but which never had the required number of staff.

13.06 We estimate that about 375 boys were admitted to Bersham Hall between April 1974 and the end of April 1980 on the basis of figures reported to the Management Committee; the average occupancy dropped from 1977 onwards because of the building work. It was intended that boys should stay at the centre for only 8 weeks but many stayed longer, usually because of difficulties in obtaining placements.

13.07 Many of the residents were referred to Bersham Hall by the courts for re-assessment following stressful court proceedings and were emotionally disturbed for this and other reasons. A report by the senior teacher in January 1979 showed that, of 27 boys admitted in the preceding 5 months, 19 were maladjusted, 20 were violent or extremely disruptive and 22 had learning difficulties.

13.08 We are aware of 19 former residents who complained that they were abused at Bersham Hall prior to May 1980, but 7 of these referred only to incidents before Clwyd County Council came into existence and the complaints of another referred partly to that earlier period.

13.09 The main subject of these complaints about the pre-April 1974 period was **Michael Taylor**, who was Deputy Officer-in-Charge from 26 September 1972 to 31 July 1973. There were 3 complainants who alleged sexual abuse by him at Bersham Hall and one other complaint by a former resident of Chevet Hey Children's Home, where Taylor was permitted to stay briefly in the summer of 1973, whilst waiting for his college accommodation. All 4 of them gave oral evidence to the Tribunal of indecent assaults by Taylor, usually committed in the witness' bedroom and we are fully satisfied that the complaints are true.

13.10 Unusually, 2 of the assaults came to the knowledge of higher management shortly after they had occurred, one via a complaint by the victim to another boy that was overheard by a member of staff and the other, at Chevet Hey, by direct complaint to a member of staff. Taylor denied both allegations, made in July and September 1973 respectively, and he left Chevet Hey after the second. No further action was taken against him then in respect of those allegations but he was convicted on 26 June 1980, in Wrexham Magistrates' Court, of 2 indecent assaults on a boy, committed in Shropshire, and asked for 2 similar offences to be taken into consideration. He was placed on probation for 2 years. The earlier allegations were investigated by the North Wales Police in 1993, whereupon Taylor made full admissions and accepted cautions in respect of indecent assaults on 6 victims, including the 4 who gave evidence to us.

13.11 The other allegations of abuse at Bersham Hall prior to May 1980[12] were much more diffuse and consisted mainly of complaints by one former resident against one member of staff only; and 7 of them were unable to identify the member of staff concerned. Overall, the complaints do not suggest that violence by members of the staff was characteristic of the home prior to 1980. However, 4 complainants, alleged that they had been physically assaulted by **Michael Barnes** and 2 alleged physical assaults by **(Joseph) Nefyn Dodd** during the period of 9 months to 1 August 1974 in which he was employed at Bersham Hall before moving to Bryn Estyn. The allegations against the latter did not add anything of substance to what we have said about him in paragraph 10.25

---

[12] We did not receive any complaints against Richard Ernest Leake, the Officer-in-Charge from 4 August 1972 to 30 June 1994, but see now para 22.07 of this Summary for details of his conviction on 24 November 1999, after the Tribunal's report was signed.

of this Summary and we consider those against Barnes in the wider context of later allegations against him.

13.12 The 2 leading figures on the staff of Bersham Hall after it re-opened were Barnes and Christopher Thomas. **Michael Barnes** was initially Third-in-Charge at Bersham Hall from September 1972 and progressed to substantive Officer-in-Charge from 1 June 1976 until he was appointed to the same position at Little Acton on 1 January 1979. Barnes then returned to Bersham Hall as Officer-in-Charge from 21 May 1980 to 31 December 1987, before being promoted to Principal Social Worker (Child and Family Services) with responsibility for the remaining children's homes in Clwyd and some other matters[13]. He was away at Keele University, however, taking the CQSW course from October 1982 to July 1984; and from 1 April 1986 he had the additional responsibility of Chevet Hey as Acting Officer-in-Charge.

13.13 Barnes' Deputy at Bersham Hall from April 1978 to February 1979 and again from May 1980 was **Christopher Thomas**, who moved back there with **Barnes** from Little Acton. He acted as Officer-in-Charge at Bersham Hall during Barnes' absence at university and then succeeded Barnes from 1 January 1988, remaining until Bersham Hall closed in September 1993. Thomas began working there in September 1974 so that he was on the staff for most of the period under review.

13.14 Although the number of children admitted was substantially larger in the second period than in the first, we are aware of only 24 former residents who made complaints that they had been abused at Bersham Hall after April 1980; and 14 of them have not renewed their complaints to this Tribunal.

13.15 Allegations of sexual abuse were made by 3 women witnesses, only one of whom gave oral evidence to the Tribunal. She alleged that a male member of staff (identified only by his first name), whom she described as "very charismatic", had had sex with her but added that it was very vague, "a snatch of memory". She did not complain because the man was her friend and she did not want to lose him for that reason.

13.16 The second witness alleged in her statement that she had been touched on her leg by a member of staff when she was in bed and the third witness alleged sexual misconduct of various kinds by several members of the staff. One of the staff whom the third witness accused was suspended on 3 March 1992 and later dismissed after disciplinary hearings in October 1992 but it does not appear that any of the charges against him were based directly on this witness' evidence: eight charges against him were found to have been proved and his name was referred to the DoH Consultancy Service for registration on the Index. Christopher Thomas said in his evidence that the man had been warned 4 times about the unwisdom of being alone with the third witness and that she too had been warned about the matter.

13.17 In the light of the evidence we have no doubt that sexual intercourse between residents did occur at Bersham Hall from time to time and that there was some

---

[13] See para 28.12 of this Summary.

inappropriate conduct on the part of individual members of the care staff. The favourable side of the picture is that the volume of complaints has been small and that no one has alleged persistent or habitual sexual abuse of successive residents. The only allegations of sexual incidents after 1981 were those of the third witness referred to above.

13.18 Varying views were expressed to us about the extent to which physical force was used against residents at Bersham Hall between 1980 and 1993. There was a conflict of attitude between Barnes, who saw himself as a disciplinarian, and Thomas, who favoured a more relaxed regime. There was some conflict also between other members of the staff, some of whom were transferred to Bersham Hall when Bryn Estyn closed. Three of the latter described the regime at Bersham Hall as oppressive and one said that it was more so than at Bryn Estyn.

13.19 Of the 10 complainants who were at Bersham Hall between 1980 and 1993 and whose evidence we received, 4 complained of physical assaults by **Barnes** involving varying degrees of force. All but one of these complainants referred to events that were alleged to have occurred within a year of his return to Bersham Hall in May 1980. Barnes himself denied all these allegations and said that he never used violence towards any resident, except in necessary restraint.

13.20 In reviewing the various criticisms of Barnes we have had to consider not only his record at Bersham Hall but also the evidence about him at Little Acton and Chevet Hey and his subsequent activities in more senior posts. He was a good communicator, with intelligent ideas, and his reports to the Management Committee were helpful and thoughtful. We have had in mind also that a high proportion of the children at Bersham Hall were seriously disturbed in one way or another and that most of them were held there on a short term basis only. We are satisfied, however, that he was viewed by some of the residents as a remote, unfriendly and arrogant figure. Although we regarded as unreliable some of the comparatively small number of witnesses who complained of physical assaults by him, we are satisfied also that he did, on occasions, use excessive force against residents, both by way of restraint and in response to impertinence or indiscipline by them.

13.21 There were also 4 witnesses who alleged physical assaults by **Thomas** and 3 of them gave oral evidence to the Tribunal. Bearing in mind that he was at Bersham Hall for nearly 20 years, apart from 2 interruptions, the volume of complaints against him is small. He admitted that, in the climate that obtained there, he did on occasions use excessive force in restraining residents. Our conclusion is that there was a small number of occasions when he did so and others when he responded with force to provocation.

13.22 One of the Bryn Estyn staff re-deployed to Bersham Hall from Bryn Estyn was **John Ilton**[14]. We know of only 3 complaints about him at Bersham Hall, however, and he remained there from September 1984 until March 1992. None of these 3 potential witnesses provided evidence to the Tribunal but one of the incidents, which occurred on 27 September 1988, was fully investigated by

---

[14] Ibid, para 10.20.

Barnes as Principal Social Worker (Child and Family Services). The boy concerned told the police in September 1992 that he probably deserved to get a slap as he could be very abusive and that he had no complaint to make against Ilton. Similar comment was made to the police in August 1992 by the second complainant and the third did not himself allege that he had been assaulted.

13.23 More serious was an incident on 15 November 1989 involving **Frederick Marshall Jones**, who was Third Officer-in-Charge (Assistant Centre Manager) from 1 October 1989 to 30 June 1990, before succeeding Stephen Norris as Officer-in-Charge of Cartrefle. Marshall Jones had previously worked for 10 years at Chevet Hey.

13.24 In brief, the allegation was that Marshall Jones had given a disturbed boy resident a "dead leg" by kneeing him in the thigh, after a minor altercation. Visible symptoms (swelling and bruising) were subsequently observed on 2 visits to a doctor. A detailed report was sent by Thomas in December 1979 to Barnes, who himself carried out an investigation but was unable to see the victim, who was by then in a psychiatric hospital. Marshall Jones denied causing the injury and the victim ultimately accepted that it had been caused accidentally but Marshall Jones was "made aware of the risk of engaging in physical play and of the need to immediately report and log details of collisions with clients".

13.25 In our judgment the quality of care generally at Bersham Hall fell below an acceptable standard. Sexual abuse was not prevalent but there was an unacceptable reliance upon physical force for the purposes of discipline and restraint, attributable in part at least to the lack of a coherent admissions policy from 1980 onwards, with the result that much too wide a spectrum of children with problems had to be accommodated. The controlled regime geared to short stays was not suitable for those children who remained there for long periods: for them the experience was damaging and the home failed to provide them with the quality of care essential for young teenagers. Some former residents in the short stay category, however, compared Bersham Hall favourably with other homes in which they had been placed.

Chevet Hey, 1974 to 1990 (Chapter 14)

14.01 This community home was a large house set in its own grounds in the centre of a residential community in Price's Lane, Wrexham, within walking distance of the town centre. It was opened as a children's home by Denbighshire County Council at least 8 years before Clwyd County Council inherited responsibility for it; and it was described in 1971 as a home for up to 18 children of school age and over. It was re-classified as a Group 1 home on 1 January 1988 and closed in June 1990, when its functions were transferred to Gladwyn Children's Centre at Gresford.

14.02 The level of complaints and the evidence of abuse at Chevet Hey have been significantly less than at the 3 other Wrexham community homes already discussed. The general picture has been that the atmosphere of the home was much better from the children's point of view; and most of the former residents would probably say that they did not suffer any appreciable damage from their detention there. Nevertheless, there are disquieting features of its history, which we discuss in the report.

14.03 The Officer-in-Charge of Chevet Hey from 1 August 1972 until 8 March 1986 was **Enoch Ellis Edwards**, who retired about 18 months later at the age of 60 years, after serving meanwhile in the same capacity at Cherry Hill Community Home. At Chevet Hey, his wife Irene, who has been described as the dominant partner, served as Matron initially and then as Deputy Officer-in-Charge from 1 July 1979 until her husband's retirement on 30 November 1987. There were 3 successive Deputies between 1972 and 1979, one of whom **Huw Meurig Jones**[15], who was Deputy from September 1973 to 20 July 1974, needs to be mentioned. There was no complaint, however, against Meurig Jones in respect of his period as Deputy at Chevet Hey or his earlier service there for 7 months in 1972 as an RCCO.

14.04 During the first 4 years of Edwards' period Chevet Hey acted as a reception centre for boys and girls in the age range of 6 to 14 years but its role gradually changed by force of circumstances. According to Edwards, a "gridlock of children" developed because there was nowhere else to put them. The home was always full and on occasions had as many as 21 children, with some sleeping on mattresses on the floor. Edwards said also that there was too wide a mix of children, most arriving via the courts without an assessment process. Many of the former residents who gave oral evidence to us, however, spoke quite warmly of it, subject only to a qualification from 1979 about the presence of Marshall Jones[16] there.

14.05 Apart from the complaint of sexual abuse by Michael Taylor whilst he was permitted to stay briefly at Chevet Hey in the summer of 1973[17], the only complaint of abuse prior to the arrival of Marshall Jones on 2 September 1979 was that Edwards made 2 boys eat "a little bit" of soap in May 1973, after they had been caught smoking, and required one of them to stand for a long time outside Edwards' bedroom.

14.06 **Frederick Marshall Jones** was referred to by 21 of the total of 33 complainants who named identified members of the staff at Chevet Hey between 1974 and 1990. He was 39 years old when he was appointed as a temporary RCCO there and had about 5 years' experience of child care. His appointment was made permanent from 17 February 1980 and he became Third Officer-in-Charge from 1 November 1981. This was his substantive rank for the following 8 years, until he was transferred to Bersham Hall, but he acted as Deputy Officer-in-Charge and then as Officer-in-Charge between October 1986 and July 1988 because of Irene Edwards' sickness and Barnes' promotion.

14.07 We heard oral evidence from 10 of the Chevet Hey complainants about Marshall Jones and the written statement of another was admitted in evidence. There was a striking degree of consistency in their descriptions of his general

---

[15] Ibid, paras 12.05 and 12.12.
[16] Ibid, paras 13.23 and 13.24.
[17] Ibid, paras 13.09 and 13.10.

conduct and behaviour; and they singled Marshall Jones out as a particular cause of unhappiness at Chevet Hey. The causes of complaint appear to have increased rather than decreased after he became Third Officer-in-Charge.

14.08 A recurring complaint was of Marshall Jones' habit of striking residents on the knuckles or fingers with a large bunch of keys that he carried round with him or of throwing the keys at them and most of the complainants alleged that they had been victims of serious assaults by him in other ways, including punching and throwing to the floor. One of the witnesses complained also of being given "dead arms" and "dead legs" by Marshall Jones with the use of his fists. His general manner also was the subject of complaint: he was described as robust, loud and verbally aggressive to the children by one member of the staff and "brusque and sergeant-majorish" by another.

14.09 Marshall Jones denied most of these allegations in his own evidence and said that he was dedicated to child care: he would listen to young people and help and advise them. He had thrown his keys on occasions but he had never assaulted anyone with them. Marshall Jones said also that he had discussed throwing the keys with Edwards and had readily accepted Edwards' advice to stop doing so because of the risk of injury.

14.10 Although Marshall Jones had some defenders, we are compelled to the conclusion, on all the evidence about him, that his disciplinary attitude and methods were very seriously flawed throughout and that he was unfitted for all the posts, particularly the senior positions, to which he was appointed. In personal mitigation for him it can be said that he was untrained for child care work and that he received virtually no effective guidance from above throughout his period of employment as a care officer.

14.11 A cause of problems at Chevet Hey during Edwards' regime was the influx of some members of staff and residents from Bryn Estyn when it closed in September 1984. One of the members of staff transferred was **Paul Bicker Wilson**[18], who accepted the posting reluctantly from 15 October 1984 until he was suspended on 15 August 1985.

14.12 There were further complaints of physical abuse by Wilson at Chevet Hey and he himself complained of difficulties in his relationship with Edwards. In view of what we have said about Wilson earlier, however, it is sufficient to say that he was suspended pending a police investigation of complaints by 2 returned absconders from Chevet Hey who alleged that they had been roused from sleep in their respective beds by Wilson and then kicked and elbowed by him. The allegations were investigated by Edwards and 2 headquarters RDCOs promptly and then referred to the police.

14.13 The North Wales Police reported on 2 October 1985 that no further police action was to be taken in the matter. Wilson did not return to Chevet Hey and it was ultimately agreed that he should be an instructor/supervisor at a day centre from January 1986. He retired on health grounds on 31 December 1987.

---

[18] Ibid, paras 8.26, 8.27 and 10.04 to 10.12.

14.14 Wilson's complaints about Edwards led to an internal investigation by Geoffrey Wyatt as Assistant Director (Residential) early in 1986. Wyatt expressed the surprising view that "we discovered nothing in our enquiries to prevent Mr Wilson immediately returning to his duties at Chevet Hey" but other comments by him were inconsistent with this opinion. More generally, Wyatt said that he did not believe that the existing management of Chevet Hey could provide the professional and management skills that were necessary to achieve clarity in its function and excellence in its performance. His main strictures were upon Edwards, for whom he recommended transfer to a less demanding post or an offer of early retirement.

14.15 This was the background to the transfer of Edwards to Cherry Hill on 8 March 1986 and the appointment of **Michael Barnes** as Acting Officer-in-Charge from 1 April 1986 to 31 December 1987. We express the view that **Edwards** was clearly not a strong leader. His major fault relevant to our inquiry was his failure to control Marshall Jones but he was probably less to blame in relation to Wilson, of whom he was critical. It is questionable whether he ever possessed the necessary attributes to be a successful Officer-in-Charge but he and his wife did at least provide a setting that most residents recognised as a home, which was a paramount need for children in care.

14.16 It seems that Marshall Jones was left in charge at Chevet Hey for 6 months or so when Barnes was promoted to Principal Social Worker. The new Officer-in-Charge appointed with effect from 27 June 1988 was **Michael Nelson** and he remained there until Chevet Hey closed 2 years later. Most of the complaints post-April 1986 related to Marshall Jones but it is necessary to mention here 2 other members of the staff, Jacqueline Thomas and David Birch.

14.17 **Jacqueline Elizabeth Thomas** was appointed as an RCCO at Chevet Hey, from 26 February 1979, when she was 20 years old. She was suspended from duty on 3 January 1986 and dismissed on 19 January 1987.

14.18 Thomas' suspension occurred because of revelations by a boy resident at Bersham Hall on returning there from Christmas home leave on 27 December 1985. The boy (G) was interviewed by Barnes, as Officer-in-Charge of Bersham Hall, and disclosed that a gold bracelet that he had sold had been obtained from Thomas' flat. This led to admissions by G about his relationship with Thomas, including sexual intercourse with her. Further investigations, in which Geoffrey Wyatt, the Area Officer and the police were involved, revealed that a social worker for the physically handicapped, **David John Gillison**, had stayed the night of 24 December 1985 at Thomas' flat in the company of G, another boy (S) not in care and a former resident of Wrexham community homes, **William Gerry**. Thomas had been on duty that night at Chevet Hey and slept the night there.

14.19 The allegation against Thomas was that she had participated in "group sex" with G, S and Gerry at her flat but she denied it. In the event the prosecution did not proceed with any charge against her in respect of that allegation. Instead, she pleaded guilty to taking part in a more limited form of group sex at her flat in August 1985, involving only G and S. For this offence of indecent assault she was sentenced on 5 August 1986 at Wrexham Maelor Magistrates' Court to 3 months' imprisonment suspended for 2 years.

14.20 Gillison pleaded guilty on 16 January 1987 in Mold Crown Court to 2 offences of gross indecency against G, for which he received 3 years 3 months' imprisonment. Gerry, who was 20 years old at the time of the offences and who had never been employed by the SSD, was sentenced to 2 years' imprisonment for buggery with G and 4 offences of gross indecency involving both G and S. Gerry committed suicide on 1 December 1997.

14.21 We heard evidence from one former resident of Chevet Hey who alleged that Thomas indulged in sexual play with him a few times in his bedroom, the bathroom and her motor car when he was at Chevet Hey for 7 weeks at the age of 16 years.

14.22 Thomas denied these last allegations but we have no reason to doubt that they are true. She admitted having sexual intercourse with G, when he was 16 years old and had left Chevet Hey, and with S, who she thought was aged over 16 years; but she does not accept now the facts relied upon by the prosecution on the charge to which she pleaded guilty.

14.23 On sentencing Gillison and Gerry, Mr Justice Mars-Jones requested that an investigation should be carried out by Clwyd SSD into the circumstances in which Thomas and Gillison had come to occupy the positions that they held. It was not until October 1990, however, that a report was presented by the County Secretary, Roger Davies, to the Social Services (Child and Family Services) Sub-Committee. His report, which acquitted everyone of blame, was in our judgment superficial because it did not probe the many closely related problems that the judge must have had in mind and underlying problems raised by the requests of some officers during Davies' investigation for greater clarity in their instructions.

14.24 **David Gwyn Birch**[19] was transferred to Chevet Hey with effect from 1 November 1984, having worked briefly at South Meadow and Park House in Prestatyn on leaving Bryn Estyn in June 1984. He remained at Chevet Hey until 14 January 1990, when his resignation took effect, and it appears that he ranked immediately below Marshall Jones in seniority there.

14.25 Of 5 known complainants about Birch at Chevet Hey, 3 gave oral evidence to the Tribunal, one of whom was a former girl resident. One of the witnesses complained that Birch had used excessive violence in restraining him on 2 occasions but we were not impressed by these allegations. Other complaints of isolated incidents of slapping and punching were persuasive and we accept that Birch was at fault on occasions. It is to be noted, however, that all 3 witnesses said that they "got on" reasonably well with Birch and one described him as "a decent bloke". None of the incidents was the subject of a criminal charge against him.

---

[19] Ibid, paras 8.25 and 10.14 to 10.18.

14.26 There was persistent conflict between Barnes and Birch: Barnes was critical of Birch's performance of his duties and the latter was suspended for a short period in October 1986 as a result. There were complaints about Birch's time keeping and alleged absenteeism on the ground of sickness whilst he was still able to play rugby. Eventually, however, Birch secured a post as the Deputy Officer-in-Charge of a community home in Sefton from January 1990, with the aid of a favourable reference in the name of Clwyd's Director of Social Services.

14.27 Disciplinary proceedings were begun against one other member of the Chevet Hey staff shortly before the home closed. This was **Andrew Humphriss**, who spent about 11 months there between 1 May 1988 and 25 September 1989, during which time there was conflict between him and Marshall Jones. Four former residents complained of physical abuse by Humphriss but none of them provided evidence to the Tribunal. Contemporary records show that several allegations against him in January 1989 were investigated and withdrawn. The disciplinary proceedings were started because, on 24 April 1989, a local councillor reported to Barnes that he had witnessed Humphriss physically assaulting one of Chevet Hey's residents outside local swimming baths. Humphriss was suspended from duty and a date was fixed for the disciplinary hearing but his resignation (on the ground that he was disillusioned with his work) was accepted without any adverse finding against him.

14.28 To sum up, Chevet Hey had serious shortcomings as a community home, apart from the incidents of abuse that we have described. Wyatt's criticisms of the Edwards' regime were justified and were confirmed in a later memorandum by Barnes, after he had become Acting Officer-in-Charge. Barnes achieved some improvements but he had great difficulties in securing an adequate response from headquarters. The most successful period was probably the final 2 years under Nelson, when the level of complaints was much reduced and those that came to light appear to have been investigated promptly.

Cartrefle Community Home, 1974 to 1993 (Chapter 15)

15.01 Cartrefle was quite a small house, of council house appearance, on a main road next door to a police station, at Broughton, east of Hawarden. It was opened as a children's home, for up to 8 children aged between 10 and 16 years, in 1966 by Flintshire County Council. By 1979 it was described as a home for up to 10 mainly older children. It was used primarily as a resource for boys until the early 1990s, when some girls were admitted, but it was closed in March 1993.

15.02 The relevant history of Cartrefle extended from 1 December 1984, when **Stephen Norris**[20] took over as Officer-in-Charge until 17 September 1992, when his successor, **Frederick Marshall Jones**[21], was suspended from duty. We are not aware of any complaint against any identified member of the staff in respect of the 10 year period from 1974 until Norris' arrival.

---

[20] Ibid, paras 8.15 to 8.22.
[21] Ibid, paras 13.23, 13.24 and 14.06 to 14.10.

15.03 **Norris** was initially transferred to Cartrefle from Bryn Estyn as a supernumerary RCCO from 9 July 1984 but he was on sick leave for most of the following 5 months. The decision to appoint him as Officer-in-Charge was apparently made at the time of his transfer: the post was not advertised and he was not interviewed.

15.04 At Cartrefle Norris pursued for over 5 years the course of sexual abuse of boy residents that he had begun at Bryn Estyn. All but one of the 24 former residents of Cartrefle between 1984 and 1990 who complained to the police and/or the Tribunal of being abused there named Norris as an abuser: twenty alleged sexual abuse by him and 7 complained that he abused them physically. The number of complainants exceeds half of the total number of boys who came under his care at Cartrefle. We received evidence from 12 of them and it is clear that the pattern of his sexual abuse was similar to that at Bryn Estyn, except that we did not hear any evidence of further visits by him with boys to his smallholding. There were repeated indecent assaults and 4 of the 12 witnesses alleged that they had been buggered by Norris.

15.05 Norris' sexual offences were brought to a halt when a boy complained to a member of the staff with whom he was on friendly terms. Norris was suspended from duty on 18 June 1990 and he appeared at Chester Crown Court on 5 October 1990, when he pleaded guilty to 5 offences of indecent assault involving 3 boy residents at Cartrefle, for which he was sentenced to $3\frac{1}{2}$ years' imprisonment. Verdicts of not guilty were entered by the Court in respect of 3 other counts and another count was left on the Court file.

15.06 A further indictment, alleging 6 offences of buggery involving 5 boys at Cartrefle, was preferred against Norris on 11 November 1993, in the Crown Court at Knutsford, when Norris pleaded guilty to offences committed at Bryn Estyn set out in a separate indictment[22]. The order of the Court was that the further Cartrefle indictment should lie on the Court file.

15.07 When Norris gave evidence to the Tribunal, he did not make any detailed admissions but said that he had taken advantage of the boys in a sexual way. He accepted that he had abused children disastrously but he attributed the boys' failure to complain at the time to his relationship with them rather than to his position of power.

15.08 We are satisfied that the evidence that we heard from the complainants of Norris' sexual abuse of them is substantially true. The result of his activities was the complete negation of the concept of care for a wide range of boys and the wider social consequences for those children and their families of his breaches of trust are incalculable.

15.09 We express deep concern also about the response of Clwyd SSD in dealing with the children who remained in their care at Cartrefle after Norris' arrest. There was an inexcusable delay of several months in providing counselling and, when it was provided, it was both unskilled and inept.

---

[22] Ibid, para 8.17.

15.10 In relation to the allegations of physical abuse by Norris, we are satisfied that there were some occasions when he struck boys at Cartrefle with his hands and rare occasions when he did so with a belt but, in our judgment, the level of physical abuse by him was almost insignificant in comparison with the gravity of his persistent sexual abuse and his more general inadequacy as the Officer-in-Charge.

15.11 We heard severe criticisms of the regime and conditions at Cartrefle whilst Norris was in charge. The home was described as a "Mickey Mouse" operation: it was neglected and run down. It was said that Norris was incapable of running the home administratively: he was almost illiterate and unable to deal with routine paperwork in an acceptable manner. There were no directions for the children and nothing for them to do other than watch television. One staff witness was also sufficiently concerned about the level of violence in the home to make a log entry to that effect.

15.12 **Marshall Jones** took over as temporary or acting Officer-in-Charge on 8 July 1990 and the appointment was made permanent from about 1 December 1990. The post was not advertised (apparently by mistake) and Marshall Jones was not interviewed; but he had been interviewed by a panel on 19 September 1989 prior to his appointment to a post at Bersham Hall.

15.13 Marshall Jones was suspended from duty on 17 September 1992 as the result of a preliminary investigation triggered by reports from a NUPE representative, who had relayed anxieties of members of the staff at Cartrefle about Marshall Jones' conduct towards the children. The general tenor of the complaints was that his behaviour towards the resident children was threatening and intimidating and that, on occasions, he would use physical force to them.

15.14 Particular incidents of which the staff spoke had occurred shortly after Christmas 1991 and on or about 10 August 1992, immediately before a trip to France. We heard evidence from 2 former residents about these incidents and also about an alleged assault on one of them whilst they were in France. Marshall Jones denied using any violence on these occasions and one member of staff gave him support in her evidence. Our conclusion about his period at Cartrefle, however, is that he was very ill-suited to the particularly difficult task that he had been set. He continued to rule by intimidation, which affected other members of the staff as well as the children, and he resorted to violence on some occasions when dealing with provocative and difficult boys. We are not satisfied, however, that he regularly used excessive force during this period and there were some positive aspects to his regime.

15.15 Marshall Jones, who died on 23 December 1998, remained in limbo following his suspension until his employment was terminated by agreement on the ground of redundancy on 30 November 1994. He was not prosecuted.

15.16 We deal with a small number of allegations against other members of the staff at Cartrefle in the period between 1974 and 1993. One woman member of staff had to resign from her post on 14 September 1990, following her admission that she had had a sexual relationship with a boy resident, who was just over

16 years old at the time. Another woman member of the staff was dismissed in November 1988 for causing a boy undue distress by the disciplinary action that she took against him, following a written warning to her 6 months earlier. The other complaints, however, do not affect the general picture that we have given of Cartrefle.

15.17 In November 1990, following Norris' first conviction and sentence, Clwyd County Council instructed John Banham, a retired senior officer of Cheshire SSD to act as an independent reviewing officer and to report on the events that had occurred at Cartrefle. Clwyd ACPC then called for agency case reviews from the Health Authority and the Education Department in an attempt to conform with procedures recommended in Part Nine of Working Together (1988)[23].

15.18 This procedure was, in our view, misconceived and the reports could not be published for several reasons that are discussed in Chapter 32 of this Tribunal's report[24]. The 3 reports were presented by June 1991 and Clwyd ACPC then appointed a panel of 5 senior professionals to provide an independent overview, which was received in February 1992.

15.19 Our general conclusion is that, despite the fact that Cartrefle was a purpose built community home, caring for quite a small number of children, its history from 1984 onwards was disastrous. At the root of the problem was unsuitable staffing but there was a wide spectrum of other failures, highlighted, in particular, by the Banham report. The consequences of all these failings were highly damaging to the individual children, many with serious problems, who were placed at Cartrefle; and there was a signal failure in 1990 to tackle the special problems of each of the children who had been affected, directly or indirectly, by Norris' persistent abuse.

The other four local authority community homes in Clwyd (Chapters 16 and 17)

Complaints of abuse at these other homes that we have examined in detail were significantly fewer than those that we have already discussed.

16.01 **Cherry Hill Community Home** is included in the report only because it provides further evidence of the failure of Clwyd SSD to tackle adequately the problems of the children who had been affected by Norris' sexual abuse at Cartrefle and other potentially abusive children.

16.02 Cherry Hill is a large house in a well established residential area on the outskirts of Wrexham. It was opened by Denbighshire County Council on 1 January 1971 as a home for up to 11 children of school age and over (usually teenagers). Later, the age range of children was widened to include youngsters from 7 years old but the number of children was reduced to 8. It remains open and is now a 6 bedded unit for young people aged 14 to 17 years.

[23] Department of Health and Welsh Office: HMSO.
[24] See paras 32.14 to 32.16 of this Summary.

16.03 We have not received directly any complaints of child abuse at Cherry Hill.

16.04 There were 9 boys, in the age range of 9 to 16 years, at Cartrefle when Norris was suspended on 18 June 1990; 2 of them, who disclosed that they had been abused, were transferred to Cherry Hill and Gladwyn respectively and 2 brothers were transferred later to Llwyn Onn; the other 5 remained at Cartrefle, where they received limited counselling some months later. Of the 4 boys who had been moved, there were 2 at Cherry Hill by May 1992, following further movements between homes.

16.05 By November 1992 there was concern that a boy was "doing things" to other boys at Cherry Hill and by March 1993 there was increased anxiety because 3 boys were said to be engaged in sexual activity with each other. Some other persons also were thought to have been involved. Child protection conferences were held but little positive action ensued. A report outlining possible treatment for the 3 boys and training for the Cherry Hill staff was obtained from a child therapist in June 1993 but desultory correspondence before and after it was received did not result in any progress being made.

16.06 In the light of the documents to which we refer in our report, it was clear by February 1993 that a major management issue had arisen. A multi-agency planning group was then established and continued in existence until January 1994, when (it was said) the group's work was completed. In our judgment, however, there were serious breaches of good practice because the local authority failed (a) to arrange a speedy investigation of the facts; (b) to hold immediate case conferences as soon as the basic facts had been determined; (c) to make firm decisions about the disposal and treatment of the children and implement them; and (d) to provide training and guidance for the residential care staff dealing with the children.

17.01 **Upper Downing Community Home** was a very large old country mansion set in secluded grounds at Whitford, near Holywell. It was opened in 1948 as a home for 48 older boys and girls but in the 1971 Regional Plan it was described as providing accommodation for up to 24 children. By then the intention was that it should be replaced in 1973 by homes in St Asaph and Prestatyn but it survived until 31 January 1977, latterly as a reception centre.

17.02 We are aware only of 5 complainants who were resident at Upper Downing after 1 April 1974.

17.03 Of these complainants, 3 alleged that they had been sexually abused by a gardener/driver at the home, who is now dead. The last of these was aged 17 years in March 1976, when she alleged that this man had had sexual intercourse with her after making her drunk during an evening trip to Holywell. A policeman came across her in the town at 2.35 am and a full investigation took place. There was no prosecution but the gardener/driver was first suspended and then dismissed on 16 June 1976 for gross misconduct in various respects. He was a shop steward of NUPE and an Industrial Tribunal subsequently upheld his claim of unfair dismissal on the ground of procedural unfairness. The Tribunal found also that he had contributed to his dismissal to the extent of 50 per cent and awarded him £507.20. He was not re-employed by Clwyd County Council.

17.04 The dismissed man reported to Geoffrey Wyatt that a probationary woman member of the care staff had been allowing a 15 year old boy resident of Upper Downing (K) to spend a lot of time in her bedroom and that she was drinking heavily. By that time K had been transferred to Little Acton and members of the staff there expressed concern that K was receiving frequent letters from the woman. The upshot of Wyatt's investigation was that the woman's period of probation was extended by 6 months on the ground that her first period of employment had not been entirely satisfactory but no other adverse finding was made against her. A coded note received by K from the woman has survived and we heard oral evidence from him of his sexual relationship with her, which she denied in a written statement to the Tribunal. We are satisfied, however, that K gave us an essentially truthful account of the relationship.

17.05 The only other relevant complaint was by a girl resident, who alleged that she was punched in the face and knocked over a settee by a young male member of the staff in the summer of 1976, with the result that she sustained a black eye and a swollen finger. Her injuries were seen by a social worker, but she did not wish to make a formal complaint. Her assailant was employed only briefly at Upper Downing and was not regarded as a suitable residential care worker; he left to work as a postman.

17.06 The former residents of Upper Downing whose evidence we have seen have, in general, described their time in the home as happy: it seems that a genuine effort was made to create a homely atmosphere, even though most of the care staff were untrained.

17.07 **South Meadow Community Home** in Ffordd Ffrith, Prestatyn, was also quite a long established children's home. It was a large house in the centre of a residential area and it was opened by Flintshire County Council as a home for up to 12 children on or about 1 January 1967. There was a cottage in the grounds providing accommodation for some of the staff but it was used later to provide residents with training for independence. The home survived until 14 September 1990, when its functions were transferred to Cefndy Hostel, Rhyl, which was re-named New South Meadow. The latter premises took over also the functions of Park House in August 1991 but the amalgamated unit itself closed in October 1993.

17.08 We know of only 9 complainants who were resident at South Meadow during the period between 1974 and 1990 and one of them was unable to identify the member of the staff alleged to have hit him.

17.09 The Officer-in-Charge for approximately the first half of this period was **Joan Glover**, against whom 4 former residents made complaints. She returned to South Meadow in that capacity on 1 January 1974, after obtaining the CRCCYP at Salford Institute of Technology, having previously served for 3 years at South Meadow as a housemother; and she remained until 27 March 1981, when she left to take up a post as a housemother with the Pentecostal Child Care Association.

17.10 There were complaints about Glover's conduct by both members of the staff and children. She received a written warning and reprimand from the Director of Social Services, dated 3 October 1975, in relation to an incident on 26 August 1975, when she caught hold of a 13 year old girl resident from behind, turned her round and slapped her in the face. By 1979, other members of the staff had become very restive about Glover's conduct towards the children and, on 21 June 1979, they reported their concerns to the Area Officer. They alleged that Glover was shouting at the children, extremely irritable and very tense, impatient and intolerant.

17.11 Glover underwent some medical treatment following this report but there was no improvement in her behaviour and she was given 4 weeks' leave from 1 September 1979. It was agreed also that she would become non-resident from that date. Unfortunately, there was no significant improvement on her return from leave and the staff were again expressing anxiety about her in the last 2 months of that year. No steps were taken to remedy the situation, however, until it resolved itself with Glover's new appointment.

17.12 Two former residents of South Meadow confirmed this general picture of Glover's behaviour. One of them described how Glover had had an obsession about her, treating her as if she had been Glover's own child, but abusing her physically on many occasions. Glover herself accepted that she had "lost her rag" at times, usually shouting on those occasions, and that she had sometimes slapped children, but only once across the face. Our conclusion is that the staff concerns about her behaviour were fully justified and that the 2 complainants who gave evidence to us gave a fair picture of her conduct. In our opinion she had serious temperamental or character defects, which disabled her from carrying out her work as Officer-in-Charge in an appropriate manner.

17.13 Clwyd SSD was at fault in failing to monitor Glover's performance after 1975 adequately and then in failing after September 1979 to remove her from her post, bearing in mind the earlier written warning that she had received.

17.14 Glover's successor as Officer-in-Charge from 3 August 1981 was **Glyn Williams** (after a short interregnum) and he remained in post at South Meadow and then New South Meadow until February 1992. The role of South Meadow changed because it became the home of 6 wards of court from the same family in or about 1981. There was a further change in 1985 when it became an adolescent unit and was re-categorised as a Group 1 home.

17.15 Numbers rose in this last period and conditions became more difficult because older residents with varied behavioural problems were admitted but there were no allegations of substantial physical abuse by members of staff in this later period and no allegations of sexual abuse throughout the period under review.

17.16 **Park House Community Home,** a large, old 2 storey building in Nant Hall Road, Prestatyn, was opened by Flintshire County Council in 1972 as a community home for up to 12 boys and girls in the age range of 10 to 17 years. It remained open until 31 July 1991, when the remaining residents moved to New South Meadow in Rhyl.

17.17 There were comparatively few allegations of child abuse at Park House but wider shortcomings were disclosed by successive reports in 1975, 1980 and 1988 and little action appears to have been taken to address them.

17.18 The first 2 of these reports were made during the period when **Mary Ellis** was Officer-in-Charge. She was appointed to that post by Flintshire County Council on 1 September 1973, when she was 46 years old, and she remained there until 31 March 1981, when she took early retirement.

17.19 The 1975 report was made by Gledwyn Jones (Deputy Director of Social Services) and Geoffrey Wyatt (then Principal Social Worker), following adverse publicity that had resulted from a campaign by a local resident to secure closure of the home, ostensibly on the ground that children were being ill-treated there. This person had, 'inter alia', instigated and drafted a letter from a girl resident at the home to the *News of the World.*

17.20 The finding of the two man panel was that there had been obvious collusion between the author and the signatory of the letter and most of the complaints in it were dismissed. The report did, however, state that there was a need for a less rigid regime and it made criticisms of the administration of Park House, particularly in relation to control and discipline.

17.21 The investigation in 1980 arose from complaints by staff that were pursued through NALGO. It was carried out by a Clwyd inspector of residential homes and his 2 reports drew attention again to many administrative failings at Park House. They showed also that considerable indiscipline was occurring and that the attitudes of staff to resident children were unsatisfactory. Record keeping was defective and the inspector commented adversely on the ways in which punishments were administered. Mary Ellis herself was described as "a somewhat over-conscientious, anxious person who was convinced that her approach to her work was appropriate and considered to be 'good child practice'".

17.22 Ellis' successor as Officer-in-Charge of Park House for most of its remaining period as a community home was **Jeffrey Douglas**. He started as Deputy to Ellis on 1 March 1981, his 39th birthday, and was then Officer-in-Charge from 1 April 1981 until 31 October 1988, when he became a social worker in the Alyn and Deeside area. Douglas was, however, absent from September 1986 to July 1988, taking the CQSW course. In his absence the Acting Officer-in-Charge was **David Evans**, who had been Deputy there and at South Meadow. He succeeded Douglas as Officer-in-Charge of Park House from 1 August 1989 to 31 July 1991 and then became Deputy at New South Meadow until he retired on 31 December 1992.

17.23 The 1988 inquiry followed a holiday visit at the end of August 1988 to Butlins Holiday Camp at Pwllheli by 5 boys and 4 girls from Park House under the supervision of 5 members of the staff. A 13 years old girl in the group became friendly with a young man at the camp and told a friend that she had had sexual intercourse with the man on the last night of her holiday. The holiday had been arranged before Douglas returned to Park House and he disapproved of it but it was thought to be impracticable to cancel it by the time that he learnt of it.

17.24 A member of staff was told of the girl's disclosure and the police carried out an investigation but the offender could not be traced. Clwyd County Council set up a three member panel "to enquire into and consider all aspects of the planning and execution" of the holiday. In the event, the panel's report did not give any account of what had occurred during the holiday but it did contain scathing criticism of the state of residential child care in Clwyd at that time. Amongst its criticisms were that staff were not familiar with child protection procedures, the lack of a county-wide policy for residential child care, the need for specific aims and objectives for each individual residential care establishment and the failure to establish individual care plans for each child resident.

17.25 The panel's report was sent to the Director of Social Services (by now, Gledwyn Jones) on 11 September 1989 but it was seen by very few others. Jones' recollection was that copies were given to Wyatt, John Llewellyn Thomas and Barnes. It seems that Barnes drafted a response but it remained a draft only. The report was never debated in either the Social Services Committee or the Council and Gledwyn Jones' explanation for this was that he "wanted to move quickly on doing something about the recommendations". It was not until 18 December 1990 that Gledwyn Jones presented his own report to the Children and Family Services Sub-Committee on group care holidays for children in community homes, saying that it was in response to "national concerns that group holidays arranged by local authorities needed to be properly planned". At the same time a code of practice for such holidays was drafted.

17.26 Shortly before this, Michael Barnes met the Park House staff with representatives of 2 trades unions to give them "feedback" on the report. They were told that the main findings were that no one person or group was to blame, that there had been a system failure, that lessons were to be learned at every operational level and that action was being taken on the recommendations.

17.27 There were a few contemporary complaints of abuse in the period between 1981 and 1991. One complaint in 1981 or 1982 was of alleged slippering of 3 girls on returning from absconding. Another, by 2 girls who alleged in November 1989 that Evans had "touched their bottoms", led to Evans' suspension from duty for about 6 weeks whilst it was investigated. But the evidence that we received in support of these allegations was too unsatisfactory for us to find them proved. A Child Protection Conference in November 1989 concluded that one of the complainants had not been abused and the CPS advised against a prosecution.

17.28 **Frederick Rutter**[25] served as an RCCO at Park House from October 1984 to 28 August 1988. His subsequent convictions in July 1991, for rapes and indecent assaults committed after 1 February 1988 at his home and a hostel, are dealt with in Chapter 26 but he was not convicted of any offence committed at Park House. One former resident of Park House with a disturbed background alleged in written statements that he had raped her twice, once in his motor car and later at the community home, but she was unwilling to give oral evidence and there were inconsistencies in her statements. Her allegations, which were

---

[25] Ibid, paras 8.28, 10.26 and 10.27.

denied by Rutter, were uncorroborated and it is unlikely that a jury would feel able to convict on her evidence, despite Rutter's record of subsequent offences.

17.29 Other allegations against Rutter at Park House were comparatively minor, although it is clear that it was his practice to kiss some girl residents goodnight and that he shared part of a tent with another girl one night on a camping holiday. Two complaints against him, one of which was of hitting a girl on the side of her face, were investigated soon after the incidents occurred and we do not criticise the way in which they were dealt with.

17.30 It is notable that some residents at Park House were prepared to complain to members of the staff even before a formal complaints procedure was initiated by Barnes very late on, probably because they were, in general, long term residents. It is likely that residents who could withstand peer pressure and accommodate a degree of turbulence felt safe there but we have grave reservations about the extent to which the needs of individual children were met and the adequacy of the guidance and training for independent living that was provided.

ALLEGED ABUSE OF CHILDREN IN CARE IN OTHER NON-PRIVATE RESIDENTIAL ESTABLISHMENTS IN CLWYD BETWEEN 1974 AND 1996 (Chapters 18 to 20)

In this part of the report we deal with 3 such establishments, namely, **Tanllwyfan** (an assisted community home), **Ysgol Talfryn** (a local authority school) and **Gwynfa** (an NHS clinic for children). In general, the level of abuse in these establishments was less than in the worse local authority community homes but we have serious concerns about the vulnerability of children to sexual abuse in the first and last of them and the quality of care in the latter two. We received complaints of physical abuse occurring at each of them.

Tanllwyfan, 1974 to 1984 (Chapter 18)

18.01 Tanllwyfan is a former farmhouse standing in 5 acres of land at Penmaen Head, Old Colwyn. It was opened in 1916 by the Boys and Girls Welfare Society and it closed on 31 December 1984. The home was operated by the Society and Clwyd County Council, under an instrument of management, as an assisted community home for up to 18 boys and girls in the junior age range. Management was vested in a local committee, including 3 county councillors, which met monthly at Tanllwyfan.

18.02 A major cause of anxiety in relation to Tanllwyfan is that 2 members of the staff there have since been prosecuted for sexual offences against young boys.

18.03 **Kenneth Scott** was a care assistant at Tanllwyfan from 1974 to 1976, rising to the position of Third Officer-in-Charge before he left. He pleaded guilty 10 years later, on 28 February 1986 in Leicester Crown Court, to 2 offences of buggery and 3 offences of gross indecency, for which he was sentenced to a total of 8 years imprisonment. The offences had been committed between 1982 and 1985 at a children's home in Leicestershire, of which Scott had been Officer-in-Charge from May 1978 until his arrest in July 1985.

18.04 Scott did not have any criminal convictions before he worked at Tanllwyfan or during his service there but 6 former residents complained to the North Wales police in 1991/1993 that Scott had sexually abused them. We heard oral evidence from 2 of these complainants of indecent assaults by Scott upon them and we have no doubt that their allegations are true.

18.05 We are perturbed to record also that Scott was employed from 1991 to 1993, on his release from prison, as a warden at a youth hostel for the YHA. According to Scott's written statement to the Tribunal, the YHA were unaware of his convictions but his work "was involved with adults in the main".

18.06 **Richard Francis Groome** was Warden of Tanllwyfan from 7 August 1976 and his wife was Domestic Bursar. They remained in their respective posts until 11 November 1982. Groome went on from there to Clwyd Hall School as head of care and then principal until he left in April 1984 to found his own therapeutic community for young people at Bishop's Castle, Shropshire.

18.07 Groome is due to be tried early in 2000 at Mold Crown Court on charges alleging sexual offences involving one former boy resident at Tanllwyfan, 4 at Clwyd Hall School and others at establishments in Shropshire between 1981 and 1989. He has no previous convictions.

18.08 We know that 5 former residents of Tanllwyfan made complaints to the police in 1991/1993 about Groome but none alleged that he sexually abused any boys there.

18.09 There were very few complaints against any other members of the staff at Tanllwyfan. Groome's predecessor as Officer-in-Charge did impose a strict regime, giving rise to some anxiety in the Welsh Office, but that had been ameliorated by 1975.

18.10 Our conclusion is that Tanllwyfan achieved some success between 1974 and 1984 in caring for an appreciable number of quite disturbed children over long periods. In general, corporal punishment was effectively prohibited: on the few occasions when physical force was used, it was usually in very provocative circumstances and the degree of force used was moderate. Such pointers as we have to the quality of care suggest that it compared favourably with that provided in local authority community homes in North Wales of similar size and purpose.

Ysgol Talfryn (Chapter 19)

19.01 This was a new Clwyd Education Authority day and residential school near Holywell, with a Board of Governors, providing education for children aged 6 to 16 years with emotional and behavioural difficulties. It was opened as a day school in April 1978 but 4 residential units, each accommodating 10 children, were brought into use between 1980 and 1982. At its peak in the summer of 1988 there were 63 pupils on the roll, of whom 31 were residents. The school was still open in 1999 but there were then only 22 day pupils and its future is uncertain.

19.02 It is clear from the successive reports of HM Inspectors that Ysgol Talfryn has had an up and down history in the first 2 decades of its existence, although it has met a widespread need.

19.03 There was only one complaint to the police, in 1992, of sexual abuse by a member of staff at the school. The complainant, who was still a minor at the time of his complaint, was then serving a sentence of imprisonment for rape and his allegation was uncorroborated. No prosecution ensued and he has not provided any evidence to the Tribunal.

19.04 Allegations of physical abuse, or complicity in such abuse, involved 10 identified members of the staff and one unidentified member but the majority of the staff named were the subject of single allegations only (there were 17 complainants in all).

19.05 We heard oral evidence from 3 of those complainants, who were all in care when resident at Ysgol Talfryn; and we saw substantial documentary evidence relating to one of the incidents described (child protection procedure was set in train in respect of it). On the limited evidence before us it would be wrong to conclude that there was regular physical abuse but we are satisfied that in the 1980s there were occasions when excessive force was used in the restraint of troublesome pupils and other occasions when improper physical chastisement occurred.

19.06 The report of HMIs in 1988 revealed that none of the teaching staff had received any training in dealing with emotionally and behaviourally disturbed children. We regard such training as essential for teachers as well as care staff in any school catering for such children.

19.07 Although the quality of care is said to have improved latterly, it was disappointing prior to 1993, particularly in the standard of residential accommodation. The school began with quite high aspirations in this respect but there seems to have been a progressive decline, mainly because of inadequate financial resources.

Gwynfa Residential Unit (Chapter 20)

20.01 This unit was established in 1961 as an NHS psychiatric hospital for children in upper Colwyn Bay. The residential unit, known as a clinic, was administered by the Health Authority (in its successive forms) and the school by Clwyd County Council from 1974. By then it was providing accommodation for up to 25 (later 18) emotionally disturbed and maladjusted children and it was described as the residential extension of the North Wales Child Guidance Clinic Service, which was responsible for offering and monitoring all admissions.

20.02 The unit closed in March 1997, when its services were transferred to Cedar Grove, on the outskirts of Colwyn Bay. Latterly, Gwynfa had provided 12 in-patient places and 6 day places.

20.03 We are dismayed to record that by the end of the Tribunal's hearings there were 27 complainants who were known to have alleged that they had been abused whilst they were at Gwynfa. A total of 23 former patients made complaints relating to the period between 1974 and 1987 and it is reasonably clear that 13 of these were in care at the time when they were resident in Gwynfa.

20.04 There were 5 internal investigations or reviews of the conduct of specific members of the nursing staff at Gwynfa between 1986 and 1996.

20.05 A 45 years old nursing auxiliary, **Robert Martin Williams**, was convicted on 14 March 1997 in Mold Crown Court of 2 offences of rape upon a 16 years old girl patient, for which he was sentenced to 6 years' imprisonment. The offences were committed in the summer of 1991, when the victim was not in care but was suffering from a depressive disorder. She had not felt able to disclose the offences to the police until January 1996 but she gave oral evidence to the Tribunal. An investigation had been carried out in 1991 by Clwyd Health

Authority, following the discovery of an incriminating letter in the girl's clothing, but Williams, who denied committing any offence, resigned then before he could be dismissed.

20.06 Another member of the staff (Z), who joined the staff in April 1974, was the subject of allegations by 10 complainants, 6 of whom alleged various forms of sexual abuse. The NHS Trust responsible for Gwynfa became aware of some of these allegations in the course of the major police investigation and suspended Z from duty in July 1993. At a later stage, on legal advice, Z was transferred to other duties not involving nursing children, but he was suspended again when further allegations were made against him. We were unable to hear evidence relating to the complaints against Z (save for one witness when Z's legal position was unclear) because of the continuing police investigations in respect of him in the course of our hearings. By March 1999 the CPS had advised that a prosecution would not be justified but, as far as we are aware, Z remained suspended, pending possible disciplinary proceedings, when the Tribunal's report was signed.

20.07 Allegations of sexual abuse were made against 2 other members of the Gwynfa staff: one was alleged to have touched a 13 years old girl indecently in 1978/1979 but she did not report the matter; and the other was alleged to have committed buggery with a 17 years old male patient in 1979/1980 but the alleged offence did not come to light until August 1992.

20.08 Allegations of physical abuse were made against about 8 identified members of the staff, including Williams and Z, but 7 of the complainants were unable to identify their assailants.

20.09 We heard evidence from 14 former patients of Gwynfa in all, 3 of whom gave oral evidence, but the picture that we received of conditions at Gwynfa was incomplete and we have not attempted to reach detailed conclusions about the regime there. It is clear, however, that sexual abuse did occur during the period under review and that on occasions unjustified physical force was used by staff members. All but one of the complaints, however, related to events prior to the end of 1985.

20.10 In the light of the evidence before us there is a strong argument for greater social services involvement in residential clinics of this kind and the introduction of some trained residential care staff. It is arguable also that senior staff should have an appropriate qualification in residential child care, whether or not they are nursing officers primarily.

ALLEGED ABUSE OF CHILDREN IN CARE IN PRIVATE RESIDENTIAL ESTABLISHMENTS IN CLWYD BETWEEN 1974 AND 1996 (Chapters 21 to 23)

In this part we give an account of alleged abuse in children's homes or residential schools run by 3 separate private organisations, namely, the Bryn Alyn Community, Care Concern and Clwyd Hall for Child Welfare. Sexual and physical abuse occurred in many of the establishments for which those organisations were responsible and the trial of one relevant officer for alleged offences has yet to take place. There is cause for public concern also about the level of physical abuse in some of the homes and the quality of care in all of them.

The Bryn Alyn Community (Chapter 21)

21.01 This Community, founded by **John Ernest Allen**, has attracted the most widespread public criticism.

21.02 Bryn Alyn was first established as a children's home in April 1969 by Allen in partnership with his wife-to-be, his parents and an uncle. He had acquired, the year before, a lease of Bryn Alyn Hall, with 50 acres, near Wrexham; and the partnership opened it as a children's home for up to 20 boys, in the age range of 11 to 16 years, with 9 care staff and one teacher with experience in remedial training. None of the care staff, apart from Allen and his future wife, had any previous experience of residential work or any formal qualification.

21.03 A private limited company, Bryn Alyn Community Limited, was formed to succeed the partnership in 1972 and it continued to trade until 1995, when restructuring into a holding company and a trading company took place. The trading company went into voluntary liquidation on 6 March 1997. Allen remained as Chief Executive until 1990, when he retired, ostensibly on health grounds.

21.04 The other person most closely involved in the business financially was **Kenneth White, senior**, an hotelier who sold his hotel to the company in July 1977. In or about 1980 he invested £300,000 in the company in return for a salary and an income on his investment, and it seems that he became Finance Director from August 1984. White senior gave evidence to the Tribunal but died at the end of 1997. It seems that Allen was "paid off" in 1991 and that White senior held most of the shares thereafter. Kenneth White senior's son, Kenneth J White or Kenneth White junior, then became increasingly prominent in the business and joined the board of directors.

21.05 From time to time Bryn Alyn Community acquired no less than 11 properties, mainly in the Wrexham area but including Marton's Camp in Cheshire and Cotsbrook Hall in Shropshire. Allen estimated that, at its peak, the Community was accommodating about 200 children and adolescents; and other evidence suggests that the total occupancy in Clwyd alone exceeded 150 at times during the 1980s. According to Allen, the aim was to provide an environment that was as close as possible to that of a family: it was to be "stimulating and responsive, a therapeutic environment".

21.06 Allen claimed that, at the height of the company's trading, which he put in the mid-1980s, its annual turnover was about £2.6m and the profit of the order of £80,000 to £90,000. Accounts between 1977 and 1990 show that the total turnover, made up almost entirely of payments by local authorities, was £28.25m. Allen's salary in 1988 was shown as £204,894 (by 1990, it was £50,000).

21.07 The vast majority of residents were in care and were placed with the Community by local authority social service departments. We understand that, initially, placements by authorities in the north east may have predominated but subsequently there were placements by authorities throughout England. However, there was no child from South Wales on the list of 172 complainants, 9 of whom were placed by Clwyd and 8 by Gwynedd.

21.08 The most deplorable fact about the Community is that 28 former male residents alleged that they were sexually abused by **Allen** whilst they were resident there, of whom 6 alleged that they were buggered by him. Of these potential witnesses, 6 gave oral evidence to the Tribunal and we received in evidence the statements of 6 others.

21.09 Allen was convicted, on 9 February 1995 in the Crown Court at Chester, of 6 offences of indecent assault committed on 6 separate male residents between 1972 and 1983. He was acquitted of 4 other counts of indecent assault, involving 4 other residents, but another 4 gave "similar fact" evidence. He was sentenced to 6 concurrent terms of 6 years' imprisonment. Allen denied all the offences and maintained his denial when he gave oral evidence to the Tribunal in February 1998 but there has not been any appeal. In all 19 former residents have given oral or written evidence at Allen's trial and/or to the Tribunal of alleged sexual abuse by him.

21.10 In the report we give an account of the evidence of some of these witnesses who described sexual offences committed by Allen against them at the various Community residences such as Bryn Alyn Hall itself, Bryntirion Hall, Gwastad Hall, Poyser Street studios in Wrexham, Gatewen Hall, Pentre Saeson and a flat at Rhosllanerchrugog. They spoke also of substantial gifts made to them by Allen of money, clothes, musical instruments, motor cycles, pedal cycles, record players and other valuable objects.

21.11 Witnesses C and G gave accounts of staying in Brighton after leaving the Community. C went there in or about 1986 at Allen's suggestion and rented a flat, which Allen paid for. The sexual relationship between them continued until the early 1990s. G received large presents of money from Allen after leaving Bryn Alyn and eventually moved to Brighton, where he saw Allen. It was G's brother who died in a fire at another flat in Brighton on 18 April 1992, in circumstances which gave rise to a police investigation. G himself died on 1 February 1995, after giving evidence at Allen's trial but before it was concluded: the inquest verdict was that the cause of his death was "non-dependent abuse of drugs".

21.12 Despite Allen's continuing denials of improper conduct, we are fully satisfied that he was rightly convicted and that those offences were merely a sample of his overall offending.

21.13 We do not have adequate material on which to reach confident conclusions about Allen's motivation in his non-sexual activities but it is fair to say that his reputation was that of a caring and generous person.

21.14 From the late 1980s Allen became less involved with the Community as financial difficulties arose and White senior assumed the dominant role. Allen then turned his attention elsewhere, to London and Brighton particularly, where he and/or the company Bryn Alyn Care Limited had acquired various properties (Allen took over that company in the 1991 financial settlement). It appears that these properties were used, probably mainly, to house young men who had been discharged from care but it has not been within the scope of our terms of reference to investigate these later activities of Allen. Such evidence as we have heard has given us some cause for concern and has underlined the vulnerability of many young persons on leaving care.

21.15 We are satisfied that there was some contemporaneous discussion or gossip about Allen's predilections amongst both staff and residents. There were rumours amongst the residents about his liking for particular boys but they did not amount to a great deal. These rumours were known to some members of the staff but they do not appear to have taken them seriously.

21.16 Two other members of the Community staff were convicted of sexual offences and a third was the subject of police investigations in the course of our hearings but he died suddenly on 8 August 1998.

21.17 **Anthony Taylor** was convicted on 6 January 1976 at Talgarth Magistrates' Court and fined. It seems probable, from what Taylor wrote to the Welsh Office, that the offences occurred during a summer holiday that he organised for the Community and that the victims were from Newcastle-upon-Tyne. He was dismissed after he had been convicted. We received evidence from 3 of 4 complainants who alleged that they were abused sexually by him and we accept that his assaults were not confined to the offences of which he was convicted but also occurred in dormitories at Bryntirion Hall, where he was on the staff, and included oral sex with one of the complainants.

21.18 **Iain Muir** was Deputy Headteacher of the Community school in the mid 1980s and he was convicted on 22 July 1986, in the Crown Court at Mold, of unlawful sexual intercourse in June 1985 with a 15 years old girl resident of Bryn Alyn Hall. Muir was sentenced to 6 months' imprisonment for the offence, which he admitted, and he either resigned or was dismissed. The offence occurred at Muir's flat in Wrexham following a weekend leave that the girl had spent with him in Hertfordshire. It came to light 4 months later, when she confided in a fellow resident, who informed her Team Leader.

21.19 The deceased former member of staff was the subject of 4 complaints of sexual abuse and 12 of physical abuse. According to Allen, he was a qualified residential care officer who worked for the Community from 1977, latterly as Officer-in-Charge of Pentre Saeson Hall from 1983, until he was suspended from duty in or about April 1992 and then dismissed in January 1993. We did not hear evidence in support of the allegations against him, of varying gravity, because of the continuing police investigation.

21.20 About 28 former residents of the Community have made complaints of indecent assaults by other members of the staff; 7 were unable to identify the staff member and the other 21 named 17 of the staff in all. Three women former residents alleged that they had been raped and 3 of the men alleged buggery. The spread of these allegations has been such that no pattern of misconduct by particular individuals has emerged. We heard evidence from 8 of these complainants, 4 of whom gave oral evidence but, in view of the passage of time and the lack of corroboration, we could not reach firm conclusions about the guilt of individuals.

21.21 The principal witness for the Welsh Office, John Lloyd, told us of 2 allegations of sexual abuse at the Community's premises that were reported to the Welsh Office between 1989 and 1992 . One of these was an allegation against a Team Leader. No prosecution ensued in either case and neither alleged abuser was dismissed.

21.22 Our conclusions are that (John Allen apart) sexual abuse by members of the Community's staff was not rife but that it did occur to a significant and disturbing extent. The comparatively few girl residents were specially vulnerable to this and, in our judgment, the organisation and structure of the Community and its premises were never suitably adapted for co-educational purposes. Paedophile activity in relation to boys was dominated by that of Allen himself. Otherwise, it appears to have been sporadic and less likely to be detected for that reason. It is a cause for grave concern, however, that so many members of staff were named in the major police investigation, even though the allegations against particular individuals were limited in number.

21.23 In paragraphs 21.58 to 21.106 of the report we discuss allegations of physical abuse made by 139 former residents with the Community, 121 of whom named a total of 49 members of staff as alleged abusers (10 of them were accused also of sexual abuse). The other 18 former residents were unable to identify the alleged aggressor.

21.24 **John Allen** himself was named by 14 of these former residents and we heard evidence from 7 of them. Most alleged that they had been punched by him. Allen denied the allegations but we are satisfied that he did punch and slap residents on occasions when he was angry about what they had said and done. We do not think, however, that he was an habitually violent man: the complaints against him of using excessive physical force are heavily outweighed in gravity by the allegations against him of sexual misconduct.

21.25 Another main target of complaint was **Peter Steen**, who was named by 19 complainants. He worked for the Community as a residential care worker (with no professional training) from 1976 to 1993, with a break of about 12 months in or about 1986. The largest volume of complaints (12) related to Steen's period at Gatewen Hall from 1987 on, where he played the role of "troubleshooter" and where, later, residents were older than before and proved to be more difficult to control. Steen, who played the same role earlier at Bryntirion Hall, said in evidence that he made several requests for training in physical restraint but was told that none was available.

21.26 In the light of the evidence that we recount and Steen's own admission that he did lose his temper from time to time, we have no doubt that he did use excessive force on occasions in restraining both boy and girl residents. The overall volume of complaints is, however, moderate (if that is an appropriate word) having regard to the nature of his role and the absence of any guidance as to how to perform it.

21.27 A more senior member of the staff who performed a similar role at times was **Keith Allan Evans**, nicknamed "Beef", who was employed by the Community from 1974 to 1996; and he too had no qualification or previous experience in residential child care, although he did undergo some in-service training whilst he was with the Community. Evans became a Team Leader at Bryn Alyn Hall in 1980, Senior Principal Officer from January 1982 and Head of Care from June 1989; but he reverted to Principal Officer in June 1994 because new regulations disqualified him from holding the higher appointment.

21.28 There were 5 complainants who alleged that they had been physically abused by Evans but we received evidence from only one of them. Evans himself said for about 10 years prior to the closure of the Community he was almost always the person who was called upon to deal with very difficult situations in which children might attack staff. In our view, the comparative sparseness of the allegations against him when measured against other factors such as his length of service, the number of children passing through his hands and the nature of his role, does not suggest that he was guilty of physical abuse.

21.29 We refer in our report to the allegations against some other named members of the Community staff but we are very conscious of the fact that the evidence that we have heard and seen about the use of force has been patchy and that we have not received a complete picture. Residents were drawn from all over England and only a small number from North Wales so that the evidence before us has been no more than a sample of what might have been heard if all the complainants to the police could have been called. An alarming statistic is that the police themselves complained of having to deal with 280 absconders from the Community in one short period alone, between 1 January and 19 June 1991.

21.30 We are satisfied that excessive force was used by members of the staff quite frequently, particularly in the early years of the Community when staff were almost wholly untrained; and it is likely that bullying also was prevalent. But we do not consider that the use of force by staff or residents was ever on a similar scale to that used in Bryn Estyn and we believe that the level receded in later years, as more staff were trained and the climate of opinion generally hardened against any form of corporal punishment.

21.31 Rather surprisingly, comparatively few of the complainants who gave evidence to the Tribunal commented on the general quality of care provided by the Community because they were pre-occupied with allegations of abuse by members of the staff and, in some cases, of bullying by fellow residents. There were, however, many other causes of concern, which we discuss in paragraphs 21.107 to 21.129 of the report.

21.32 The Community's facilities were intended to be for long term care. Of the 172 complainants known to the Tribunal, it appears that only 6 stayed for 6 months or less whereas the large majority were there for periods of 2 or 3 years and upwards, the longest for 10 years. However, many emergency placements were accepted without consideration by the placing authority or the Community of the suitability of the placement or preparation of the child; and, once accepted, the child would remain with the Community for months. We were told also that the Community was paid more to cope with difficult youngsters with the result that, when staff advised that the Community was not the right place for a particularly difficult or troubled child, they would nevertheless be encouraged to persevere: many children, or at least some, were retained when they ought to have been placed elsewhere. For a similar reason, it was decided to admit girls to the Community, according to one staff member, because the charge for girls was twice that for boys.

21.33 Despite Allen's claims about the management of the Community and its aims, the overall picture is of an organisation that developed rapidly far beyond its capabilities. The pressure, at least until about 1986, was to increase numbers. Staff/resident ratios were low and staff were unlikely to be released for training purposes before **Stephen Elliott** became responsible for it in or about 1986. Former members of the staff were critical also of the management and supervision of the various units: they said that very little support was given, until Elliott arrived, to those on the ground who were running the units. Corporal punishment was not permitted but there was no policy on punishments.

21.34 In October 1983 a mature student, who was attached to the Community briefly, produced a highly critical report about Bryn Alyn Hall, in which he concluded that emotional care was non-existent. He thought that standards of care were very low, that physical and emotional abuse were standard practice and that all future operations of the Community should be looked into in some depth by the relevant authorities. Very few people saw this report. The author was told later by a senior officer of Manchester SSD that his concerns had been fully investigated and that "they" were satisfied that the report was both unfounded and unprofessional.

21.35 The affairs of the Community occupied the attention of the Welsh Office from 14 November 1975, when there was a brief inspection by an HMI and an SWSO, until May 1997, when the school was removed from the register of independent schools, following the liquidation of the trading company. In their report on their first visit the inspectors expressed concern about the Community's expansionist tendency and the dangers attendant on size and dispersal.

21.36 The school, located at Bryn Alyn Hall, was provisionally registered on 18 July 1977 and substantive registration as an independent school for 60 socially maladjusted boys was eventually granted on 30 April 1980 (it had been refused on 1 June 1978). Exceptional permission was later granted by the Secretary of State on occasions for the admission of individual SEN children but it was not until 19 February 1985 that general approval for the admission of such children was granted under section 11(3)(a) of the Education Act 1981. This general SEN approval was withdrawn on 3 February 1997.

21.37 During the 22 years of the school's existence there were quite frequent visits by HMIs; and SWSOs/SSIWs joined in some of these visits to inspect the Community's residential facilities. Initially, there were substantial criticisms of both the classroom facilities and the teaching and, although some improvements were effected, there were recurring criticisms of both the school's educational performance and some aspects of the social provision. From 1988 onwards, the Welsh Office was requiring specific improvements to be made and there were at least 8 further visits by inspectors before the SEN approval was withdrawn.

21.38 Prior to the coming into force of the Children Act 1989 on 14 October 1991, Clwyd SSD did not have any direct responsibility for any of the Community's units: the SSD's concerns were limited to its role as a placement authority in relation to a small number of the children there and its responsibility as the local authority charged with child protection in its area. From 14 October 1991, however, it became responsible for the registration of private children's homes and acquired powers of inspection.

21.39 Clwyd County Council received applications from the Community in or about October 1991 for the registration of Pentre Saeson Hall and Gatewen Hall as private children's homes (Bryntirion Hall had ceased to operate as a children's home in 1986). Eventually, the Community appealed against deemed refusals of registration because Clwyd had not made decisions on the applications within the statutorily prescribed period. The appeals were heard in September 1993 and dismissed by a Registered Homes Tribunal on the ground that the proprietor of the Community was not a fit person to run a children's home.

21.40 The evidence before us has disclosed many reasons for public anxiety about this history in addition to the allegations of sexual and physical abuse. The heart of the matter is that a group of unsuitable and ill-trained persons was able to establish, with official sanction, a mushrooming centre for the care and education of behaviourally disturbed children when they had virtually none of the resources necessary to cope adequately with the task. The basic problems were allowed to persist for over 20 years and, throughout that period, local authorities from far afield were able to consign "difficult" children to the Community for long stays, cut off from their families and local environments, with little prospect that they would eventually return better equipped to take their place in society. A harsh but fair assessment would be that local authorities, acting in good faith, were persuaded by Allen's blandishments and the Community's advertising documents, to use the Community as an apparently safe dumping ground for children in care, for whose needs they did not feel able to provide themselves.

Care Concern's schools in Clwyd (Chapter 22)

22.01   Care Concern was the name given in 1976 to an organisation conceived by David Rattray, a former Deputy Director of Social Services for Denbighshire. It had opened a new independent residential school for boys 2 years earlier in 1974. This school, **Ystrad Hall**, was on the A5 road, on the Corwen side of Llangollen; and it comprised 2 residential units, that is, the Hall itself and Eirianfa, a former hotel, in the same grounds of 14 acres. There was a separate free-standing demountable block of classrooms.

22.02   Ystrad Hall School was registered provisionally in September 1974 and fully in October 1975 as a school catering wholly or mainly for handicapped pupils in the socially maladjusted category. The permitted number of pupils was not specified but there were usually 50 to 55 boys in residence. The school did not have general SEN approval but exceptional admissions of statemented pupils were authorised from time to time.

22.03   The bulk of the teaching was undertaken by 2 senior teachers, a remedial specialist and 6 class teachers. On the care side, each residential unit had a house warden, 3 senior care officers and 6 assistant care officers.

22.04   Ystrad Hall School ceased to be registered in May 1981, when it closed. The boys left at the school on its closure were offered places at another Care Concern school, Cartref Melys in the Sychnant Pass near Conway[1].

22.05   A factor in the closure of Ystrad Hall School was a major fire at Eirianfa at the end of the 1970s. The 20 or so residents of that unit were transferred for about 8 months to St David's College at Carrog, near Corwen, which had been acquired by Care Concern, but we have not received any complaint of abuse there. Ystrad Hall itself closed soon after the exiles' return.

22.06   The principal reason for public concern about Ystrad Hall School is the extent of the sexual abuse that occurred there and it is unfortunate that we were only able to investigate some of the allegations.

22.07   The reason for our own limited investigation was that the first Principal of Ystrad Hall, **Richard Ernest Leake**, was the subject of continuing inquiries by the police and has now been convicted of 14 offences of indecent assault on boys alleged to have been committed between 1972 and 1978. Four of the offences, involving one boy only, were committed at Wrexham between 1 August 1972 and 30 June 1974. The other 10 charges related to periods between 30 June 1974 and 5 May 1978. The same boy was named in 3 of these later charges and another boy in 5 of them. Eight are said to have been committed at Llangollen and 2 at Wrexham. Leake denied the charges but he was convicted on 24 November 1999 in the Crown Court at Chester. Sentencing was adjourned to 17 December 1999.

---

[1] See para 5.06 of this Summary.

22.08 Leake was recruited by Rattray from Bersham Hall, where he had been Officer-in-Charge from 4 August 1972 and he joined Rattray, at the age of 33 years, on 1 July 1974 (3 months only after the beginning of our period under review). He remained with Care Concern until 31 January 1987 but he ceased to be Principal of Ystrad Hall in 1976, when Cartref Melys was acquired and the organisation adopted the name of Care Concern. Leake became Assistant Director (Director from 1980) of Professional Services, with management responsibilities for both establishments and then for Hengwrt Hall School at Dolgellau as well, which continued until January 1986.

22.09 Another senior officer at Ystrad Hall School was **Bryan Davies**, who was Deputy Principal and Warden of Eirianfa, which housed the younger boys, aged 11 to 14 years. He was appointed in or about 1975, having had some previous experience of residential care work, but he remained for only 3 years, until 25 May 1978, when he was arrested.

22.10 Davies was convicted on 4 September 1978, in Llangollen Magistrates' Court, of 3 offences of indecent assault, involving 2 residents at Eirianfa. He was placed on probation for 12 months, with a condition requiring him to undergo hospital treatment, and ordered to perform 160 hours community service. Davies did not return to the school after his arrest.

22.11 The North Wales Police received 8 complaints of sexual abuse by Davies at Ystrad Hall School in the course of their later major investigation. However, we received evidence from only 2 of these complainants and it was not possible to serve notice of these on Davies so that we did not receive any evidence from him. We do not know, therefore, the extent of his express admissions. We have no reason, however, to doubt the correctness of his convictions and we accept the evidence that we received of his additional indecent assault on the witness referred to as B in Chapter 22 of our report.

22.12 Allegations of sexual abuse were made also against 4 other members of the staff (one unidentified) and a resident by 5 different former residents. Police officers investigated these allegations but none was corroborated and no prosecution ensued. The evidence that we received from one of these complainants against an unidentified member of staff contained too many conflicting statements for it to be accepted as reliable.

22.13 The main target of allegations of physical abuse was **Christopher Williamson**, who was Deputy Officer-in-Charge of the Eirianfa Unit from the autumn of 1976 until 1981 and who had previously worked at a remand centre. He remained with Care Concern until 1986 and then went to South Glamorgan as an SRCCO.

22.14 We received evidence from 3 of the complainants against Williamson but, for reasons that we explain in the report, there was no basis on that evidence for a finding that he physically abused children and we are not satisfied that he condoned such behaviour. In his own evidence to us, Williamson denied all the allegations.

22.15 Complaints of physical assaults of varying gravity by 11 other members of the staff were made in statements to the police by former residents but only one was named by as many as 3 of them. Most of them named only one member of staff and few of these complainants provided statements to the Tribunal. We are unable to reach any firm conclusions on this limited evidence but we draw attention to the case of one 13 years old child, D, whose injuries were investigated by Leake in May 1978. That investigation disclosed that D, who was hyperactive and intrusive, had been physically chastised by 3 members of staff, who were cautioned about their conduct. Leake's view was that D had suffered excessive physical abuse because of the inexperience of staff, who were unable to understand the depth of his problems, and the frustration of his peer group, who were unable to cope with him. It is reasonable to infer from the dates before us that physical abuse became less frequent after this investigation.

22.16 HMIs visited Ystrad Hall School on 5 occasions, the last being a formal inspection on 3 December 1979. Their findings varied to a surprising extent. Substantial improvements were made in the educational block in 1979 and were described as quite remarkable but the reporting inspector wrote that "these 2 visits" in 1979 "illustrate the absolute necessity for regular and close monitoring of independent schools of this kind. With our present manpower we are unable to do this and will, therefore, always be to some extent 'at risk' with these establishments".

22.17 **Berwyn College for Girls** was established by Care Concern in the Ystrad Hall unit of Ystrad Hall School when the latter closed. It was provisionally registered on 13 August 1981 but it closed on 31 March 1985 before full registration had been granted. At the time of provisional registration there were 17 resident pupils in the age range of 13 to 16 years, 12 of whom had been transferred from St David's College.

22.18 Care Concern planned to operate the college as a co-educational school from 1 December 1983, with about equal numbers of boys and girls in separate residential units, but this plan was never implemented and there were only 12 resident pupils when it was decided to close the school.

22.19 We know of one boy who went to Berwyn College at the end of 1983, at the age of 16 years, after being expelled from other schools. It appears that he was only admitted (from Coventry), because of the national industrial action by social workers, until a place could be found for him in his home area; and he remained for 6 months.

22.20 This boy and 7 former girl residents complained to the police in or about 1992 of physical abuse by **David Tinniswood,** mainly in the form of excessive restraint, but only the boy gave evidence to the Tribunal. Tinniswood was a certificated teacher who worked for Care Concern from the late 1970s until 1981. He was an assistant teacher at Berwyn College initially but became a Group Leader on the care staff. He had no qualification in residential care work.

22.21 The allegations against Tinniswood illustrate the problems that are likely to arise if an untrained care worker is placed in charge of disturbed children, who may have to be restrained physically from time to time. The dangers are likely to be aggravated if the children are girls and the care worker is a robust man. In the absence of any evidence to the Tribunal from the former girl residents, however, it would be inappropriate for us to make any finding about their complaints.

22.22 The boy had many problems, having been in care from the age of 9 months, and we suspect that he is more bitter now than he was at the time, even though he never wanted to be at Berwyn College. He told the Tribunal that he did not get on with any of the staff there, that he was a regular glue sniffer and that he ran away every day. Contemporary documents confirm his problems and suggest that he was handled quite sensitively. In one review reference was made to his "nice rapport" with Tinniswood, who had suggested that work should be arranged for him on the local railway.

22.23 Tinniswood denied all the allegations made against him when he gave evidence to the Tribunal and we found his evidence persuasive. In the circumstances we are not satisfied that he was guilty of abusing the boy.

22.24 We are not aware of any complaint of sexual abuse at Berwyn College.

22.25 Berwyn College took upon itself the difficult task of looking after emotionally disturbed girls far from their own homes and appears to have achieved a degree of success, despite the shortcomings in training of most of the staff. However, although the basic quality of care was probably adequate, it was formal and rather rigid, lacking much of the quality of homeliness, which is an important aspect of a young girl's training for life.

Clwyd Hall School (Chapter 23)

23.01 This residential school for children with behavioural and emotional problems was established by **William Carman** and his wife in 1958 and it closed finally on 27 July 1984. The Carmans were the joint headteachers until they retired in or about January 1972.

23.02 The school was housed in "a delightful building of historical interest, aesthetically pleasing both inside and out, set in about 18 acres of grounds"[2]. The setting was described as a joy to the eye and the views as breathtaking.

23.03 The Carmans retained control of the school until July 1982 and William Carman remained the Principal until 13 October 1982. At that point he took in 3 partners, of whom one, **David Edge**, succeeded him as Principal until 26 February 1983. The last relevant Principal from then on until April 1984 was another partner, **Richard Francis Groome**[3].

---

[2] Report by Senior HMI (Staff Inspector) in December 1977.
[3] See paras 18.06 to 18.08 of this Summary.

23.04 Clwyd Hall School was recognised as efficient under former education legislation until that status ended in April 1978. It is not clear from the documents before the Tribunal whether it ever achieved final registration subsequently. It is clear, however, that it did not receive general SEN approval and it may have remained provisionally registered only, although Edge referred to the school in 1982 as "recognised by the Department of Education and Science".

23.05 From the reports about Clwyd Hall School that we have seen, it would seem that the number of resident pupils reached a peak in or about the autumn of 1977, when there were 32 boys and 12 girls. In addition to the headteacher, there were 4 teachers and a riding instructor at week-ends (the post of deputy headteacher was vacant). There were 5 resident care staff but only one of them had a child care qualification. There were also a housekeeper and about 6 domestic staff.

23.06 Unhappily, the history of this school during the period under review was disfigured by persistent sexual abuse of residents that did not come to light until after it had closed.

23.07 **Noel Ryan**, who was employed as a houseparent from about 1968 until he resigned in 1981, appeared before the Crown Court at Chester on 4 July 1997, when he pleaded guilty to 14 of 22 counts alleging sexual offences against 10 boys at Clwyd Hall School committed between 1 January 1970 and 30 June 1981. The offences admitted were 3 of buggery, one of attempted buggery and 10 indecent assaults. Ryan asked the Court to take into consideration also when sentencing him 7 similar (specimen) offences of indecent assault committed within the same period, which he admitted. Thus, he confessed to serious offences against a total of 17 boys over a period of about 10 years. He was sentenced to 12 years' imprisonment and the sentencing judge ordered that the 8 counts to which he had pleaded not guilty should lie on the Court file. An order under the Sex Offenders Act 1997 was also made.

23.08 The Tribunal itself is aware of 13 male former residents who complained to the police that they had been abused whilst they were at Clwyd Hall School and all 13 named Ryan as an abuser. Twelve of them alleged sexual abuse by him and 4 complained that he had abused them physically.

23.09 Ryan was aged 37 years when he went to the school and he was described by his Counsel at his trial as "untrained, unskilled and untutored": he was a naive individual, who himself had been the victim of abuse as a child, and he had no other sexual experience. The evidence relied upon by the prosecution showed that there was a pattern to his behaviour. He was attracted to some of the boys and would groom them for subsequent sexual misconduct. They would be shown favours and later touched intimately in the bathroom or showers. Ryan occupied a bed-sitting room above the staff room in the main building and was able to take advantage of this and his quasi-parental status to progress to graver offences.

23.10 Ryan's employment at Clwyd Hall School ended with his resignation on 27 May 1981, following complaints by a parent to the headteacher about Ryan hugging her son and by a boy of Ryan holding his hand.

23.11 In view of the impending prosecution of Ryan during the first part of our hearings and then his admissions, we did not hear full evidence about his activities and Ryan himself was not called to give evidence at the trial. We did, however, hear harrowing evidence from 2 of his victims and the evidence of 2 others was read to us.

23.12 We did not receive any complaints about **Richard Francis Groome** in respect of his period at Clwyd Hall School but we were aware of the continuing police investigation in respect of him. He went there from Tanllwyfan in November 1982 and left in or about April 1984, during which period he was Head of Care and then Principal. Some of the 24 charges that he now faces relate to 4 former boy residents of Clwyd Hall School[4].

23.13 Apart from Ryan, only 4 other members of the staff were named in other complaints by 4 former residents and only one staff member was named by more than one resident. Only one complainant to the police named another member of the staff as a sexual offender and we did not receive any evidence from him.

23.14 There were visits to the school by HMIs in November 1977, May 1982 and October 1983. The first of these followed a complaint to a Minister of State at the Department of Education and Science by a senior teacher, who had left after only a few days there. The report of the inspectors, however, was complimentary and they concluded that they had neither seen nor heard anything to make them uneasy or to indicate any kind of emergency situation, which might have endangered either recognition or registration. The report in 1982 was much less favourable and the inspectors were critical of the state of the premises and of the staffing, both for care and teaching purposes: they thought that it might be necessary to recommend that Clwyd Hall was no longer a school for which exceptional SEN admissions could be approved. Improvements were carried out by October 1983 but the future remained uncertain and a further inspection would have been made but for the closure of the school in July 1984.

23.15 Other criticisms of Clwyd Hall School pale in comparison with the allegations of sexual abuse and its central failure to provide a safe home for the children. Its short history within our period of review does, however, underline the need for frequent and effective independent inspection, bearing in mind the deterioration that occurred between 1977 and 1982. We are dismayed also that the Welsh Office did not (apparently) think it necessary to investigate a parent's complaint 'inter alia' of a physical assault on her son by a teacher at the school in November 1977[5].

---

[4] Ibid, para 18.07.
[5] See paras 23.15 and 23.16 of our report.

ALLEGED ABUSE OF CHILDREN IN FOSTER HOMES IN CLWYD BETWEEN 1974 AND 1996 (Chapters 24 to 27)

In this part of the report we give an account of the general fostering arrangements in Clwyd and deal with 7 foster homes in respect of which there are known to have been complaints. The 2 cases that attracted the greatest public attention, those of Roger Saint and Frederick Rutter, are dealt with in Chapters 25 and 26 respectively.

The overall provision of foster care in Clwyd, 1974 to 1996 (Chapter 24)

24.01 Between 1974 and 1992 the number of children in foster care in Clwyd rose by only just over 50 to about 250. The number of children in care had declined, however, from 577 to 328 so that the percentage of them in foster care rose from about 34 to 76. The comparable percentages for Wales as a whole were about 31 in 1974 and 75 in 1992.

24.02 The latest figures that we have for Clwyd show that on 31 March 1995 about 78 per cent (190) of the looked after children (244) were in foster care; and in 1995 Clwyd had access to 300 foster carers. Both the number of children being looked after and the actual number in foster care had diminished appreciably in the preceding 3 years.

24.03 Alleged abuse of children in foster homes in Clwyd did not play any significant part in the events that led to the appointment of this Tribunal. However, in the course of our hearings, the conviction on 7 March 1997 of Roger Saint gave rise to nationwide publicity.

The case of Roger Saint (Chapter 25)

25.01 **Roger Saint** was convicted on 9 June 1972, at Neath Magistrates' Court, of an indecent assault on a boy aged 12 years, to which he pleaded guilty. The offence had been committed on 6 March 1972 when Saint had followed the boy, who was a stranger, and had then seized him, touching him indecently. Saint was fined £15 and ordered to pay an advocate's fee of £8 as well as a contribution to the cost of his own legal aid.

25.02 At the time of this offence, Saint, who was nearly 25 years old, was working as the Deputy Superintendent of a children's home in Salisbury.

25.03 The facts of the offence were reported to the Home Office Police Department (F1 Division) by the Chief Constable by letter dated 19 June 1972, in which Saint's current appointment was specified.

25.04 Saint was initially suspended from this appointment but he resigned just before his conviction, according to his own statement to the Tribunal.

25.05 Saint had various appointments after his conviction, including at least 2 in children's homes, but he was dismissed after 2 or 3 months as Officer-in-Charge of a children's home in Barry, South Glamorgan, when his employers became aware of his conviction.

25.06 Saint's connection with Clwyd began in December 1976, when he bought a house in Holywell, following his marriage to his wife Carol earlier that year. He was by then "Officer-in-Charge of Childcare" (his description) at a residential establishment for children in West Kirby, a post that he retained for 10 years. In the documents before the Tribunal he was described as an RCCO at this home and school, where there were 160 children and 40 staff.

25.07 Saint has persistently denied that there was any indecent intent or motivation on his part in the 1972 assault and has sought to explain his plea of guilty then by saying (apparently incorrectly) that he was not legally represented. Nevertheless, on 7 March 1997, in the Crown Court at Mold, Saint pleaded guilty to 9 counts of indecent assault on boys out of 16 counts contained in 3 indictments against him. The victims of the 9 offences were a step-son, 2 pupils at the West Kirby home and school, a foster child and 5 adopted children; and they were alleged to have been committed between March 1975 and December 1987. Saint was sentenced on 23 May 1997 by Mr Justice Laws to 6½ years' imprisonment on all 9 counts. The other 7 counts were ordered to lie on the Court file.

25.08 In Chapter 25 of the report we give a full account of the Saints' dealings with Clwyd SSD from their first approach to the department in June 1977. We refer here to only the main relevant features of the history.

25.09 In October 1978 the Saints completed the standard application Form F to adopt up to 2 children aged 8 years or under. They provided 2 personal referees in Neath, who could not be traced; and Roger Saint failed to disclose his conviction, although he authorised the SSD to check with the North Wales Police whether any convictions were recorded against him. Saint made no reference to his employment at Barry, from which he had been dismissed: to cover that period he gave incorrect details of his employment record and we are satisfied that he did so deliberately to reduce the risk that Clwyd might become aware of his conviction.

25.10 The North Wales Police replied by letter to the enquiry made by Clwyd SSD, stating incorrectly (but in good faith) that nothing detrimental was known in respect of either Roger or Carol Saint. The explanation given for this lapse is that "in 1978 there was no readily available facility to check a person against a national collection of persons with criminal records held at New Scotland Yard". In view of the fact that Roger Saint had no connection with North Wales in 1972, his conviction at Neath had not been communicated to them. Clwyd SSD was not informed, however, of the limited scope of the check made by the North Wales Police.

25.11 Clwyd SSD did not make further efforts to trace the Saints' nominated referees after receiving a negative response from West Glamorgan County Council in December 1978 and they did not ask for substitute referees.

25.12 Clwyd SSD remained ignorant of Saint's 1972 conviction until 10 February 1988. At that point Devon SSD became aware of it through a check made following an approach by the Saints to adopt 2 Devon children. The Director of Social Services for Devon informed Clwyd SSD, who asked the North Wales Police to make a further check, which confirmed the connection. The national police computerised record base had been established in 1981.

25.13 There had been a missed opportunity to learn of the conviction in the intervening 10 years because Clwyd SSD had been asked in November 1982 by Tower Hamlets SSD to make a fresh check with the North Wales Police in connection with another adoption application by the Saints. The evidence before us indicates, however, that Clwyd failed to request the check by the police and that Tower Hamlets failed to pursue the matter.

25.14 In the event, 11 children were placed with the Saints between December 1978 and February 1988, although only 2 of these were placed by Clwyd SSD. The total does not include short term placements, of which there appear to have been at least 5 in 1979 and 1980. The Saints moved from Holywell to a larger house in Llanarmon-yn-Ial in December 1984 and thence to a village near Bala in September 1990.

25.15 It is unnecessary for the purposes of this Summary to give details of all these placements. One of the boys placed by Clwyd was adopted by the Saints on 13 July 1979 and was still living in their household in September 1997: he did not allege that he had been abused. We received evidence from 2 other boys, who are brothers, both of whom complained of physical and sexual abuse by Roger Saint. One of them stayed for only a year but the other stayed with the Saints from 26 April 1979 to 27 July 1981. Roger Saint pleaded guilty in 1997 to a specimen count of indecent assault against the latter in that period. The boy told the police about this in March 1996.

25.16 The social worker for this last boy prepared a report about the placement that was critical of the Saints in some important respects but it was seriously defective because it contained only indirect reference to repeated allegations by both boys of physical punishment that had caused them to run away from the Saints twice.

25.17 Although there is no documentary evidence to indicate that Clwyd SSD had any further discussions about the suitability of the Saints as foster parents or adoptive parents, it seems that they were not on Clwyd's active list at the end of 1981 and we do not know of any further placement by Clwyd with them after that date. Roger Saint was, however, appointed as a member of the Adoption and Foster Care Panel for Clwyd South on 26 October 1987 on the nomination of Clwyd's Adoptions Officer.

25.18 When the Director of Social Services learned about 4 months later of Saint's 1972 conviction, he rightly took the view that it would be unwise for Saint to continue to be a member of the panel. On 11 March 1988 he wrote to the County Secretary, Roger Davies, expressing that view and seeking the latter's advice. Astonishingly, the County Secretary did not reply to that letter, despite a belated reminder 19 months later. In the event no action was taken and Saint remained on the panel until 31 March 1996.

25.19 From 1981 onwards the Saints sought fostering and adoption opportunities further afield. A young disabled child was placed with them by Cheshire County Council on 5 March 1982 through Clwyd's Adoption Agency and they adopted the child about 3 months later. But from 1982 to 1990 the Saint's main involvement in respect of new placements was with Tower Hamlets.

25.20 Between February 1983 and September 1987, 7 children were placed with the Saints by the London Borough of Tower Hamlets, of whom 5 were adopted by the Saints. All 5 of these subsequently adopted children were boys in the age range of 9 to 14 years at the time when they were first boarded out with the Saints. All of them complained, after they had left the Saints, that they had been sexually abused by Roger Saint. Moreover, 4 of the boys, who were brothers, were adopted on 11 January 1989, after Roger Saint's 1972 conviction had come to light and had been confirmed to Tower Hamlets by the Metropolitan Police, by letter dated 8 March 1988. Saint pleaded guilty in March 1997 to indecent assaults upon each of the 5 boys.

25.21 The Tower Hamlets social worker who dealt with the adoption applications in 1988/1989 was aware of Saint's conviction but appears to have accepted his lame explanation that the "bother" was the result of a broken engagement and that he did not recall that the incident had been a sexual assault. We have neither seen nor heard anything that indicates that the County Court was informed of the conviction.

25.22 The unanswered request from Tower Hamlets to Clwyd for a further check with the police on Saint's record was made in connection with an adoption application by the Saints in respect of the 2 other boys, who were also brothers. Clwyd SSD did not give any warning against the placement in the light of its previous experiences with the Saints and the latter were formally approved as foster parents by Tower Hamlets on 3 December 1982. One of them was adopted by the Saints on 23 June 1987, just before his 18th birthday, but the other left them in or about September 1985, when he was 17 years old. Both alleged sexual abuse by Saint, who pleaded guilty to 2 counts of indecent assault in respect of the boy who was adopted.

25.23 Roger Saint was arrested in March 1996 following complaints made by 2 of the boys to social workers in Wrexham the previous month. He persistently denied abusing any of the children until Christmas of that year, when he made admissions by telephone to his wife and 3 of their adopted children.

25.24 There were at least 5 further placements by local authorities in the years preceding Saint's arrest and one of the children became their 8th adopted child. The authorities making the placements were North Yorkshire County Council, North Tyneside MBC and the London Borough of Greenwich. It was said at Saint's trial that North Tyneside had received from him an exculpatory account of the 1972 offence: the judgment made by North Tyneside was "that the conviction was not so significant and that he had successfully cared for so many children in the past and no person had made a complaint against him".

25.25 To sum up, it is regrettable both that the enquiry by the police in 1978 was limited to their local records and that this was not made clear to Clwyd SSD.

There are, however, many other causes for concern about the Saint case. Clwyd's main shortcomings after 1981 were their failure (a) to make a further check with the police in 1982 when asked to do so and (b) to terminate Saint's membership of the Adoption and Foster Care Panel in 1988 on learning of his 1972 conviction. There appears also to have been defective liaison between Clwyd and other local authorities.

25.26 The history generally illustrates the dangers and confusions that may arise when prospective foster parents are permitted to apply for placements to a variety of local authorities or other agencies. These should now be lessened by the requirement in Regulation 3 of the Foster Placement (Children) Regulations 1991 that there shall be only one approving authority in respect of any specific foster parent, although others may place children with the foster parent with the approval of that authority; and the "usual fostering limit" is now 3 children[1].

25.27 We criticise also the response of Tower Hamlets to the discovery in 1988 of Saint's conviction. Once that conviction became known it was plain that he had seriously deceived both Clwyd and Tower Hamlets; it was most inappropriate to rely upon one social worker's assessment of his explanation of the offence and, if the County Court was not informed of the conviction, the omission was lamentable.

25.28 Following critical reporting of the Saint case, the Department of Health issued the Children (Protection from Offenders)(Miscellaneous Amendments) Regulations 1997[2]. These regulations prohibit (subject to very limited exceptions) the approval as a foster carer or adoptive parent by adoption agencies, local authorities or voluntary organisations of any person who is known to have been convicted of, or cautioned for, any one of a list of specified offences, including indecent assault. There are provisions also in relation to other convicted members of the relevant household and for the removal of children already placed.

Frederick Rutter (Chapter 26)

26.01 **Frederick Rutter** was employed as a temporary RCCO at Bryn Estyn from 5 June 1982 to 19 November 1983 and then at Park House, where he became a permanent RCCO, from October 1984 to 28 August 1988[3]. His last relevant employment was by Clwyd Housing Association Limited from the latter date as Warden of their Pen-y-Llan hostel for young people at Connah's Quay: he was suspended from duty on 18 May 1990 and resigned from the post on 12 June 1990.

26.02 Rutter and his wife first applied to become foster parents on 28 December 1984. The application was to foster a boy, who was then living at Park House, but it was discontinued in March 1985 because of the proposed rehabilitation of the boy with his mother.

---

[1] Schedule 7 to the Children Act 1989.
[2] SI 1997 No 2308.
[3] See paras 8.28, 10.26, 10.27, 17.28 and 17.29 of this Summary.

26.03 On 28 February 1986 the Director of Social Services approved the Rutter's home as lodgings for another boy in residential care, who had already spent many week-ends and the Christmas period with them. However, the placement broke down by September 1986.

26.04 In 1987 the Rutters moved their home from Flint to a larger house in Connah's Quay; and they applied again on 8 January 1988 to become foster parents. The application, which was approved on 12 May 1988, was in respect of one of 2 girls (A) subsequently raped by Rutter at the house. A, who was 15 years old at the time of the application, had previously been a school friend of the Rutter's younger daughter and she had been placed at Park House in January 1988.

26.05 When the application to foster A was approved, 2 boys were already placed at the Rutter's new home as approved lodgings. A was raped once, in 1989, when she was 16 years old, but she was too embarrassed to tell anyone then. She moved out to a flat in 1989, after she had become pregnant by a boyfriend.

26.06 The second girl, B, was another resident of Park House who went to live with the Rutters in 1988. She was 17 years old and had been told by the SSD that she had to move into approved lodgings. B remained with the Rutters for only a month or so because she was raped and sexually assaulted by Frederick Rutter.

26.07 Rutter's offences came to light on 3 April 1990 because an 18 years old woman resident at the Pen-y-Llan hostel complained to the police that he had behaved improperly towards her there. In the course of the wider investigation that followed, she and other residents at the hostel made more serious allegations against him, as did A and B. The residents at the hostel were not in care at the time. Rutter was arrested on 22 October 1990 but he denied all the allegations.

26.08 Rutter was tried in July 1991, in the Crown Court at Chester, on an indictment alleging 5 offences of rape, one of buggery and 3 indecent assaults involving 5 residents at the hostel as well as A and B. On 30 July 1991 he was found guilty of raping both A and B. He was convicted also of 2 rapes and 2 indecent assaults upon 3 of the hostel residents but he was acquitted of the offences alleged by the other 2 hostel residents. Concurrent sentences of 12 years' imprisonment were imposed for each of the 4 rapes proved and of 12 months' imprisonment for the 2 indecent assaults.

26.09 It appears that the very serious offences against A and B would only have been avoided if the Rutters had not been approved as foster parents and their home had not been approved as lodgings. We do not think that Clwyd can be realistically criticised for granting these applications on the basis of the information available at the time. However, with a degree of hindsight, it can be said that, if a full record had been kept (and entered on Rutter's personal file) a less favourable picture of him might have emerged.

26.10 This history provides yet another example of the dangers that arise when children in residential care are permitted to visit and stay with care staff in the latter's homes. We emphasise also that employees of SSDs should not be assessed as potential foster and adoptive parents by social workers who have worked closely with them.

Allegations against other foster parents resident in Clwyd (Chapter 27)

27.01 In this chapter we discuss events at 5 other foster homes in Clwyd during the period under review. In 3 of them serious sexual abuse occurred whereas the complaints against the foster parents in the other 2 cases were mainly of physical abuse and inappropriate living conditions and the evidence was less reliable.

27.02 The foster father identified as **Mr B** was convicted successively of sexual offences against 3 sisters, who had been placed with him and his wife from the end of November 1977, when the girls' grandmother had died. Mr and Mrs B were approved as foster parents for the girls and their brother on 10 January 1978 and Clwyd County Council assumed parental rights in respect of the 4 children on 17 December 1980.

27.03 Mr B was first convicted on 13 March 1987, in the Crown Court at Mold, of an attempted rape of the youngest girl, for which he received a sentence of 18 months' imprisonment suspended for 2 years. Over 11 years later, on 9 September 1998, in the Crown Court at Chester, Mr B pleaded guilty to 4 indecent assaults upon the eldest girl, and to 3 rapes and 6 indecent assaults upon the next in age. He was sentenced to concurrent terms of 3 years' imprisonment for the rapes and of 12 months' imprisonment for the indecent assaults. The full time span of the offences alleged in the indictment was alleged to have been from October 1975 to October 1985. From this it will be apparent that they were alleged to have begun before the girls were placed with Mr and Mrs B but to have ended over a year before Mr B's first conviction.

27.04 The second eldest girl gave oral and written evidence to the Tribunal. She alleged that the sexual abuse of her began when she was 4 years old and that Mr B had had sexual intercourse with her for about 10 years, beginning when she was 7 years old. She had not complained when her youngest sister had first complained in August 1986 because she had been threatened with "going into homes" and "because of Mrs B". In 1997 she complained also of physical abuse by Mr B, who had punished her with a belt. At the time of our hearings, Mr B could not be traced.

27.05 Having reviewed the available evidence in this case, we do not think that Clwyd SSD can be validly criticised for placing the children with Mr and Mrs B or for failing to discover the sexual abuse earlier. Appropriate action was taken after the youngest girl had complained in October 1986. There were complaints about "belting" and of being physically struck before that, which probably ought to have been investigated more fully, but such further investigation would probably not have revealed the sexual abuse.

27.06 The 3 foster children of **Mr and Mrs C** were placed with them as an emergency arrangement on 26 July 1978 and were the subject of a care order made in matrimonial proceedings on 10 May 1979. Mr and Mrs C had 3 children of their own and fostered 4 other children contemporaneously with the 3 about whom we heard evidence.

27.07 One of those 3 children, who was disabled, complained in April 1991 (when she was 19 years old) that **Mr C** had sexually abused her over a long period, beginning with gross indecency and culminating in rape. On 5 August 1991, Mr C was committed for trial on the strength of these complaints on one representative charge of rape and 4 of indecent assault, alleged to have occurred between July 1982 and April 1991; but he was found dead on 27 August 1991, having hanged himself. When interviewed by the police, he had denied having raped the girl but had admitted the other offences.

27.08 The documents show that Mr and Mrs C were carefully vetted in accordance with approved practice before becoming foster parents. It is troubling to record, however, that on 16 March 1982 (before any alleged offences against the foster child) the C's natural daughter had complained that Mr C had made sexual advances to her, leading to a fight between them, in which both had been injured. The incident was investigated quite fully by a social worker after the girl's headmaster had referred the matter to the SSD; and the girl withdrew her allegations the following day, after the social worker had interviewed Mr and Mrs C. The social worker thought that it was almost certain that the parents were telling the truth and the Area Officer decided that no further action need be taken.

27.09 If the Child Protection procedures formulated later in the 1980s had been in existence in 1982, the police would have been involved in investigating the matter and the outcome might have been different.

27.10 The circumstances in which a girl aged 15 years was placed with **Miss E** were unusual. The girl in question E1, had been in conflict with her mother and stepfather and was found by them at the home of E, a friend of hers of a few months' standing. It was an address that the police had visited on previous occasions with the result that they had sent several "at risk" reports, in respect of specific children, to the SSD.

27.11 The initial decision of Clwyd SSD was that E1 should live at home with her mother and stepfather but the couple refused to allow E1 to do so. E1 refused a foster placement and decided to stay with E. Clwyd County Council then placed E1 with E on 29 April 1994 as an immediate placement with a friend under Regulation 11(3) of the Foster Placement (Children) Regulations 1991[4]. The SSD paid E an allowance and began the process of approving her as a foster parent.

27.12 On 27 May 1994 E1 presented herself at a social services office, where she was advised to talk to her mother and stepfather. Police were called to her in a shopping precinct later that day and found her in a distressed state. She complained of rape and serious sexual assault whilst living at E's house. The Clwyd Child Protection Procedures were set in motion and a full joint investigation by the police and social workers followed.

27.13 As a result of the investigation, E was convicted in March 1995, in the Crown Court at Chester, of keeping a disorderly house and of permitting unlawful

---

[4] See also section 20(1)(c) of the Children Act 1989.

sexual intercourse with E1. E was placed on probation for 12 months for these offences. Two young men were conditionally discharged for having unlawful sexual intercourse with E1 and a third was made subject of a probation order for 12 months for indecently assaulting her.

27.14 A Part 8 Management Case Review was conducted in 1994/1995, under Part 8 of the Working Together guidance; and the Review Sub-Committee expressed serious concerns about the judgment of several senior officers of Clwyd SSD because "at no time was E1 seen as a child in need of protection". Other major critical findings are listed in paragraph 27.51 of the Tribunal's report: they included criticism of the placement without inspection beforehand, lack of consultation and the harshness of the response of the office to E1 on 27 May 1994. A perturbing concluding comment was that managers within the SSD, East Division, still believed that there had been no significant errors.

27.15 One of the other 2 foster homes also provided some evidence of defective practice. We do not consider that we would be justified in accepting the allegations of various forms of abuse between 1977 and 1979 made by 2 foster daughters against **Mr and Mrs A** and other members of their household. It is probable, however, that the As' way of life was unsuitable for damaged foster children. Mrs A herself complained in her evidence of lack of support from the SSD, lack of communication with social workers and that visits by social workers had been too infrequent and brief. She complained also of inaction by the SSD when the family routine had been upset by threatening telephone calls from the natural father of the foster children. Our conclusions are that there is substance in Mrs A's allegation of lack of support and that there was insufficient social worker input into the placement, bearing in mind the girls' troubled upbringing and other obvious factors.

27.16 Foster child D1 was unfortunately an unreliable witness for reasons that we state in our report. He complained of persistent physical abuse by **Mr and Mrs D** during the period of 2 years (to April 1991) when he was placed with them, but the length of the placement, in comparison with other fostering attempts with this highly disturbed boy, suggests that the Ds at least provided him with some necessary stability and security. We have insufficient documentary evidence before us to justify comment on the quality of supervision by social workers responsible for visiting him.

27.17 Overall the histories underline the need for vigilant monitoring of all placements. We emphasise also the need for social workers to see foster children on their own and individually when a foster home is visited. Unless this precept is observed it is unlikely that an adequate picture of a child's response to a placement will be obtained. We recognise that sexual complaints are particularly difficult to elicit but, if a child is seen alone, the social worker is more likely to discern symptoms of anxiety or unease.

THE RESPONSIBILITY OF HIGHER MANAGEMENT IN CLWYD (Chapters 28 to 32)

Management structures and responsibilities for Clwyd Social Services from 1974 to 1996

28.01 There were 3 successive Directors of Social Services during the period under review, namely:

(Joseph) Emlyn Evans, the former Director for Denbighshire, from 1 April 1974 to 31 January 1980.

(Daniel) Gledwyn Jones, who had been the first Deputy Director, from 1 February 1980 to 14 April 1991.

John (Christopher) Jevons, who became the Deputy Director in October 1984, from 15 April 1991 to 30 March 1996.

Of these 3, only Gledwyn Jones was a former child care specialist.

28.02 During the period of 22 years there were 3 major changes in the structure of the Social Services Department.

28.03 In the first structure that was adopted there were 2 relevant Assistant Directors: one was responsible for residential and day care and the other for fieldwork.

28.04 In short, the Assistant Director responsible for residential and day care had under him a Principal Officer (Residential and Day Care Services) and, from September 1975, a Principal RDCO, Veronica Pares, whose responsibilities included advising heads of homes and staff supervision by means of monthly visits to all the residential homes. There were also 4 RDCOs responsible for such matters as staffing, supplies, children and the elderly.

28.05 The Assistant Director (Fieldwork), **Raymond Powell,** was responsible for the work of 6 Area Offices, the areas corresponding to the local government districts. Under him the person nominally responsible for children was the Principal Officer (Fieldwork) but the effective responsibility appears to have been shouldered by the officer below, the Principal Social Worker (Children), **Gordon Ramsay,** whose job description included advising on all aspects of child care and considering residential and day care facilities.

28.06 When the Assistant Director (Residential and Day Care) retired in 1976, his responsibilities were merged with those of Powell, who became Assistant Director Operational (Fieldwork Services). **Geoffrey Wyatt,** who was to be a key figure for the next 16 years, became Principal Officer (Residential and Day Care Services) at this time, reporting to Powell.

28.07 The first major change on the residential and day care side took place on 1 April 1977 when immediate managerial responsibility for the residential homes was transferred to the 6 Area Officers, each with a small complement of RDCOs. None of the Area Officers had any experience of the management of children's homes. However, 2 inspectors, Veronica Pares and Ivor Hughes, were appointed. Their responsibility was to inspect every social services establishment in the county and to report to the Assistant Director Management Services.

28.08 This change was said to have been part of a 10 year plan, devised in response to Welsh Office Circular 195/72, but it proved to be a failure for reasons that we discuss in paragraphs 28.15 and 28.16 of the Tribunal's report. A result was that effective day to day responsibility for children's services fell upon Geoffrey Wyatt and Gordon Ramsay.

28.09 The second major change in structure occurred in 1980 and 1982, when the recommendations put forward in March 1980, in a highly critical O & M report on the Social Services Department, were implemented in part. The first phase of this was the transfer back from the Area Offices to headquarters of responsibility for residential and day care services, which took place in 1980. Wyatt's direct responsibilities as Principal Officer Residential Services were then clarified and the range of his responsibilities was recognised by his promotion to the new post of Assistant Director (Residential) in December 1982.

28.10 At first, Wyatt had only one Principal Social Worker (Ivor Hughes) under him with various RDCOs but, from 1984, there were 3 Principal Officers under Wyatt, one of whom, **John Llewellyn Thomas,** was specifically responsible for children. The line of command was then from the heads of children's homes through 2 RDCOs to Thomas and thence to Wyatt. This lasted only until 1986, however, because Wyatt was made Assistant Director (Adult Services). Powell became the Assistant Director responsible for children and family services, until his retirement in October 1989, with Thomas working under him and also Gordon Ramsay, until the latter's own retirement in 1987.

28.11 The major recruits to headquarters in the 1980s were **John Hubert Coley**, who was Deputy Director from July 1980 to February 1984, in succession to Gledwyn Jones, and **John Jevons**, who was appointed initially as Assistant Director with responsibility for policy and resources from 9 January 1984 but who then succeeded Coley as Deputy Director in October of the same year. Despite the recommendations of the O & M report, however, the Deputy Directors in the 1980s were not closely involved in children's services; and both Coley and Jevons were assigned to specific other tasks.

28.12 The most relevant newcomer to headquarters was **Michael Barnes**[1], who was appointed Principal Social Worker (Child and Family Services) from 1 January 1988. According to Barnes, his duty was to manage the remaining children's homes, reporting to Thomas and through him to Powell. He was also

---

[1] See paras 12.16, 13.12, 13.18 to 13.20, 14.15 and 14.28 of this Summary.

given some responsibility for policy, the appointment of staff, training and support and "gatekeeping"[2].

28.13 The third major upheaval occurred in October 1990, when a divisional structure was adopted on the recommendation initially of Clwyd County Council's Systems and Efficiency Unit. Under this, responsibilities for operational services were transferred from headquarters to 3 divisional offices, each with a divisional director. No new Deputy Director was appointed to replace John Jevons: in effect, the 3 new Divisional Directors replaced the Deputy in the hierarchy.

28.14 The proposals were that, within each division, a service manager would head a team responsible for services to one client group, except in respect of children, for whom work was so large in volume that it was to be split between a child care social work manager and another manager responsible for the resources to assist and protect children. The remaining smaller headquarters team was to be responsible for policy and resources matters plus the inspection and support of the services delivered from the divisions.

28.15 Geoffrey Wyatt remained at headquarters until his retirement on 30 September 1992, in the non-operational role of Assistant Director (Operational Support and Inspection) with responsibility for the registration and inspection of children's homes and of residential homes for adults. He had responsibility also for setting up a complaints procedure. Thomas went to the East Division as Children's Resources Manager but was also given lead responsibility for children's services policy and development throughout the county, until he moved back to Mid Glamorgan as an Assistant Director in April 1991. Barnes became Children's Resources Manager in the North Division.

28.16 Before Thomas left Clwyd, he wrote to the Director of Social Services on 20 March 1991, proffering criticisms of the new decentralised structure. In Thomas' view, Children and Family Services needed a recognised post centrally with adequate administrative and professional support and with sufficient status to give it credibility in relation to the Senior Management Team and others, including the Welsh Office.

28.17 The limited response to these criticisms was the appointment of a Principal Officer (Children) at headquarters from January 1992 but she was suffering from a long term illness: her appointment ended in April 1994 and she was not replaced. Instead, Barnes was invited by the Director, in December 1994, to accept secondment from the North Division to the Strategic Planning Division at headquarters to assist the Assistant Director (Strategic Planning). His tasks were expected to include 8 matters specified in paragraph 28.44 of this Tribunal's report; and he took up his duties in January 1995.

28.18 We comment that the frequent structural changes imposed additional burdens on hard pressed staff, who were already having to cope with the major changes in social services departments generally. The changes tended also to dissipate

---

[2] Examining the need for a child to be taken into care, which was mainly the responsibility of Area Officers and social worker teams.

Clwyd's limited resources in child care expertise or at least to diminish their impact on the delivery of operational services. Moreover, there were striking anomalies in the various structures from time to time, most notably in relation to Ramsay's position. It is a strong criticism of the senior management that this unsatisfactory situation was allowed to continue for such a long time.

28.19 Other criticisms are that the structural changes were ill-timed and inadequately supported and that the abilities of newcomers such as Coley, Jevons and Thomas were not fully exploited at a practice level in the 1980s in relation to child care. Finally, all the evidence that we have heard suggests that, between 1974 and 1991, the period of major abuse, there was little effective accountability or monitoring of performance at the higher levels of Clwyd SSD.

28.20 In the penultimate section of Chapter 28 of the report we discuss the role of the Chief Executive of Clwyd in the light, particularly, of a 1985/1986 job evaluation report. The County Secretary was the monitoring and compliance officer.

28.21 The Chief Executive for most of the period under review, that is, from 1977 until 31 July 1992, was **Mervyn (Hugh) Phillips**, the former Deputy. He was succeeded by **(Edward) Roger (Llewellyn) Davies**, who had been Deputy from 1982 and County Secretary from 1980.

28.22 It is clear from the evidence that Phillips relied heavily upon the Director of Social Services and County Secretary and expected to be informed by one or both of them of any significant problems. He expected a reference to be made to him if it was "the sort of thing that might need the attention of the County Council as opposed to the Social Services Committee".

28.23 Although there were seeds of confusion and misunderstanding about this (and in the Job Evaluation), we have reached the conclusion that successive failures to inform the Chief Executive of criticisms of the management and practice of the SSD, discussed elsewhere in the Tribunal's report, were part of a pattern of deliberate non-disclosure; and the result was that monitoring of the performance of the SSD and its officers by the Chief Executive was ineffective.

The failure to prevent sexual abuse or to detect it earlier (Chapter 29)

29.01 Our findings are that serious sexual abuse was committed by 6 (and quite possibly more) members of staff in 5 Clwyd County Council community homes. In relation to other residential establishments our findings are necessarily less clear because of continuing police investigations and impending prosecutions but the general picture of sexual abuse is similar to that found in the local authority homes.

29.02 Public concern has understandably focussed on revelations about Bryn Estyn and Bryn Alyn because of the number of victims, the positions held by the abusers and the persistence of the abuse but they should not be regarded as unique or even special cases. The lessons to be drawn are of wide significance and apply to a broad range of institutions providing accommodation for children and young persons.

29.03 In relation to fostering the picture is quite different. Although we have given accounts of 3 proved cases of grave sexual abuse in Clwyd that occurred in the course of fostering, the number of complaints has been very much less, despite the increasing emphasis on fostering during the period under review. Nevertheless, the risk of such abuse in foster care and the problem of detecting it combine to present social workers and senior officials with onerous responsibilities that are similar in kind to those that they carry in respect of children's homes but arguably more difficult to discharge successfully.

29.04 In this chapter of the Tribunal's report we discuss the circumstances of the appointment and the subsequent careers in residential care of the main sexual abusers; the incidence of, and response to, complaints; the absence of any complaints procedures; the awareness of staff; the role of field social workers; and monitoring, inspection and rota visits.

29.05 None of the sexual abusers referred to in the report was or is known to have a previous conviction for a relevant offence, except for Roger Saint, the foster parent whose case is dealt with in paragraphs 25.01 to 25.29 of this Summary.

29.06 We do not believe that the Principal of Bryn Estyn (Arnold) had any knowledge of the sexual proclivities of Howarth and Norris at the time that they were appointed to posts at Bryn Estyn.

29.07 There is good reason to criticise the subsequent advancement of Norris but we do not suggest that Arnold became aware of, or suspected, Norris' sexual abuse. Norris should not have been appointed head of Clwyd House or subsequently transferred to Cartrefle to become Officer-in-Charge there, having regard to his limited abilities and his general coarseness, which were known to other members of the staff. Arnold, Howarth and Wyatt must each bear some of the blame for these errors of judgment.

29.08 The woman member of the staff at Upper Downing whose probationary period was extended should have been dismissed on that occasion. In the event, she formed a similar relationship later at Cartrefle, where she was appointed Deputy Officer-in-Charge, and resigned just before a disciplinary hearing. The error of judgment in her case was mainly that of Wyatt.

29.09 It is dispiriting that consultation with the police and with other centrally held records, such as those held by the Departments of Health and Education, would not have revealed anything adverse about the abusers. However, we emphasise the importance of such consultation whenever an appointment is made and the equal importance of re-checking when another occasion to do so, such as a further appointment or application, occurs. This is well illustrated by what happened in Clwyd in respect of Roger Saint. The same principle applies to all those responsible for other residential establishments for children and for the selection of other persons involved in the care of children.

29.10 Other evidence indicates that consultation by Clwyd SSD with the police and other record holding agencies was, at best, sporadic.

29.11 The most discouraging fact in relation to complaints of sexual abuse is that very few children in residential care in Clwyd complained to anyone in authority of being sexually abused at or about the time when the abuse was occurring.

29.12 The evidence is clearest about complaints made by 3 boys. Two of these boys complained about Norris to a member of the staff at Cartrefle, Stanley, who dealt with them sensitively. Stanley, to whom great credit is due, reported the complaints appropriately and the first prosecution of Norris followed. The third boy complained at Chevet Hey to a member of staff (or direct to the Officer-in-Charge) of an indecent assault by Taylor in or about September 1973; but Taylor was permitted to leave without any other action being taken in relation to him, despite the fact that a similar allegation against him by another boy had been overheard and reported at Bersham Hall 2 months previously, when it was not believed.

29.13 The negative response to the complaints about Taylor occurred shortly before Clwyd County Council came into existence but that form of response was to become typical in Clwyd in the following 15 years, especially in relation to reports of physical abuse, and justified the pervading cynicism of most residents in care about the likely outcome of any complaints that they might make.

29.14 The failure of the victims of abuse by Howarth and Norris to complain at the time is understandable for a wide range of reasons that we spell out in the report, including the abusers' dominant positions at Bryn Estyn and Cartrefle. In the event, 5 witnesses told the Tribunal that they did complain about Howarth whilst they were at Bryn Estyn and another said that he complained about both Howarth and (less clearly) about Norris. One other witness, who was at Cartrefle, alleged that he complained of Norris' sexual abuse there before June 1990.

29.15 We discuss this evidence in detail in the Tribunal's report but we cannot be confident that any of the alleged complaints was made in comprehensible form for reasons that we explain. The evidence does, however, underline the importance of listening to, recording and taking seriously any complaints of this kind made by children.

29.16 A similar picture has emerged in relation to other residential establishments, particularly those of the Bryn Alyn Community, where John Allen was the dominant figure. One former resident of the Eirianfa unit at Ystrad Hall claimed that he complained to a member of staff of being buggered by another member of the staff and alleged that he was physically assaulted for his pains but we explain in paragraph 22.19 of the report our reasons for doubting this evidence. As for the abuse by Ryan at Clwyd Hall School, there were only minor complaints by a parent of hugging a boy and by another boy of Ryan holding his hand.

29.17 The picture in relation to foster care is not dissimilar. Saint's offences came to light as a result of complaints by 2 of his adopted children in February 1996 but by then the abuse in the foster home had been occurring for many years. In Rutter's case, there were complaints but they were made by mature girls in a hostel; and sexual abuse in foster home B persisted for nearly 8 years before one of the children first made allegations against Mr B.

29.18 The sparseness of contemporary complaints of sexual abuse is typical of many cases that came before courts throughout the United Kingdom but it does not exonerate from responsibility staff and officers in Clwyd who were charged with the duty of looking after these children in care. Quite apart from the general constraints on making this type of complaint, there were additional factors in Clwyd militating against the early discovery of sexual abuse when it occurred.

29.19 One of these factors was the absence of any complaints procedures, which was a serious defect nationally until well into the 1980s. In Clwyd there was no recognised complaints procedure from 1974 until about 1991. The absence of such a procedure confirmed, in effect, the general view of residents that it was pointless to complain. Moreover, in practice, when a resident did pluck up courage to complain, he/she was rarely believed and was almost invariably asked if he/she wished to make a formal complaint (being warned of the seriousness of the matter for the member of staff impugned). If he/she went on to make a written statement, the complainant would rarely be seen subsequently by anyone with disciplinary authority and in most cases he/she would be transferred to another (usually less congenial) home.

29.20 We are critical also of the lack of awareness of residential care staff, with particular reference to the staff at Bryn Estyn. We discuss again their knowledge of Howarth's flat list practice and gossip about it. Whilst some sympathy is due to them, in view of Arnold's attitude to the matter and his threat of dismissal for anyone who gave currency to the rumours about Howarth, they must share some of the blame for the failure to discover Howarth's abuse earlier.

29.21 Only one member of the Bryn Estyn staff, Paul Wilson, claimed to have spoken to Wyatt about his suspicions of Howarth and that was as late as February 1984. According to Wilson, Wyatt's response was to ask whether he was making a formal complaint and to warn him that the repercussions could be quite serious. We have no reason to doubt Wilson's evidence on this point but we add that, if Wyatt was unaware by that late date of Howarth's flat list practice, it exemplifies the inadequate monitoring of Bryn Estyn by the SSD.

29.22 In succeeding paragraphs of the report we refer to the cult of silence that prevailed at Bryn Estyn and emphasise the importance of "whistleblowers" who are prepared to speak up. We comment also that awareness on the part of staff depends not only upon their own observation but also upon confiding relationships between staff and residents, illustrated by the example of Stanley at Cartrefle[3]. In this context we stress the importance of dealing with absconders sensitively because their reasons for absconding may disclose abuse.

29.23 Very few of the many complainants who gave evidence to the Tribunal said that they had a confiding relationship with any member of the residential care staff or with their field social worker. In a separate section of Chapter 29 we

---

[3] See para 29.12 of this Summary.

stress the importance of the field social worker's duty to establish and maintain a close relationship with children in residential care.

29.24 There were no statutory regulations specifying a required frequency of visits by field social workers to children in residential care for whom they were responsible but Clwyd (like many other local authorities) accepted the requirements of successive Boarding Out Regulations (applying only to children in foster care) as the appropriate standard to be followed. In general, this involved a visit within one month of a placement and thereafter every 2 or 3 months.

29.25 It is unlikely that the overall record of visiting by field workers was as bad as most of the complainants now recall and some of the latter were shown by contemporary records to be incorrect. Nevertheless, the record overall was, at best, very patchy and this was a matter to which Ramsay drew attention on several occasions at meetings of senior managers.

29.26 This problem affected most local authority homes in Clwyd but was felt most acutely by residents in Bryn Estyn. We point out also that a high proportion of residents in Bryn Estyn were from far away so that visits by their field workers were comparatively rare. It is very credible, therefore, that most of the residents felt that they were unsupported and largely forgotten unless they behaved in such a way that further local authority or police action was triggered.

29.27 A notable feature of the evidence before the Tribunal has been the lack of any personal contact between the children in residential care in Clwyd and anyone from the outside world. The Management Committee for the 3 Wrexham community homes of Bryn Estyn, Little Acton and Bersham Hall, did meet quarterly at each of these homes in turn between about 1976 and 1984 but none of the former residents of these homes recalls meaningful contact with any councillor on these occasions.

29.28 Provision was made for members of the Social Services Committee to visit all the community homes in accordance with a rota but it cannot be said that the arrangements made any substantial contribution to the welfare of the children. We have been left with a lasting impression of councillors' unease and uncertainty about their role as visitors. They were encouraged by senior officials to perform this duty and given guidance but their unhappiness with it was reflected in diminishing attendance. In 1992 it was reported to the Director of Social Services that no Wrexham children's home had been visited by senior officers or senior elected members in the past 12 months; and in 1995 attendance at a training day for rota visitors was so bad that plans for further training were abandoned.

29.29 There was no formal structure for inspection of the local authority community homes, except during the period of delegation to the areas from 1977 to 1980, when there were 2 inspectors based at headquarters[4]. Their remit, however, covered all 65 social service establishments in the county and their work load

---

[4] Ibid, para 28.07.

was too heavy to enable them effectively to monitor the many community homes still in existence.

29.30 Outside this period from 1977 to 1980, visits to the community homes by senior officials seem to have been largely random. In paragraphs 29.72 to 29.85 of the report we trace the history of these visits through the evidence of Powell, Wyatt, Ramsay, Thomas and Barnes.

29.31 Our conclusion is that, although the identification of potential sexual abusers often presents insurmountable difficulties and young victims are usually extremely reluctant to complain when it occurs, the failings discussed in this chapter of the report must have played a part cumulatively in prolonging the sexual abuse that occurred and may have encouraged the abusers, before it began, to think that they would escape detection.

29.32 Our discussion in Chapter 29 is focussed mainly on the community homes for which Clwyd County Council was directly responsible but our comments are relevant to the agencies responsible for other residential establishments for children within the county.

29.33 The issues that arise in relation to the avoidance or early elimination of sexual abuse in foster care are rather different but the quality of the relationship between field social worker and child, awareness on the part of the former and regular monitoring of the placement are all of the utmost importance.

The failure to eliminate physical abuse (Chapter 30)

30.01 Many of the criticisms made in Chapter 29 are equally relevant to the prevalence of physical abuse in the community homes within Clwyd but some different issues arise. On the evidence presented to us we have found that physical abuse on a significant scale occurred in 6 of the local authority community homes in Clwyd and in 4 of the other establishments.

30.02 Corporal punishment in community homes was prohibited by Clwyd County Council from 1974 onwards, following the policy of its 2 predecessor councils. A memorandum to this effect was addressed to staff in residential establishments for children and young people by the Director of Social Services on 20 June 1974. The memorandum stated that corporal punishment included "striking, slapping, pushing etc".

30.03 It was not until 1987 that corporal punishment was banned in state schools and the statutory ban was not extended to community homes until 1990 but we are satisfied that the staff in community homes in Clwyd, with few exceptions, knew from about mid 1974 that they were not permitted by their employing authority to inflict corporal punishment, even by slapping or pushing. It ceased to be permissible in voluntary homes in 1990 and in registered private children's homes in 1991.

30.04 There was much less certainty about the degree of physical restraint that was permissible. We are not aware of any national or local guidance on the subject that was readily available to members of staff during the period under review and none of them received any training directed to this problem. The foreseeable results were that there were wide variations in practice and that many of the complaints of physical abuse that we received related to alleged excesses by members of staff in restraining residents.

30.05 The failure of Clwyd SSD to deal effectively with the problem of physical abuse in its community homes stemmed mainly from shortcomings in its recruitment policies, the absence of adequate complaints procedures, the failure of staff to record and report untoward incidents accurately and lack of appropriate training.

30.06 Two aspects of Clwyd's recruiting procedures caused us particular concern, namely:

    (a) the frequent appointment of unqualified staff without advertising and without other conventional procedures;

    (b) the use of a pool of unqualified staff to fill casual vacancies.

30.07 The first of these defects was a particular feature of recruitment at Bryn Estyn and illustrates the extent to which Arnold was permitted to run that major community home as he saw fit.

30.08 This informal method of appointment (without any structured guidance or induction) does not appear to have been adopted generally in Clwyd but the use of a pool system to fill vacancies gathered momentum from about 1976 and remained in use until 1996. It appears that, when responsibility for the homes reverted to headquarters in 1980, Officers-in-Charge were given responsibility for staff appointments from the pool without reference to headquarters. Appointees were vetted but only by the provision of 2 personal references and a check with the police.

30.09 Temporary appointments from the pool were regarded as a useful means of checking the suitability of the persons chosen and avoiding the need for formal dismissal procedures, but Thomas and Barnes criticised the system in a review of staffing in the Spring of 1989 and Jevons told the Tribunal that all the staff concerned were unhappy with the pool system. He wanted to replace it when resources would allow him to do so, but it was not seen to be a high priority.

30.10 We recognise, however, that throughout the period under review there were very real difficulties about recruitment: there was no national pool or reserve of trained and experienced care workers on which a county such as Clwyd could draw and conditions generally for residential care workers were so unfavourable that the response to advertising of vacant posts was poor, even at times of high unemployment.

30.11 Despite the absence of any formal complaints procedures, residents in community homes did complain from time to time of physical abuse, as we recount in the report, but it was rare for a complaint to reach a formal stage because the complainant would be discouraged in the ways outlined in paragraph 29.19 of this Summary. The relevant incident would rarely be recorded in any log book in appropriate terms so that an uninformed reader would not surmise that an alleged assault had occurred. Even more perturbingly, on some occasions when the complaint was plainly true in substance, records would be distorted.

30.12 The inadequacies of the system are fully illustrated by the history of Paul Wilson[5], in respect of whom not less than 6 serious complaints came to the notice of headquarters during his period at Bryn Estyn.

30.13 Quite apart from reluctance to believe complainants, at least 3 other factors had an important influence on the outcome of investigations. These were:

(a) reluctance to set in train formal disciplinary procedures and misunderstanding of what had to be proved to justify written warnings and/or dismissal;

(b) persistent weakness in dealing with trades union representations on behalf of individual members of staff; and

(c) the impact (but not an unavoidable effect) of a "containment" agreement with the trades unions.

30.14 We have heard of quite a large number of complaints which were reported to the police but which did not result in a prosecution. Invariably, it seems, the decision not to prosecute was regarded by Clwyd SSD as an end of the matter and no disciplinary investigation or similar action followed. The result was that the member of staff who had been reported emerged unscathed, whatever the rights or wrongs of the matter might have been, and no remedial action was taken to deal with any underlying causes of conflict or unrest.

30.15 In our judgment this approach to disciplinary matters was fundamentally flawed. It was based on a mistaken belief that the criminal standard of proof applied to all complaints of misconduct by staff and it ignored the duty of the Council to investigate complaints thoroughly. The SSD adopted a mistaken rule also that complainants and witnesses in care, of whatever age or capability, should not be heard in disciplinary proceedings because it was contrary to the best interests of children to be called to do so.

30.16 We have not found anything in Clwyd County Council's disciplinary code to explain or justify these errors of approach and it was an abdication of the Council's duties to rely upon police investigations of matters that involved important employment and welfare issues.

30.17 We do not criticise the trades unions for the representations that they made and we are not persuaded that they went beyond the legitimate bounds of their duties. They were very powerful, exercising influence at all levels of management, but the evidence suggests that both senior and middle management adopted an unduly timorous approach to staff problems within the SSD and were too ready to accept what appeared to be an easy solution.

30.18 The "containment" agreement made in or about October 1980 between Clwyd County Council and the trades unions was intended to achieve a rational process for a reduction in staff costs without compulsory redundancies. We do

---

[5] Ibid, paras 10.04 to 10.12.

not consider, however, that this agreement should have inhibited proper disciplinary action or that it justified the transfer of unsuitable care staff to senior positions in community homes.

30.19 Examples of inadequate responses to complaints of physical abuse are legion throughout our report and they were probably the major factor in Clwyd's failure to eliminate such abuse in their community homes. In the end physical abuse could only have been stamped out if a new culture had been established through vigorous monitoring of both standards and practice, coupled with appropriate disciplinary action.

30.20 One of the difficulties of obtaining an accurate picture of the extent of physical abuse long after the event has been inadequate recording of incidents by staff of the community homes. The general standard of the records varied a great deal from time to time and from home to home. But the evidence points clearly to the conclusion that misleading recording and even, on occasions, falsification of records were part of a deliberate system intended to suppress the truth.

30.21 The inadequacy of the training of staff employed in residential establishments in Clwyd is a recurring theme of the Tribunal's report but it requires special mention in the context of physical abuse. Bad practices were by no means unique to Clwyd or North Wales in the 1970s and 1980s and the need for appropriate training was stressed in a number of reports commissioned by central government during that period.

30.22 Whereas the percentage of qualified field social workers in Clwyd advanced from 48 to 89 between 1975 and 1985, there was no similar progress in respect of residential child care staff. A training strategy was formulated in 1984 and periodically reviewed but comparatively little was achieved in the training of residential child care staff. Thomas told the Tribunal that it was known from the mid-1970s that only 10 to 15 per cent of residential child care staff for the whole of Wales were qualified. In his opinion, the position in Clwyd could only have changed "around the margins" by the 1990s in view of national policy towards residential child care training.

30.23 The comments that we have made, in relation to the prevention of sexual abuse, about the awareness of staff and their willingness to report abuse, the potential role of field social workers in discovering it and the need for effective monitoring, supervision and visiting apply with even greater force to the elimination of physical abuse because it is usually more easily detectable.

30.24 Although our analysis of the failure to eliminate physical abuse is somewhat different from that in relation to sexual abuse, the differences are only of emphasis. As a result of the failures that we have identified, the community homes were left in the main to run themselves; where physical abuse was occurring, it was allowed to continue; and the responsibility for these homes lay with senior management throughout.

30.25 The lessons to be learned in respect of other residential establishments for children are the same. It is essential that children in care placed in such establishments should be visited regularly by persons they trust, that there should be an adequate complement of trained care staff and that the practices and performances of the establishments should be closely monitored. Without such safeguards, there will always be a risk that physical abuse may occur and the children will be inadequately protected from harm.

Basic failings in the quality of care (Chapter 31)

31.01   The evidence that we heard from complainants and others demonstrated that, for many children in care in Clwyd, the quality of care provided fell far below an acceptable standard. The cumulative effect of the SSD's various failings in this respect amounted, in our judgment, to abuse of those children; and the lamentable result was that many of them emerged from care unfitted to meet the demands of adult life, without adequate continuing support and filled with resentment about their treatment in care.

31.02   The major failings that we have identified were:

      (a)   The lack of adequate planning of each child's period in care.

      (b)   The absence of any strategic framework for the placement of children in residential care.

      (c)   Ineffective reviewing processes and lack of consultation with the child.

      (d)   Intermittent and inadequate surveillance by field social workers.

      (e)   Failure to establish any co-ordinated system for preparing residents for their discharge from care.

31.03   Elaine Baxter, who carried out a review of files and interviews with social workers, confirmed the lack of structured assessment and planning. Social workers commented to her that there was no structured proforma for individual care planning in the 1980s and that the only planning mechanism was the review, the form for which provided a space for future plans. Moreover, the views of the child were not obtained in any formal sense before the Children Act 1989. The result was that many children in residential care had no coherent picture of their likely future in care and were not given any clear idea of how they might progress positively.

31.04   One of the reasons for the lack of individual care plans may have been the absence of any clear framework for the placement of children after their reception into care. Ramsay's role as Placement Officer was formalised in 1975 and he retained this responsibility until he retired in 1987 but he seems to have had little effective discretion in the matter. The reality was that the number of available places in residential care was limited throughout and that, in many cases, admissions were treated as emergency cases when they need not have been. Thus, many (perhaps most) placements were decided on the basis of availability rather than suitability.

31.05   From the point of view of the child in care, he/she was liable to be moved for reasons unconnected with his/her welfare and might be placed far away from his/her home of origin and friends. Financial constraints became a factor from

1980 onwards, particularly in relation to the closure of Bryn Estyn. Thus, it was difficult for many children to foresee their future or even to retain any realistic immediate aims.

31.06 We received evidence of divergent practice in carrying out the reviews of children in care required by statute[6]. Whichever procedure was followed, however, the direct contribution of the child was very limited in the 1970s and 1980s. It was not normal for the child to be consulted or directly involved in reviews.

31.07 A further serious problem was delay in carrying out the reviews in some areas. In one area in 1982, 209 (including 80 supervision order cases included by Clwyd in the system) out of 267 reviews were reported to be overdue. In another area, in the previous year, 42 reviews had been missed, some were 12 months late and 2 of the teams had each been late in completing 35 reviews.

31.08 Although we heard some evidence of good practice in visiting and of the general availability of social workers at, for example, Park House and South Meadow and early on at Bersham Hall, for most children contact with social workers was insufficient. Once children were placed in residential care, they became a low priority and social workers tended to concentrate on work with their families. One of the consequences was considerable disaffection between social workers and residential care staff: the former Area Officer for Wrexham, for example, described the relationship as "abysmal". This was not necessarily the fault of social workers. Some children did not have a social worker allocated to them and others were placed so far from their own homes that visiting by social workers, with high case loads and limited mileage allowances, was difficult.

31.09 The failure to prepare young persons for their discharge from care was a striking criticism made by many complainants. The evidence suggests that greater sustained efforts were made in this respect in the earlier part of the period under review than later, when the boarding out of children predominated. As unemployment increased, work training for residents seems to have faded from the picture and we heard very little of positive training, even in the domestic sphere, once residents had passed school age.

31.10 On the initiative of the Director of Social Services (Gledwyn Jones), who had to address a conference called to discuss housing homeless young people at risk, a survey was carried out in Clwyd of young people who had left care between 1 April 1983 and 30 September 1984. Some of the results of that survey are summarised in paragraph 31.25 of our report. Amongst the findings were that only 10 out of 27 in temporary accommodation were receiving any planned follow up and 37 of the total of 62 who responded were unemployed. The report on the survey concluded that most children in care were offered few opportunities to learn basic "survival" skills.

---

[6] Section 27(4) of the Children and Young Persons Act 1969. There was a parallel requirement in successive Boarding Out Regulations.

31.11 This survey and report did not lead to any very positive action but the Children Act 1989 imposed a wide range of duties on local authorities in relation to young people leaving care. Clwyd did then respond swiftly and a leaving care strategy, embodying 11 policy statements, was approved by committee on 3 May 1995.

31.12 In November and December 1992, Clwyd was one of 3 Welsh counties selected by the SSIW for an inspection of outcomes for children leaving care. The overall picture presented by the report on the inspection was dismal, although Clwyd did not compare unfavourably with the other 2 counties. The situation in Clwyd was much the same as it had been 8 years earlier. Of the 8 young persons seen (in the South Division), who had all left care in the preceding 14 months, only one was undergoing training and the other 7 were unemployed. All were dependent on State benefits and top up payments made by the SSD. The inspectors stressed the need for Clwyd to produce a statement on leaving care policy and the high priority that should be given to education, training and employment in all reviews of children looked after.

31.13 It is likely that many of the failings of the Clwyd care system were common to other local authorities, at least until the requirements of the Children Act 1989 began to concentrate minds. Some officers in Clwyd were, however, aware of the need for action well before the Act of 1989 and the major fault in responding to that need lay with senior officers, most of whom had inadequate skill in management and who made little effort to overcome their initial lack of expertise in child care matters. It was they who should have given the necessary strategic impetus and directions for reform.

The response of higher management to investigations, including the Jillings inquiry (Chapter 32)

32.01 It is of some relevance to the relationship between Clwyd county councillors and the Social Services Department that from 1974 to 1989 no political party had overall control. Until 1987 committee and sub-committee chairmanships were shared between groups, in which the group of independents was prominent. Apart from a small number of prominent figures, according to the first Director of Social Services, they had neither the inclination nor the ability or experience to give a firm lead; and this last comment applied to successive chairmen of the Social Services Committee. Members saw the Director of Social Services rather than themselves as the employer and the staff as his employees.

32.02 This relationship changed from 1989 when the Labour group became a majority of the elected members. From 1987 Labour members had conducted themselves as the opposition to a coalition of the other groups and, when they became the majority, management of the Council's affairs changed quite quickly.

32.03 Two relevant leading figures emerged. **Councillor Dennis Parry**, who had been a county councillor from 1981, became chairman of the Labour group in 1990 and its leader in 1991, whereupon he became Leader of the Council, with his own office at Shire Hall. The second leading figure was **Councillor Malcolm King,** who had been employed by the Council as Centre Manager/Area Organiser of an Intermediate Treatment Centre at Wrexham from 1977 to 1982 and had then become manager of a community project for children and families in Wrexham. King was elected to the County Council in May 1989 and became Chairman of its Social Services Committee from January 1990, after serving as Vice-Chairman for 6 months. The result was that these 2 men played leading roles with John Jevons in all major decision making in relation to the county's social services from 1990 until the County Council ceased to exist.

32.04 There were 6 relevant investigations before 1990, all of which have been referred to earlier in this Summary. There were 3 into events at Park House (1975, 1978 and 1988), one each into Little Acton (1978) and Chevet Hey (1986), and the sixth was, at the request of Mr Justice Mars-Jones in 1987, into the circumstances in which David Gillison and Jacqueline Thomas had come to be employed by the SSD.

32.05 It is unnecessary to refer again here to the contents of these reports. All except the Gillison/Thomas report were severely critical of aspects of the management of the individual homes and some contained highly relevant criticisms of senior management. None of the critical reports, however, was made known to the Social Services Committee. It appears that each report was given very restricted circulation and the only one that was mentioned even indirectly to the Social Services Committee was the 1988 report on Park House, which was dealt with in a very misleading way 2 years later, as we have explained in paragraph 17.25 of this Summary.

32.06 As for the response to Mr Justice Mars-Jones' request, the investigation was superficial and there was an extraordinary delay of 3 years before the report was presented to a sub-committee[7]. We do not believe that the report would have been presented then but for a journalist's comment on the matter at the time of Norris' first conviction.

32.07 It is clear also that neither copies nor summaries of the critical reports were given to senior members of the residential staff such as Michael Barnes, who took over as Acting Officer-in-Charge at Little Acton in 1978 and Chevet Hey in 1986 following adverse reports on those homes. In August 1986 Barnes and Christopher Thomas presented a document entitled "Report on Child Care - Draft Policies", which contained a number of the criticisms of senior management that are made in our own report. In one passage they said:

> "As a result the role of HQ in setting policy and in maintaining practice has become so blurred to the point that some Areas (and some residential settings) find it easy "to do their own thing" regardless of policy. We are not quite sure whether this cavalier attitude is the cause or the effect of uncertain management."

32.08 No effective administrative or other action appears to have been taken in response to any of these reports.

---

[7] See para 14.23 of this Summary.

32.09 There were 4 more investigations into specific homes between 1990 and 1995. These were into Cartrefle (1990 to 1992), Frederick Rutter (1992), Cherry Hill (1994) and Foster home E (1995). Of these, the most important and wide-ranging was the investigation into Cartrefle. There were unsatisfactory aspects about each of the 3 others.

32.10 The Rutter report, apparently drafted by Wyatt, was presented to a sub-committee on 21 October 1992 but it was far from thorough: the investigation of the supervision and support of children boarded out or in lodgings was little more than cursory and one member of the sub-committee commented on its inadequacy.

32.11 The Cherry Hill investigation appears to have been inconclusive[8].

32.12 Despite the serious concerns and criticisms expressed by the Review Sub-Committee in its report on the placement in Foster home E, managers within the East Division were said to believe that no significant errors were to be learned from the handling of the case.

32.13 The reports by John Banham and the panel, forming part of the overall review of Cartrefle following Norris' conviction, contained many criticisms of the SSD, some of which had been voiced in the reports on Little Acton (1975) and Park House (1988). They were highly critical of the lack of leadership and direction shown by senior management and its lack of awareness of its responsibility to safeguard and promote the welfare of the child. In their view, a change of style and attitude was needed to develop an ethos which put the interests of the service user first. Amongst their recommendations was the appointment of a new headquarters Officer-in-Charge of Child Care Services, equivalent in rank or senior to Divisional Directors. The weakness of management arrangements was seen as a significant contributing factor to both the poor quality of care at Cartrefle and the failure to protect children living there from abuse.

32.14 The panel presented its report in February 1992 but it was not until 27 October 1992 that a report of its conclusions, together with the response of the Director of Social Services, were put before the Social Services Committee. In the interim period there had been discussions with the Council's insurers and the County Solicitor about the extent to which the report could be published, if at all. Discussions had taken place also with representatives of the CPS, who said that the report must not be published because publication might prejudice forthcoming or contemplated criminal proceedings.

32.15 The difficulties were resolved by an agreement that there should be limited publication of conclusions and recommendations extracted from the report. Discussion by members of the council was to be confined to "the general principles disclosed". Thus, the Social Services Committee and the ACPC received a much censored and anodyne version of the panel's findings and recommendations. The recommendation that there should be a senior post at Assistant Director level or equivalent for child care services within

---

[8] Ibid, paras 16.05 and 16.06.

headquarters was rejected by the Director on the ground that it reflected "a centralist approach directly contrary to the aims of the new department structure".

32.16 The proposal to set up the Jillings inquiry was approved by the Social Services Committee on 12 January 1994. The stated reason for it was that the police investigations had been protracted and that considerable further time was likely to elapse before any public inquiry could start: it was felt that the Council needed to review the past more quickly than a public inquiry could in order to learn whether anything else needed to be done by the Council to ensure the proper care and protection of children. The Council's insurers were not consulted about the proposal.

32.17 John Jillings, a retired Director of Social Services for Derbyshire and former President of the Association of Directors of Social Services, agreed to act as chairman of the three member panel of inquiry.

32.18 The investigation lasted 16 months longer than had been expected and the report was completed in February 1996. It covered the period in Clwyd from 1974 to 1995.

32.19 This Tribunal decided at an early stage that the Jillings report should not be admitted in evidence before us. Major reasons for this decision were that the report consisted substantially of expressions of opinion on matters that we were required to investigate afresh and to reach our own conclusions and that the report had been presented less than 2 months before the demise of the Council so that there had not been sufficient time for any positive action in response to it. Other important reasons were that the contents of the report were largely hearsay in relation to the issues that we had to decide, on which we were to receive direct evidence. Moreover, the form of the report was such that it could not helpfully be used in cross-examination of individual witnesses.

32.20 The members of the Tribunal were, however, supplied with copies of the Jillings report to enable us to consider the action that had been taken in respect of it after it had been presented. It was helpful also to Counsel to the Tribunal in advising as to the evidence that ought to be placed before us.

32.21 The report was given very limited circulation within Clwyd County Council when it was received.

32.22 The Council sought the advice of the Hon Michael Beloff QC and Paul Stinchcombe on 3 main problems attendant upon publication of the report, namely:

(1) whether publication might avoid the Council's insurance policy;

(2) the potential liability of Clwyd for defamatory comments in the report;

(3) whether there was any risk to the proper administration of justice through the impact of the report upon any pending trials.

32.23 In the light of their views on these questions, Counsel advised that the report should only be made available to members under strictly controlled conditions, observing safeguards suggested by the Council's insurers.

32.24 The advice of Counsel was accepted and the Policy, Finance and Resources Committee received the report at its meeting on 22 March 1996, 9 days before Clwyd County Council ceased to exist. The decisions of the committee were approved by the Council at its last meeting on 26 March 1996.

32.25 It was almost inevitable that there should be allegations of a "cover up" in the following months but they receded once the setting up of this Tribunal was announced in June 1996. The Welsh Office and the successor authorities canvassed the possibility that the successor authorities might publish an edited version of the Jillings report but we agree with the conclusion of those authorities that it was impracticable to do so.

32.26 In our judgment leading members and senior officers of Clwyd County Council were bound, in the exercise of reasonable prudence, to accept the authoritative legal advice that they received and to act accordingly in the short space of time left to them.

32.27 We have been given full information about the discussions with the insurers and the representations on the question of publication made by the CPS and the North Wales Police; and we discuss the issues raised by these events in paragraphs 32.52 to 32.60 of our report. We are satisfied that the various parties to the discussions and correspondence about publication all acted in good faith.

32.28 We reach the conclusion that the legal and contractual issues that arise in relation to the conduct of inquiries such as the Jillings investigation and the earlier inquiry into Cartrefle and the publication of reports on them are matters of public concern that deserve further consideration at a high level. We list the specific questions that we have in mind in paragraphs 32.61 and 32.62 of the Tribunal's report and these are reflected in recommendation 71.

32.29 We recommend also that advice to local authorities in relation to ad hoc inquiries in local government should be up-dated when these questions have been considered (recommendation 72).

ALLEGED ABUSE OF CHILDREN IN CARE IN LOCAL AUTHORITY HOMES IN GWYNEDD BETWEEN 1974 AND 1996
(Chapters 33 to 37)

In this part of the report we deal in successive chapters with 5 community homes in Gwynedd. The most important, overshadowing the others, is Tŷ'r Felin, because a majority of the complaints of abuse related to this home and because the longest serving Officer-in-Charge was (Joseph) Nefyn Dodd, whose influence permeated residential child care in the county for a dozen years from 1978.

Tŷ'r Felin, 1974 to 1995 (Chapter 33)

33.01 Tŷ'r Felin was a long 2 storey building in a large council estate on the northern outskirts of Bangor. It was planned and built as an observation and assessment centre at a cost of £48,000; and up to 12 children were to be accommodated at a time, 5 for assessment and 7 for short stays. Education was provided on the premises in one classroom and one teacher was employed.

33.02 It was said initially that the categories of children to be accommodated at Tŷ'r Felin were those needing to be detained in secure or semi-secure accommodation but no special facilities of this kind appear to have been planned or provided. By the time of the 1979 Regional Plan it was categorised merely under the head of "Other homes"; and it was described as a community home for boys and girls aged 3 to 17 years, with 6 places for local assessment and 6 residential places.

33.03 This home opened in or about January 1974 and it remained open until the autumn of 1995. It was demolished in March 1997.

33.04 Most of the evidence that we heard about Tŷ'r Felin related to the period between 1 January 1978 and 23 May 1990, when the Officer-in-Charge was **(Joseph) Nefyn Dodd**[1]. During this period his wife, **June Dodd**, whom he married in 1961, was also employed at Tŷ'r Felin. She had worked as an assistant domestic supervisor at Bersham Hall for 5 years and she became an assistant housemother at Tŷ'r Felin in April 1978, progressing to Senior RCCO from 1 August 1982, after taking the CSS course. She and her husband lived in a flat forming part of Tŷ'r Felin until 1988.

33.05 Dodd's health deteriorated in the late 1980s and June Dodd became Acting Officer-in-Charge of Tŷ'r Felin on 1 December 1989. On Dodd's retirement, at the age of 54 years, his wife became the established Officer-in-Charge from 1 September 1990, but she herself took early retirement on 31 December 1992.

---

[1] For earlier references to him, see paras 10.25 and 13.11 of this Summary.

33.06 In the period prior to the appointment of Nefyn Dodd the most relevant event was the arrival of **Alison Taylor** as Deputy Officer-in-Charge from 6 September 1976. She remained there until July 1980, when she left to take the CQSW course at Cartrefle College, Wrexham, before becoming Officer-in-Charge of Tŷ Newydd.

33.07 Whilst Taylor was at Tŷ'r Felin, she was Acting Officer-in-Charge for about a year because Dodd's predecessor was away sick. During that period Taylor lived on the premises with her husband, son and adopted daughter.

33.08 There were very few complaints of abuse at Tŷ'r Felin prior to 1978 and we did not receive any acceptable evidence of physical or sexual abuse by any member of the staff. One complaint by a girl resident of sexual abuse by a senior male member of the staff was investigated by the Deputy Director of Social Services, D A Parry, who was "completely satisfied" that the allegations were unfounded.

33.09 Unlike Clwyd County Council, Gwynedd County Council did not prohibit corporal punishment in its community homes until 8 February 1983. Before that, it was permitted at the discretion of the Officer-in-Charge. Taylor told the Tribunal that Parry instructed her that a cane should be on display.

33.10 There were signs of conflict between Dodd and Taylor soon after his arrival. She received without warning a letter of reprimand from Parry dated 1 February 1978, following strangely soon upon a letter of thanks from him for her work as Acting Officer-in-Charge. The strong inference is that this letter was inspired by Dodd.

33.11 Almost from the beginning, Dodd was given additional responsibilities outside Tŷ'r Felin. In the absence of the Community Homes Officer on sick leave, it was agreed that, from 9 October 1978, Dodd would spend 15 hours per week fulfilling part of her duties referable to children's homes. The arrangement apparently ended on 28 February 1979 but Dodd was then asked by Parry (probably in 1980) to assist in supervising the running of Y Gwyngyll at Llanfairpwll. This responsibility was enlarged into full responsibility for all the community homes in August 1982.

33.12 In his new role Dodd was accorded the title of Supervisor/Co-ordinator and his position as line manager for the Officers-in-Charge of the other community homes was confirmed in a memorandum from the Officer-in-Charge of the Children's Section at headquarters, Owain Gethin Evans, dated 23 November 1983.

33.13 The final stage in this process of advancement for Dodd, whilst he remained Officer-in-Charge of Tŷ'r Felin, was his promotion to Principal Officer (Residential Care - Children) from 1 October 1985. This was said to be in recognition of the work that he had carried out from 1982 onwards: his new job description was broadly in line with his earlier responsibilities.

33.14 It follows that Dodd became progressively less involved in the daily running of Tŷ'r Felin during the 1980s. Nevertheless, it remained his own domestic home during the week until 1988 and his wife was effectively his Deputy Officer-in-Charge from 1982. When he was not at headquarters or visiting other community homes, he would work in the office at Tŷ'r Felin from 9 am to 5 pm before retiring to their flat.

33.15 The extent to which the Dodds have dominated the evidence that we have heard about Tŷ'r Felin may be judged from the fact that, of the 84 former residents known to have complained of abuse there, 65 alleged abuse by one or both of the Dodds. In all we heard oral evidence from 15 former residents and we received in evidence the written statements of 12 others: of these 27 witnesses, only 3 did not complain about one or both of the Dodds and one of these 3 left a year before they arrived.

33.16 We deal with the complaints about Nefyn Dodd under 2 main headings, namely, the disciplinary climate at Tŷ'r Felin under him and the allegations of physical abuse made against him. Complaints of sexual abuse at Tŷ'r Felin did not figure prominently in statements made to the police or in evidence received by the Tribunal and we deal with these briefly at paragraph 33.22 below.

33.17 We received conflicting evidence about Dodd's regime at Tŷ'r Felin. Many complainants painted him as an aggressive and dictatorial man, who did not hesitate to use physical force when dealing with children and who imposed a tyrannical and unreasonable regime upon child residents and the staff. In short, it is said that he ran Tŷ'r Felin as "a little Bryn Estyn". Some other witnesses described him, as a gentle giant, who believed in running "a tight ship" in the interests of the children themselves and who was able to establish a good rapport with them.

33.18 We examine the evidence on these issues in paragraphs 33.31 to 33.55 of the report. Although an SWSO's report on a visit in November 1978 was favourable, a very different view was expressed by Dewi Evans, now Director of Social Services for Carmarthen, who visited Tŷ'r Felin in August 1981, as a member of an inquiry team investigating complaints about Y Gwyngyll. Evans told the Tribunal that Tŷ'r Felin had the atmosphere of an army camp for small soldiers: the kerbstones were painted white, the youngsters were in uniform and were required to wear a tie with Tŷ'r Felin written on it, and every time they went to a shop for sweets they had to bring back a receipt. He referred also to an atmosphere of fear and likened the children to mice "scurrying here and there".

33.19 Evidence in support of Dodd's regime came from senior officers of Gwynedd SSD, some neighbours and interested persons in the locality and some former staff and residents; and we have received persuasive evidence that, in his first years as Officer-in-Charge, Dodd did effect improvements to the appearance of Tŷ'r Felin and involved himself with the children to the extent, for example, of eating with them. However, to many of the children and at least some of the staff, he was an intimidating figure and a bully. He was a large man with a powerful presence, who frequently raised his voice to impose himself. Moreover, he was dictatorial to those under him, brooking no disagreement; and his approach to residential child care was no doubt influenced by his early experience at Bryn Estyn and Bersham Hall.

33.20 It may be said that in his first 2 years or so at Tŷ'r Felin the balance of achievement was in Dodd's favour in the sense that, although he imposed an inappropriately repressive and regimented pattern of life upon residents, he did show some interest in them, and did provide a degree of security for children placed there. As time passed, however, his external duties grew, as did his powers; and he became a more awesome figure, to whom June Dodd would report for punishment any misdemeanours that had occurred during the day.

33.21 Our view of Dodd and his regime is strongly supported by numerous entries in the Tŷ'r Felin log books in which Dodd addressed homilies and instructions to members of the staff, some of which we quote in our report; and it reflects also the oral evidence to the Tribunal of 2 senior members of the staff. It is a reasonable inference, however, that Dodd's behaviour became more circumspect from about 1986 onwards because of the investigation by the police into Alison Taylor's complaints about him and his promotion to the status of Principal Officer towards the end of the previous year.

33.22 Of the 84 known complainants of abuse at Tŷ'r Felin, covering a period of nearly 22 years when the community home was open, 12 alleged that they had been sexually abused by a member of the staff; and the total number of staff against whom these allegations were made was 6 (including the member of staff referred to in paragraph 33.08 of this Summary). We heard evidence from 4 of these complainants and we are satisfied that the other potential witnesses would not have added significantly to the overall picture. There were 5 complainants (3 female, 2 male) who alleged that Dodd abused them sexually, but there was no discernible pattern to his alleged misconduct on separate occasions between 1979 and 1985 and none of the allegations was corroborated either directly or indirectly. Dodd himself vehemently denied all of them and we are unable to find that any sexual abuse by him or by any other identified member of the staff at Tŷ'r Felin has been proved.

33.23 We received evidence from 17 former residents alleging physical assaults of varying gravity by Nefyn Dodd but 2 of them do not appear to have been at Tŷ'r Felin when he was there. Of the other 15, 8 gave oral evidence to the Tribunal and, 10 alleged substantial assaults and threats by him. We describe these various assaults in our report and they included caning, head-butting, punching, kicking and severe slapping. Dodd denied all the allegations in his evidence to the Tribunal and, when interviewed by the police, he made only one admission about the use of physical force, saying that he had grabbed a boy by the shoulders and pinned him against the wall, when telling him not to do something. He was then asked by the police officer whether that was a regular thing and he replied "Yes, I'm ashamed of it now but it happened".

33.24 Assessing the allegations of physical abuse made against Dodd has been one of the more difficult tasks that we have had to face. We accept that some of his aspirations as Officer-in-Charge were well meant. We are satisfied, however, that the regime that he imposed upon both children and staff at Tŷ'r Felin was unduly oppressive and that many of his methods of working were inappropriate. We are satisfied also that he did frequently use excessive force to the children in his care. Such conduct was not, in our view, habitual but it did reflect frailties in his temperament and his determination to stamp upon behaviour that cast a reflection upon the home or appeared to challenge his authority in any way. Thus, he would inflict inappropriate physical punishment upon absconders and was prone to do so for illicit smoking or other breaches of his rules that he regarded as flagrant or impertinent.

33.25 There were many complaints of physical abuse also against 2 other members of the Tŷ'r Felin staff, namely, June Dodd and the teacher, John Roberts.

33.26 Of the 10 former residents who complained to the police of being physically abused by **June Dodd**, only one gave oral evidence to the Tribunal but we received written evidence from 3 others. One witness alleged a serious assault, by kneeing in the groin, but this was said to have followed a very nasty incident in which someone had "set light" to Nefyn Dodd's dog. We discuss these complaints in paragraphs 33.87 to 33.92 of the Tribunal's report but, in our judgment, it would be inappropriate on the evidence to find that June Dodd was guilty of physically abusing children in her care either at Tŷ'r Felin or elsewhere.

33.27 June Dodd's position was inevitably difficult because she was employed in the community home of which her husband was Officer-in-Charge, contrary to generally approved practice. One of the many adverse consequences of this was that she was distrusted as a spy; and nothing that we have heard has cast doubt on the soundness of the rule against employing a spouse or partner in the same home as the other party to the relationship.

33.28 The number of complainants of physical abuse by **John Roberts** was similar to that in respect of June Dodd but they alleged much severer abuse. He became teacher-in-charge at Tŷ'r Felin in September 1979, when he was 32 years old, and he remained there until July 1985, after which he was transferred to the special unit of a primary school. During his Tŷ'r Felin period he was absent for the academic year 1981/1982, whilst attending a full time course for an advanced diploma in the education of children with special needs.

33.29 We heard oral evidence from 6 of the complainants against John Roberts, all of whom said that they were resident at Tŷ'r Felin at the time, and we received written evidence from 2 others, who were resident at Tŷ Newydd but who attended daily at Tŷ'r Felin for schooling. There is insurmountable difficulty about the allegations of one of the "live" witnesses, despite his apparent sincerity, because the documentary evidence suggests that he was only at Tŷ'r Felin for about 8 weeks at the beginning of 1978, over 18 months before John Roberts was posted there. However, the evidence of the other witnesses was persuasive and one of the incidents, referred to by a witness who gave written evidence, was the subject of a written report by Alison Taylor to the Director of Social Services on 26 May 1984.

33.30 The allegations against Roberts, which he denied, were almost wholly of assaults in the classroom at Tŷ'r Felin. They included throwing a blackboard duster, striking boys on the head with the revolving blackboard, hitting a boy on the head with a snooker cue and hitting another in the face, causing a nose bleed. One boy alleged also that he was chased and pursued by Roberts from the dining room, and then knocked to the floor and kicked and punched in the face.

33.31 In his evidence to the Tribunal, Roberts accepted that he had shouted at some pupils. He said also that, when he was at Tŷ'r Felin, he believed that there was a place for corporal punishment, but he had never used it. He dealt with each of the alleged incidents and said, of the one reported in May 1984, that the boy had been out of his place and disrupting others but that he had merely put his hand on the boy's head and directed him towards his seat.

33.32 Roberts was ultimately suspended in July 1992, in view of the allegations made against him in the major investigation by the North Wales Police. He had earlier received an informal warning as the result of complaints by the mother of a boy at his primary school arising out of 2 incidents earlier that year. The decision not to prosecute Roberts in respect of the Tŷ'r Felin complaints was taken early in 1993 but he remained suspended until a disciplinary hearing, which eventually took place on 9 November 1994. The outcome of the hearing was that Roberts was given a formal written warning "regarding (his) work as a teacher arising from the alleged incidents during (his) time at Tŷ'r Felin". He resigned from his teaching post and was appointed as an administrative officer with the pupils' service unit from 1 January 1995.

33.33 Our firm conclusion is that Roberts did use inappropriate and excessive physical force to some of his pupils at Tŷ'r Felin. The total volume of complaints against him has not been specially high and the proportion of his former pupils who have come forward to give evidence against him is comparatively small but we reject any suggestion that there has been an orchestrated conspiracy against him. Although he may have been under the influence of Dodd and lacked professional training in dealing with disturbed children, apart from the course referred to, these disadvantages do not excuse his excesses or his failure to recognise and admit that he was at fault.

33.34 Allegations of physical abuse by about 11 other members of the staff were made to the police but little evidence in support of them was received by the Tribunal and one of them was expressly withdrawn. **Mari Thomas**, who was a Senior RCCO at Tŷ'r Felin and later Officer-in-Charge of Cartref Bontnewydd, was named by 4 witnesses who gave evidence to us and 2 of them alleged that they had been assaulted by her, one with slaps to the face and the other by lashing out at him and dragging him from his bed by his hair, after both had misbehaved. Thomas denied these allegations but she accepted that she had been strict and she agreed in cross-examination that she had been forced to follow the regime laid down by Dodd.

33.35 We accept that, for some, Mari Thomas and some other members of staff were part of the overall oppressive atmosphere of Tŷ'r Felin and did use physical force to residents on occasions but the evidence falls far short of establishing persistent physical abuse by Thomas or the other members of staff referred to.

33.36 In the last section of this chapter we deal with other deficiencies in the quality of care provided at Tŷ'r Felin. Many of these failings were similar to those that we found in the Clwyd community homes.

33.37 A basic failing was that Tŷ'r Felin never fulfilled adequately its role as an assessment centre because it did not have the trained staff to do so. This appears to have been recognised gradually because the home's role changed to that of a holding centre; and it became indistinguishable in its purpose from the other community homes in Gwynedd. Moreover, many of the admissions were emergency cases; there was a general lack of care planning for each child; and many of them were allowed to drift.

33.38 A second failing was in the quality of education provided on the premises, which was described by SWSOs in 1988 as "basic in the extreme". Tŷ'r Felin merely provided a classroom and the teaching staff were provided by the Gwynedd Education Department on secondment. The scale of the service provided depended on the number of children receiving education and was at the rate of 2 hours per child per week. The education component of a child's care at Tŷ'r Felin was not formally integrated with any other part of it. Successive teachers there appear to have received no briefing as to their role and were required to function, in general, without supervision or professional support.

33.39 Other failings that were common to all the Gwynedd community homes included:

(a) the absence of any complaints procedures until a handbook for children in residential care was drafted by Dodd and approved by Gethin Evans before being circulated to heads of homes on or about 25 October 1988;

(b) the absence of any key worker system before 1985 and lack of clarity about it after it had been introduced;

(c) the lack of adequate assessment prior to the admission of a child to care;

(d) an unacceptably low level of fieldwork contact with children in residential care;

(e) the practice of Dodd, who was responsible for all placements within the county, to preside over all case conferences with the result that his view prevailed, and the individual social worker was marginalised once a child entered residential care;

(f) the lack of any effective county strategy so that placements were haphazard and too often depended on availability rather than suitability, many children being placed far from their home communities.

33.40 Despite the difficulties, a few residents did make complaints at the time but the evidence before us indicates that the response to them, even when they filtered through to higher management, was invariably negative. Complainants were discouraged from pursuing their complaints and were usually not believed. We cite a number of the responses that emerged in the evidence before us, including one case in which the record of an incident was suppressed on Dodd's initiative.

33.41 The general atmosphere at Tŷ'r Felin appears to have improved in the later stages of the Dodds' regime and it was described as "relaxed and friendly" by SWSOs during their visit in September 1988. However, the departure of the Dodds did not lead to a period of tranquillity.

33.42 The new Principal Officer (Children's and Adolescent Services) from March 1993, Dafydd Ifans, soon became aware of major difficulties at Tŷ'r Felin, where the Officer-in-Charge (by then called Residential Team Manager) was enthusiastic but inexperienced. There were divided loyalties amongst the staff, some of whom misbehaved, and a Senior RCCO was warned for misconduct. In or about early March 1994 the personal diary of a young woman resident was reported to be missing and it was established later that 3 pages of this diary had been passed a month earlier to the Chairman of the Social Services Committee.

33.43 The diary pages contained many shocking allegations of misconduct at Tŷ'r Felin, including drug abuse, sexual intercourse between residents and thefts of valuable property. A report by O & K Associates was commissioned in September 1994 and presented in February 1995; and it was probably the crucial factor in the decision by the Children's Committee in September 1995 to recommend the closure of Tŷ'r Felin.

33.44 In conclusion, we do not think that Dodd's initial appointment as Officer-in-Charge can fairly be criticised because it is likely that he presented himself well and he received a strongly favourable reference from Arnold of Bryn Estyn. It was a grave error, however, to give him additional and increasing responsibilities thereafter, despite the adverse report in 1981, to which we refer again later, and his wife should not have been appointed to a senior position in the same community home.

33.45 The combined effect of these errors was to facilitate the suppression of legitimate complaints about the regime at Tŷ'r Felin and to confer on Dodd excessive powers and responsibilities beyond his capacities. In any event, however, effective monitoring and supervision of the community home ought to have revealed defects in Dodd's attitudes and practices and to have led to a re-appraisal of him even before the police investigation in 1986.

Tŷ Newydd, 1982 to 1987 (Chapter 34)

34.01 Tŷ Newydd is a rather forbidding stone building on the A5122 road leading into Bangor, about a mile south-east of the Maesgeirchen Estate in which Tŷ'r Felin was located.

34.02 It was opened in 1978 as a hostel for up to 10 boys aged 16 to 21 years but was closed in 1981, by which time it was in a dilapidated state, which was severely criticised by the inquiry team referred to above in paragraph 33.18.

34.03 Tŷ Newydd was re-opened as a community home on 16 August 1982, to provide for up to 12 (but more usually 9) boys and girls in the age range of 5 to 18 years, who attended local schools or Tŷ'r Felin for education. The home closed on 31 January 1987 and the building is now a bail hostel.

34.04 The number of complaints of abuse at Tŷ Newydd in relation to the period from 1982 to 1987 would not justify its inclusion as a separate chapter but it is of some relevance because **Alison Taylor** was Officer-in-Charge from its re-opening until she was suspended from duty with effect from 1 December 1986.

34.05 According to Taylor, Tŷ Newydd was still in a state of considerable disrepair when she re-opened it. In her view, the physical conditions were such that it was barely fit to house children. It seemed to her that the home was being deliberately run down in anticipation of its replacement by Cartref Bontnewydd.

34.06 We know of only one complaint of sexual abuse by a member of the staff at Tŷ Newydd. It was not corroborated and no evidence in support of it has been presented to the Tribunal.

34.07 There were 5 complainants who alleged that they had been struck by members of the staff. Only one of these, however, gave oral evidence to the Tribunal. This witness alleged that X used to push people around and abuse them vocally without threatening them physically. On one occasion X did, however, grab him by the throat and pin him against the wall for giving cheek. In consequence, the boy stole a tin of petty cash.

34.08 Taylor made a log entry on the day of this incident, which was 12 August 1985. The entry indicated that the boy had absconded after an argument with X: after being returned by a policeman he had been abusive and threatening to both Taylor and X and had assaulted X finally, before running off. The witness, however, repudiated this account and said that it was completely inaccurate. A petty cash box was recorded as missing on 9 and 10 August 1985. When it was recovered about £20 was said to be missing.

34.09 Other allegations by complainants to the police who did not give evidence to us were of slapping incidents only and the overall position is that we have not received any persuasive evidence that physical or sexual abuse occurred at Tŷ Newydd during Taylor's regime or in the short period of its continued existence as a community home after she had been suspended.

34.10 In the following section of Chapter 34 of the report we give an account of the events that led to Taylor's suspension. At the outset she received a memorandum from Gethin Evans emphasising that Dodd was to be her line manager; and a practical, and unacceptable, consequence for her was that she frequently had to report to June Dodd or a more junior member of staff at Tŷ'r Felin in Dodd's absence elsewhere on his "extra mural" duties.

34.11 In the 4 years following Taylor's appointment to Tŷ Newydd there were 2 parallel developments of complaints by her to headquarters about the system and some cases of alleged maltreatment and criticisms from headquarters of Taylor's own conduct, some of which she attributed to Dodd as instigator.

34.12 Taylor eventually approached Councillor Keith Marshall, a member of Gwynedd Social Services Committee, early in 1986 to complain of maladministration in the SSD and violence by staff to children in residential care. Councillor Marshall consulted another councillor, who advised that the allegations should be reported to the police. The head of the CID of the North Wales Police met Taylor and Councillor Marshall at the latter's home on 20 February 1986 and the first of the investigations outlined in Chapter 51 of the report ensued.

34.13 Taylor became increasingly isolated from management during her period as Officer-in-Charge of Tŷ Newydd. On 8 June 1984 she received a formal warning from Gethin Evans for failing to meet a group of magistrates a month earlier and there were persistent criticisms of her by Dodd during 1985.

34.14 The Chairman of the Social Services Committee, Councillor Eric Davies, visited Taylor at Tŷ Newydd on 2 October 1986 and discussed her complaints and concerns. His report 3 days later alleged that she was unfit to be in charge of a children's home and that she was a blatant troublemaker.

34.15 On 1 December 1986 the Director of Social Services, Lucille Hughes, instructed Taylor to remain off duty pending an investigation of an alleged breakdown in "the spirit of professional trust and co-operation" between Taylor and her colleagues.

34.16 It was subsequently alleged 'inter alia' that Taylor's behaviour and attitude had created insecurity, anxiety and mistrust of her amongst a substantial number of colleagues; that her management of Tŷ Newydd had been seriously deficient, including failure to pull her weight in respect of time-keeping and duties; that she had consistently failed to co-operate with management; and that she had attempted to create rifts and tensions between Dodd and other colleagues by untruths and deceit.

34.17 Taylor was summarily dismissed following a meeting of the County Council's Disciplinary Panel on 2 November 1987, which she did not attend. She appealed against that decision and began proceedings for unfair dismissal. Before a hearing of either took place, a compromise was agreed on 25 August 1989, under which Taylor accepted voluntary redundancy together with financial compensation and costs in full settlement of her claim.

34.18 It is clear that Taylor was a thorn in the side of higher management from the moment when she returned to Gwynedd after professional training. In our view this was attributable to a substantial degree to the decisions to give Dodd wider responsibilities and retain him as Officer-in-Charge of Tŷ'r Felin. There were faults on both sides but Taylor's complaints about Dodd and John Roberts, although at times exaggerated, have been substantially vindicated by our own findings.

34.19 There is no persuasive evidence that Taylor acted contrary to the interests of the children in her care and there is some evidence that her relationship with them was good. It seems likely, however, that she had failings as a manager and leader of staff with the result that she did not endear herself to many of her colleagues, who were not prepared to support her when major disciplinary proceedings were taken against her.

Y Gwyngyll, 1979 to 1986 (Chapter 35)

35.01 Y Gwyngyll was a purpose-built community home in a small private housing estate at Llanfairpwll in Anglesey, intended to provide accommodation for 16 boys and girls in the full age range up to 18 years plus bed-sitting accommodation for 2 school leavers. Although the building was selected for an architectural award, its appearance, layout and amenities were criticised by independent social services officers; and it lacked warmth and a homely feeling.

35.02 The home opened on 1 January 1979, when the staff and residents from a small children's home at Llangefni were transferred to it, and it closed on or about 21 July 1986. The first Officer-in-Charge was **R A Dyson**, a man in his early 50s, who had previously been in charge of a voluntary children's home for 17 years.

35.03 The first SWSO report on Y Gwyngyll, based on a visit in October 1979, was quite favourable and the atmosphere in the home was said to be relaxed, despite its physical shortcomings. The report was critical, however, of the extent of the involvement of the Deputy Director of Social Services (D A Parry) in the running of the home, fettering the Officer-in-Charge's discretion, and of the case conference/review system, based at Tŷ'r Felin, which was already dominated by Dodd as chairman of all case conferences.

35.04 In the summer of 1981 an inquiry team from Dyfed was invited by the Chief Executive of Gwynedd County Council, Ioan Bowen Rees, to investigate complaints made by current and former members of the staff of Gwynedd County Council about the running of Y Gwyngyll[2]. The inquiry team of 3 visited Y Gwyngyll and other Gwynedd community homes in July and August 1981 and they produced a robust and critical report.

35.05 The complaints investigated, which were substantially endorsed by the Dyfed team, included inappropriate placement of children at Y Gwyngyll, inadequate managerial control and staffing arrangements, the absence of a co-ordinated policy for the management of children in care, the involvement of Dodd and noise and disturbance to neighbours. The team were critical of unplanned admissions and the absence of individual care plans and they regarded the involvement of Dodd in the running of Y Gwyngyll as an error of judgment.

35.06 A conclusion drawn by the Dyfed team was that the Gwynedd Children's Section was poorly administered at headquarters and within individual homes and that this was reflected in lower standards of provision for children.

35.07 This was the situation that faced **David Bayley Hughes**, when he took over as the second Officer-in-Charge of Y Gwyngyll on 14 September 1981, having previously worked in Tŷ'r Felin and other Gwynedd community homes. He was not shown a copy of the Dyfed team's report but he found the home to be in a mess when he arrived. The premises looked unfinished and did not have the feel of a home. Most of the staff were quite junior and were in a state of despair, although there were only 6 residents when he arrived. Hughes remained as Officer-in-Charge until 27 January 1986, but he was absent because of sickness from late 1985.

---

[2] See paras 33.18 and 34.02 of this Summary.

35.08 We have not received any evidence of habitual or persistent abuse at Y Gwyngyll.

35.09 Apart from 2 complaints of being punched by a member of staff, we are not aware of any allegations of abuse during Dyson's period as head of the home. Neither complainant alleged that he was injured by being punched and one of them said that he was fairly treated at Y Gwyngyll.

35.10 Complaints were made to the police by 11 former residents of Y Gwyngyll who were there between 1981 and 1986, when Hughes was in charge. One male former resident and one female alleged that they had sexual intercourse with a member of the staff of the opposite sex. The male said that he was 16 years old when he was seduced by a student member of the staff, who had been "giving him the eye". The former girl resident said that she had sexual intercourse on 2 occasions but she did not complain until about 8 years later. There was no corroboration then of her allegation and she did not provide the Tribunal with any evidence in support of it. These various incidents may have occurred but we cannot, in the circumstances find that they have been proved and there is no suggestion that persistent sexual abuse occurred at Y Gwyngyll.

35.11 The other 9 complainants alleged physical assaults of one kind and another and we received evidence from 7 of them (4 gave oral evidence). Each of the 4 "live" witnesses claimed to have been struck by **Nefyn Dodd**: they alleged serious physical punishments such as smacks and punches in the face and "belting" in the stomach for various misdemeanours, including smoking in the boot room. Dodd denied all the allegations and they were not supported by Hughes or any other member of the staff at Y Gwyngyll. We accept, however, that there were occasions when Dodd did use excessive force to residents at Y Gwyngyll but that this was on a much lesser scale than at Tŷ'r Felin.

35.12 It is unlikely that allegations against other members of the staff would have surfaced but for the allegations against Dodd. The evidence generally suggests that the regime under Hughes was very relaxed; he said in evidence that he did not impose punishments because he believed in counselling and thought that it worked excellently. One former senior member of the staff said that there were few rules under Hughes and that sometimes you would think that the residents were running the home. Only 2 former residents made allegations against Hughes: one said that Hughes "beat him up" a few times for being naughty, but was not more specific, and the other said that Hughes threw him to the floor on one of 3 or 4 occasions when residents barricaded themselves in.

35.13 The general quality of care at Y Gwyngyll left much to be desired and no effective steps were taken in response to the adverse report of the Dyfed team. Day to day control remained vested in Dodd: there was little direction from above and no strategic planning. Hughes told the Tribunal that he felt a lack of both support from headquarters and professional supervision. His impression was that residential care staff were being left "to keep a lid on" the problems surrounding troublesome youngsters whilst senior management washed their hands of them.

35.14 Hughes voiced some of his dissatisfactions at the end of 1984 and Dodd responded with a memorandum on the main difficulties with the management of Y Gwyngyll in January 1985, in which he was critical of Hughes' leadership. Hughes was then sent on 7 March 1985 a list of areas of concern and the action to be taken to deal with them. The exchanges underlined the lack of progress in improving the quality of care after the Dyfed report.

35.15 The most serious shortcomings, as in other Gwynedd community homes, were the lack of individual care planning and the failure to prepare residents for a meaningful future, including their discharge from care, with appropriate liaison with field social workers. In the end, a significant number of residents were left mouldering there and all too many of them went on to more rigorous forms of detention under the penal system.

5 Queen's Park Close, Holyhead (Chapter 36)

36.01 This community home, in a fairly large council estate near the centre of Holyhead, was opened by the former Anglesey County Council in 1960 as a family group home. It was later designated as a community home for up to 8 boys and girls aged 0 to 18 years, but only up to 5 children were accommodated there after the Children Act 1989 came into operation in October 1991. Our latest information is that it has remained in use as a community home by the new Anglesey County Council but its future appears to be uncertain.

36.02 The Dyfed team's report was again strongly critical of the condition of Queens Park (as this home is commonly referred to) in the summer of 1981, describing its physical state as deplorable. The report went on to say "The playroom was a disgrace; the kitchen unkempt and disorderly; the downstairs toilet was dirty and out of use; the laundry room was unkempt; the inadequate grounds were unkempt and did not provide for outdoor recreation".

36.03 Queens Park was one of the homes visited by SWSOs in the autumn of 1988 and they expressed more favourable views on the physical state of the premises, although they were critical of some aspects of it, including the furniture. There were 4 children in the home at the time and the report commented that children were admitted for the stated purpose of assessment but that it could not be carried out by the number of staff (3 care workers under the Officer-in-Charge) even if they were all professionally qualified.

36.04 Three former residents complained to the police that they had been sexually abused whilst they were resident at Queens Park but the first witness was unable to identify the older male resident who had twice attempted to bugger him.

36.05 In the Tribunal's report we give extended accounts of the other 2 allegations of sexual abuse. The first was by a boy, who was nearly 16 years old at the time and who alleged that he had had sexual intercourse several times with a young female member of the staff and had spent the night with her on 2 occasions. His allegations came to light some months afterwards, by which time the boy had been transferred to Tŷ Mawr Community Home at Abergavenny, and we are strongly critical of the subsequent investigation that took place, in which the Director of Social Services (Lucille Hughes) and the Deputy Director (Glanville Owen) claim to have been involved as well as Gethin Evans, Larry King and Dodd. The allegation came to the knowledge also of the Area Officer for Arfon, who saw the boy himself, and he made highly critical comments on the response to it in a memorandum that he addressed to the Director on 26 February 1986. The upshot was that no adverse action was taken against the woman member of staff.

36.06 A dozen years later it is impossible for the Tribunal to reach a firm conclusion about the truth of this complaint in the absence of any corroborative evidence either way. What is clear is that there should have been a full investigation of the allegations in the course of disciplinary proceedings and that questioning of the boy should not have been delegated to the Principal of Tŷ Mawr. We are critical also of the insensitive way in which the boy was transferred to Tŷ Mawr.

36.07 The other complaint of sexual abuse at Queens Park had an unhappy background and involved more complicated issues of fact. The complainant (C) was admitted to Queens Park when she was 14 years old in August 1990 and remained there as a resident until March 1994. She was highly disturbed and an unusual factor was that she was the beneficiary of quite a substantial trust fund, to which she was to become absolutely entitled at the age of 18 years, as the result of the death of her father at sea. It is clear that a close relationship developed between C and a woman member of the staff at Queens Park (Y) but C complained subsequently that she was abused sexually by Y on occasions by being forced to touch Y indecently, usually after they had been drinking together.

36.08 This allegation did not come to light until C made contact with the Tribunal in late 1996. It was then investigated by the police but the CPS advised that there was insufficient evidence of any criminal offence to justify a prosecution. Y denied that any indecency with C had occurred or that she had drunk alcohol with C when she gave evidence to the Tribunal and we are not aware of any other allegation of sexual misconduct by Y.

36.09 In these circumstances we think that it would be inappropriate to find against Y on the evidence before us but the history illustrates the perils that may arise from too close a relationship between a member of staff and a child within a small children's home, which may be exacerbated if (as here) the staff member herself is suffering from emotional problems.

36.10 Other aspects of C's history at Queens Park and afterwards gave us cause for considerable concern. One of these was that Y, who has now left the County Council's employ, borrowed £2,000 from C in 1994, although the sum was eventually repaid. More worryingly, C remained very disturbed throughout her period in care. Her medical and other records show that she persistently took alcohol and drugs and that she was admitted to hospital on at least 6 occasions, twice following overdoses. Although she was seen by a psychiatrist on 6 occasions between January 1991 and June 1992, she does not appear to have received any consistent treatment; and she emerged from care to spend her capital, at least initially, on her boyfriend and drugs.

36.11 We know of only 7 former residents who allege that they were physically abused at Queens Park and their complaints relate to a short overall period between 1 January 1984 to 16 October 1987, during most of which the Officer-in-Charge was **Beryl Condra**, who was not professionally trained. There was no allegation, however, that Condra herself was guilty of physical abuse of residents. Most of the witnesses spoke highly of her and described the regime at Queens Park favourably.

36.12 The allegations of physical abuse made to the police involved 4 members of staff and only one, **Peter Gadd**, who was a Senior RCCO, needs to be mentioned. Most of the few allegations against him related to minor incidents. One complainant gave oral evidence to the Tribunal of being punched a couple of times in the chest by Gadd after he had sworn at Gadd; and he alleged to the police that Gadd had "thumped" him on 3 occasions when he had been caught smoking. But this witness also told the police in his first statement that he had enjoyed his stay at Queens Park on the whole.

36.13 Gadd denied these allegations and told the Tribunal that he did not have any problems with the witness, whom he used to take fishing. Gadd did, however, remember telling the boy off for smoking.

36.14 It follows, in our judgment that there is no evidence of persistent physical abuse by any member of the staff at Queens Park. No doubt there were occasions when a hand was raised by a member of the staff but the regime was non-violent and corporal punishment was not resorted to. Gadd has been the subject of few allegations arising out of his 10 years' service in residential child care in Gwynedd and we acquit him of any suggestion that he was guilty of physical abuse of residents in care.

36.15 Nevertheless, we have serious misgivings about the quality of care generally at Queens Park, based partly on the evidence presented to us directly and partly on the findings of the SWSOs who examined the care and career of 4 children in residence there (and of 8 children at Tŷ'r Felin) in the autumn of 1988. The failings and deficiencies mirrored those that we found at Tŷ'r Felin and Y Gwyngyll. Queens Park became gradually a repository for a small group of older children, who were in care for a wide variety of reasons and who led largely separate lives within the home. Their physical needs were met and there was a great deal of freedom but the staff were inadequately trained to provide the kind of guidance and framework of rules that adolescents needed, if the experience of being in care was to provide positive benefits for them and to equip them for independent living.

Cartref Bontnewydd, 1988 to 1996 (Chapter 37)

37.01 Cartref Bontnewydd was established as an orphanage in 1907 in the village of Y Bontnewydd, about 3 miles south of Caernarvon, on the main A487 road to Porthmadog. It was administered by a Methodist Trust and remained open until 1983, latterly as a voluntary children's home.

37.02 The Trust decided to establish a Fostering Placement Centre in place of the community home and this fostering unit opened on 11 October 1984. The agency entered into a partnership arrangement with Gwynedd County Council to provide fostering services and the arrangement continued until the demise of the County Council at the end of March 1996.

37.03 The fostering unit does not occupy the whole of the premises and part of the building was re-opened by Gwynedd County Council as a community home for up to 7 boys and girls on 10 April 1988, occupying it under licence from the Trust. The first Officer-in-Charge was **Mari Thomas**[3], who remained there until early 1995, when she took maternity leave before embarking on a full time course for a Diploma in Social Work. In her absence temporary appointments were made but she has now returned as Officer-in-Charge.

37.04 Cartref Bontnewydd remains a 7 bedded unit, accommodating boys and girls aged between 13 and 17 years. It is managed jointly with Queens Park under an agreement made between the successor authorities of Anglesey and Gwynedd and the line manager for both is one of 4 Children's Services Managers appointed by the new Gwynedd Council.

37.05 We are not aware of any complaint of sexual abuse at Cartref Bontnewydd.

37.06 Only 4 former residents made complaints to the police of physical abuse at the home and their complaints were relatively minor. Most of them alleged that they had been slapped across the face by Mari Thomas or another member of the staff for offences such as absconding and, in one case, spitting on the floor near the staff member. The evidence of 2 of these complainants was read to the Tribunal and it was clear from their statements that they bore no grudges about their treatment at Cartref Bontnewydd. One of them said that he was happy at Cartref Bontnewydd for most of the time (over 2 years) that he was there and the other told the police that she did not wish to pursue any complaint.

37.07 Mari Thomas denied striking any of the complainants. She did, however, tell children off when they ran away. Her view of herself was that, as a result of her experiences at Tŷ'r Felin, she was strict initially at Cartref Bontnewydd but that, subsequently, she could not see the point of it.

37.08 To sum up, it is clear that neither physical nor sexual abuse occurred at Cartref Bontnewydd when it was operating as a local authority community home during the period under review. It may be that Mari Thomas administered slaps or the like to absconders on one or two occasions in the early days but we have no reason to think that she persisted in doing so.

37.09 We have no doubt that some of the deficiencies in the quality of care that were pervasive in the residential child care system in Gwynedd affected Cartref Bontnewydd too in its first years. Mari Thomas said in her evidence, however, that many improvements have been effected in the past 7 years. There is now much closer scrutiny of admissions. There are planning meetings beforehand and no emergency placements are accepted at Cartref Bontnewydd. A further detailed plan is formulated at a planning meeting shortly after a child is

---

[3] See paras 33.34 and 33.35 of this Summary.

admitted and the Children Services Manager who is line manager presides over that meeting. Moreover, the Independent Reviewing Officer in the Independent Inspection Unit presides over all reviews. Other procedural improvements are listed in paragraph 37.13 of the Tribunal's report.

ALLEGED ABUSE OF CHILDREN IN CARE IN PRIVATE RESIDENTIAL ESTABLISHMENTS IN GWYNEDD BETWEEN 1974 AND 1996 (Chapters 38 and 39)

In this part of the report we give accounts of the establishments in Gwynedd of Care Concern[1] and of Paul Hett, a native of Clwyd, who set up 3 residential schools successively in the Dolgellau area during the period under review. They are included because of the complaints about them from time to time and the Welsh Office's persistent concerns in relation to their registration.

Hengwrt Hall School and its successor, Aran Hall School (Chapter 38)

38.01 Hengwrt Hall at Rhydymain, between Dolgellau and Bala, was built in or about 1870 as a large country house. It was opened as a residential school by Care Concern in 1976 and it remained in the same ownership until it was sold to new owners in November 1991. The new owners re-named it as Aran Hall School and formed a limited company in that name to run it.

38.02 The main hall, a 3 storey building, housed the residential part of the school, the main kitchen and offices. A separate school block was located in the coach house to the rear of the main building and included 2 demountable classrooms. There were also hard and grass play areas and rooms for additional activities, such as arts and crafts and domestic science.

38.03 The history, in brief, of the school's registration begins with its provisional registration as an independent school on 12 August 1976. It was granted full registration on 24 January 1977 as a residential special school for up to 25 "physically and mentally handicapped children categorised as ESN(S)". This was changed on 12 December 1983, under the new provisions of the Education Act 1981, to approval under section 11(3)(a) of that Act as a residential school to which SEN children could be admitted. However, on 6 March 1989 notice was sent to Care Concern of the intention of the Secretary of State for Wales to withdraw this approval and it was duly withdrawn, after the 21 days allowed for representations had elapsed. It was not until 15 July 1996 that the approval by the Secretary of State was restored, this time under section 189(5)(a) of the Education Act 1993.

38.04 A remarkable feature of the history is that, despite the withdrawal of general SEN approval in or about April 1989 because of numerous concerns about the physical condition of the premises, the quality of life experienced by pupils, inadequate staffing and the school's educational programmes, the owners were permitted to continue to accommodate the existing pupils on the basis of individual consents for their admission granted under section 11(3)(b) of the Act of 1981. This was stated to be subject to a proviso that the Secretary of

---

[1] See paras 22.01 to 22.25 of this Summary for an account of this organisation's establishment in Clwyd.

State would wish to withdraw the consents if the requirements imposed by him upon the owners were not complied with to his satisfaction.

38.05 Whilst we are conscious of the practical difficulty of placing existing pupils satisfactorily elsewhere at short notice, there are 2 major objections to the procedure of individual approvals that was adopted. The first is that the jurisdiction of the Secretary of State of Wales under section 11(3)(b) of the Education Act 1981 was limited to approving placements made by Welsh local authorities; and when general approval was withdrawn only one of the 21 remaining pupils had been placed at the school by a Welsh local authority. This difficulty was not recognised until the following year (1990), when further admissions to the school were made. In respect of placements by English local authorities, the approval had to be by the Secretary of State of Education and, for Scottish local authorities, by the Secretary of State for Scotland.

38.06 The second objection is that it is difficult to rationalise umbrella specific approvals of this kind in respect of a school that was regarded as unfit for general approval, except perhaps as a very temporary expedient. In the event, we are not aware of any subsequent withdrawal of consent in respect of an individual pupil or of any attempt to place the pupils elsewhere on the ground that the school was unsuitable, despite the fact that 7 years (a school generation) elapsed before general approval was granted again.

38.07 The Tribunal has not received directly any allegation of abuse at this school from a complainant and we have no evidence of any alleged abuse there since it became Aran Hall School. There was a complaint in 1988, however, by the mother of a pupil at Hengwrt Hall School, which was taken up by the Spastics Society and by her Member of Parliament and which led ultimately to the withdrawal of general SEN approval the following year.

38.08 A report by staff of a Spastics Society School in Preston, based on observations at Hengwrt Hall School between 10 and 14 October 1988, was highly critical. It criticised the physical environment of the school, many aspects of the quality of care that it provided and its educational standards. It alleged also physical and verbal mistreatment of pupils by members of staff, itemising 13 observed incidents. The authors had been specifically charged with investigating the treatment of A, whose mother had complained, but they said that their concern in writing the report was not only for the welfare of A but for all the children at the school and any who might be enrolled in the future.

38.09 This adverse report led to an inspection of the school by HMIs and SWSOs in November 1988, when there were 31 pupils in the age range of 11 to 18 years, who had been placed there by 18 different local authorities. The inspectors confirmed many of the criticisms made by the Spastics Society team and noted that little had been done to improve the accommodation since a previous inspection by them in 1986. They did not consider, however, that pupils were "at risk" in the sense that they were likely to be subjected to abuse or serious neglect.

38.10 The inspectors reported also that A presented many behavioural and educational problems, making inordinate demands upon the time and resources of the teaching and care staff. They concluded that it was unlikely that the school could meet his needs in its present situation and commented that it had accepted pupils presenting difficulties that it did not have the staff and expertise to deal with.

38.11 Nevertheless, A remained at Hengwrt Hall (after a temporary withdrawal) for at least another 5 years and Cheshire LEA (who had placed him there) expressed satisfaction with the school. There was another complaint about A's treatment in the Spring of 1990, when it was alleged that he was kicked in the testicles or stomach by a member of staff (X) during a week's holiday in Devon. It was alleged also that X had kicked another child similarly and had thrown a rock at the head of a third child. The allegations were properly reported to a Team Leader at the end of the holiday and X was severely reprimanded; but the Team Leader was dissatisfied with the leniency shown to X and resigned shortly afterwards.

38.12 On 16 March 1989 Hengwrt Hall School was one of 3 schools featured in an edition of the "This Week" television programme. It referred to the allegations made by the Spastics Society and to the profit being made by the proprietors but it did not allege ill-treatment of pupils: the programme's criticisms were of alleged management failings, bad practice and staff inadequacies.

38.13 In all, there were not less than 9 visits to this school between January 1986 and February 1996 by HMIs and SWSOs/SSIWs and we outline in the report the slow progress made in remedying the deficiencies that caused general approval to be withdrawn in 1989. These deficiencies encompassed such basic matters as the water supply (from a well), the coldness of the premises, the furniture and the state of decoration as well as the educational and care regimes. When general approval was granted again in July 1996, an action plan was still necessary because some failings still had to be remedied.

38.14 Whilst this school was almost free of abuse of residents, as we have indicated, its history underlines a number of the causes of anxiety that we expressed in relation to private residential care establishments in Clwyd. A major concern is the fact that children from so far afield should have been placed at Hengwrt Hall because of the scarcity of appropriate accommodation in more accessible locations. At times 3 Secretaries of State and up to 18 local authorities were responsible for satisfying themselves that Hengwrt Hall was a safe and appropriate school at which to place specific pupils; but the only practical monitoring was carried out by the Welsh Office, which concerned itself mainly with the performance of the school as a whole rather than the extent to which the specific requirements of individual children were being met.

38.15 The evidence suggests also that assessment prior to admission was often inadequate and that local authority staff played very little part in subsequent reviews. Overall care planning for individual children was thus a theoretical exercise rather than a meaningful and practical process.

38.16 Having regard to the large income received by private schools of this kind, derived mainly from public funds, surprise may legitimately be expressed that it took so long to remedy obvious physical defects at Hengwrt Hall. We do not think that it would be an unwarranted invasion of privacy to require a proprietor receiving public funds on this scale for such high risk services to disclose annual accounts and other relevant financial information to the regulatory authorities.

The residential establishments of Paul Hett (Chapter 39)

39.01 **Paul Hett,** who was born at Shotton in Clwyd on 17 April 1941, worked as a draughtsman and junior engineer at Hawarden Bridge Steelworks before marrying the daughter of the proprietor of The Poplars residential special school at Newnham-upon-Severn , where John Allen[2] was employed until he moved to Holywell in 1965. Hett taught at The Poplars from 1965 to 1969, whilst obtaining O and A levels, and then left to study for the Certificate in Education at Bristol University. On qualifying, after a 3 year course, Hett taught in a comprehensive school for 2 years before purchasing Ynys Fechan Hall, near Arthog, about 7 miles from Dolgellau, in 1974.

39.02 Hett subsequently owned successively 2 other residential educational establishments and his activities in this field occupied the attention of the WOED and SWSOs/SSIWs for the next 17 years until 1991. The later establishments were Dôl Rhyd School and Hengwrt House.

39.03 **Ynys Fechan Hall** had a chequered history. It opened on 28 June 1974 as a home for boys aged 11 to 14 years in need of long stay accommodation with rehabilitation and education. Apart from the Hetts, however, the staff were untrained, inexperienced and unqualified. Nevertheless, within the first 5 months of its existence 57 boys had either passed through it or were still resident there. It was described by an SWSO in November 1974 as a speculative venture and he added "The dangers of the situation are compounded by the isolation of the home and its freedom from inspection by a locally based responsible body".

39.04 In the event, Ynys Fechan Hall was provisionally registered as an independent school for only a very short period, from 21 April 1975 to February 1976. During this period the former Arthog primary school was rented for teaching purposes. The reason for the ending of its registration was that the Hetts had acquired Dôl Rhyd House in Dolgellau, which had been a residence for senior girls, housing up to 50 girls and staff, forming part of Dr Williams' School for Girls. This was opened on 5 January 1976 as Dôl Rhyd School and the intention was that Ynys Fechan Hall should be a boarding house for older boys attending this school: within a month 30 boys had been enrolled at Dôl Rhyd School, of whom 12 were resident at Ynys Fechan Hall.

39.05 Ynys Fechan Hall was a converted farmhouse with 6 bedrooms and 3 reception rooms. There were also coachhouses and a stable suitable for conversion. The premises remained in use as a boarding house until the end of 1980, when it was replaced by Hengwrt House, which Hett acquired in December 1980.

---

[2] See paras 21.01 to 21.15 and 21.24 of this Summary.

39.06 Ynys Fechan Hall remained in Hett's ownership until it was sold in September 1986. In the intervening period it was destroyed by fire in September 1981 and rebuilt at a cost of £350,000. It was then re-opened as a school for dyslexic children in October 1984 but it closed finally as a school in May 1985, when the pupils were transferred to Dôl Rhyd School.

39.07 The new owner of Ynys Fechan Hall in September 1986, Barry Young, ran it as a private children's home for up to 11 resident boys and girls, which was ultimately registered under the Children Act 1989 with Gwynedd County Council.

39.08 **Dôl Rhyd School** remained open under Hett's management from 5 January 1976 until July 1987. It was provisionally registered as an independent school on 12 October 1976 and the registration was granted to Dôl Rhyd/Ynys Fechan on the footing that the latter was a boarding house. Full registration was granted on 15 February 1979, after numerous visits by HMIs, as a school for up to 34 emotionally and behaviourally disturbed boys in the age range of 11 to 16 years, with Ynys Fechan Hall as a residential annexe. The school was never granted general SEN approval: applications for this were refused in April 1984 and again in April 1987. The WOED was then informed by Hett on 15 July 1987 that the school had closed and it was removed from the register of independent schools on 12 August 1987.

39.09 In its latter years under Paul Hett, it appears that Dôl Rhyd School catered wholly or mainly for dyslexic boys and girls and the children in this category at Ynys Fechan Hall in May 1985 were transferred to Dôl Rhyd.

39.10 After Dôl Rhyd School had closed in July 1987, it was re-opened by Hett's first wife, from whom he was divorced in 1982 or 1983, and her sister as a unit for young adults with learning difficulties; and it was registered as such with Gwynedd County Council. Hett himself remarried in 1984 or 1985.

39.11 **Hengwrt House** at Llanelltyd, about a mile from Dolgellau, was bought by Hett in October 1980, with the intention that it should be a boarding facility for Dôl Rhyd School, housing the younger pupils. It closed, however, in 1983 for extensive alterations, by which time the number of pupils at Dôl Rhyd had fallen. Hett then formed the idea that Dôl Rhyd/Ynys Fechan should become a school for dyslexic pupils and that non-dyslexic pupils should go to Hengwrt House, which should itself become a school. In May 1985 he applied for Hengwrt House to be registered as an independent school for up to 20 boys and girls aged 11 to 18 years and provisional registration was granted on that basis on 14 April 1986 in the name of **Ysgol Hengwrt.**

39.12 Ysgol Hengwrt survived for only 5 years and was never granted full registration. It was removed from the register in March 1990 (because Hett had referred to the "demise" of the school in a letter to the Welsh Office), then provisionally restored in September 1990 and finally removed on 9 December 1991. By October 1987, Hett was no longer acting as head of the school and had delegated the responsibility to a teacher. The Welsh Office began drafting a Notice of Complaint at the end of that year, following an adverse report by inspectors, but it was never served. From 1989, Hett ran it through a manager and staff whilst he attended Exeter University, obtaining the degree of Master of Education in 1993. He has retained ownership of Ysgol Hengwrt and currently describes himself as "headmaster of a residential special school with no pupils since 1993".

39.13 We are not aware of any complaint of sexual abuse at Ynys Fechan Hall and only one former resident of Dôl Rhyd School made a complaint of sexual abuse to the police. He complained of being buggered by another resident and referred to other consensual relationships with boys there from the age of 13 years. His only complaint against the staff, however, was that a male had indecently assaulted him briefly by hand: the boy did not report the incident but the offender was dismissed within a week for other reasons. This incident was said to have occurred in 1983 or 1984 but HMIs had been informed in November 1981 that one of the care staff had been dismissed summarily following an allegation by a pupil of sexual interference.

39.14 There were more serious allegations of sexual abuse at Ysgol Hengwrt by 3 former residents. Of these complainants, 2 were girls, one alleging that she had been abused by a male member of the staff and the other by a woman member of staff. The first of these, A, said that she had been forced to have sexual intercourse on many occasions with a senior member of the staff, X, after her arrival at the school on 2 June 1987 until she ran away on 11 March 1988. A complained to another member of the staff, who, with his wife, helped her to escape. She then made a statement to the police in Manchester but was later told that "there was no evidence".

39.15 A's case was unusual in that both relevant SSDs (Gwynedd and Trafford), the North Wales Police and the Welsh Office were all made aware of her complaint. A reported it initially at the Dolgellau Area Office of Gwynedd SSD and Trafford SSD agreed to collect her when she refused to return to the school. X was head of care at Ysgol Hengwrt at the time and he denied A's allegations, saying that they had been investigated and rejected 2 months earlier by Hett. However, he was suspended when A made or renewed her complaints on running away and resigned in the course of the same month.

39.16 B's case, in or about 1989, was also unusual because she had previously been moved from a Bryn Alyn home, Cotsbrook Hall in Shropshire, as a result of concern about her relationship with a woman member of staff, Y. She was transferred at that time to a home in Birkenhead but, after just over 6 months, was moved on to Ysgol Hengwrt, where Y had become a member of staff. B alleged that Y resumed abusing her sexually at Ysgol Hengwrt until it was realised that they were together again, whereupon B was moved again, this time to Gatewen Hall.

39.17 The other complainant was another resident who ultimately ran away from Ysgol Hengwrt, late in 1988, but he did not make a statement to the police until 1993. He complained of being indecently assaulted and buggered persistently for about 2 years, from the age of 14 years, by a member of the staff. He did not make a complaint at the time because he was threatened with an "unruly certificate" if he did so[3]. After running away, he was placed with his grandmother.

39.18 We do not have sufficient evidence to adjudicate firmly upon these allegations but, on the material that we do have, it is likely most of them were true. In most of the cases the complainant and the source of abuse were separated quite early on but the response of Hett to the case of A gives rise to justifiable misgivings about his ability to look after children in care; and inspectors had drawn attention earlier to the potential vulnerability of girl pupils because of the layout of the accommodation in Ysgol Hengwrt.

39.19 Although former residents of the Hett establishments are now widely dispersed in the United Kingdom, 15 are known to have made allegations to the police of physical abuse by identified members of the staff. Most of their complaints (10) related to Ysgol Hengwrt in the period between 1986 and 1990 but the 2 witnesses who gave oral evidence to the Tribunal were former residents of Ynys Fechan Hall and Dôl Rhyd School.

39.20 Both these witnesses complained of beatings by **Paul Hett.** The first of them alleged that there were 4 or 5 such beatings during his 4 years at the 2 establishments between 1976 and 1980. The second, who was there during the first 2 years of this period, complained of beatings by Hett about once a week, which started about 10 months after his arrival. There were similar complaints to the police in 1993 about Hett by 2 other former residents of Dôl Rhyd/Ynys Fechan and by 2 who had been at Ysgol Hengwrt. There were serious complaints to the police also about another qualified social worker in the earlier period and about 2 other members of the staff at Ysgol Hengwrt in the late 1980s.

39.21 The Welsh Office also received a number of complaints of ill-treatment of residents at the Hett establishments in the course of the 1980s. One complaint by an Islington parent that her son had been injured by Hett led to a visit by Gwynedd SSD to Dôl Rhyd School on 22 September 1980, but the conclusion by Gwynedd was that the injury had been inflicted accidentally in the course of restraint. Just over a year later, following the dismissal of 2 members of the care staff, representatives of 16 London boroughs that had placed children at the Hett establishments met to discuss conditions at the school and imposed a number of requirements, including a policy for the phasing out of corporal punishment. In March 1982 there were further allegations from pupils, a care worker and a teacher alleging ill-treatment, mainly by Hett, at Dôl Rhyd; and in 1984 concerns were again expressed about the running of Dôl Rhyd School and harsh treatment of pupils (3 senior members of staff were dismissed in December 1984).

39.22 Hett denied all the allegations of assault made against him when he gave evidence to the Tribunal and emphasised that his successive schools had had to deal with exceptionally disturbed children, who had had to be restrained. According to him, control had been exercised on "a family basis" and the only

---

[3] See section 22(5) of the Children and Young Persons Act 1969 and the Certificates of Unruly Character (Conditions) Order 1977, SI 1977 No 1037.

corporal punishment had been infrequent use of the slipper. Hett alleged also that, at one stage in 1989, Ysgol Hengwrt was receiving mainly 16 to 19 year olds because of the refusal of the Welsh Office to approve the admission of younger SEN children.

39.23   It is impossible for us to reach a satisfactory conclusion about the extent of physical abuse at the Hett establishment or the allegations against Hett personally on the limited evidence before us. We accept that the staff had to deal with many difficult and disturbed adolescents and that physical restraint had to be exercised quite frequently. Hett was, however, an unimpressive witness and we certainly do not accept that corporal punishment was limited to the use of the slipper. We have no doubt that excessive force was used to residents from time to time by largely untrained staff in the absence of any clear guidelines but this was but one respect in which the quality of care provided fell below an acceptable standard.

39.24   What is most striking about the history of these establishments is the fact that they occupied the close attention of the WOED and SWSOs/SSIWs for a period of 17 years. In that period only Dôl Rhyd School was granted full registration as an independent school and none of the 3 schools achieved general SEN approval. The blame for the prolonged existence and use of these schools does not rest upon the Inspectorates, who reported fully and frequently upon the deficiencies of management, staffing and organisation of the schools and who consistently pointed to their failure to achieve acceptable standards of care and educational provision. In our judgment, the fault lies, firstly, with the inadequate regulatory system and its over-elaborate procedures for de-registration and, secondly, with the Welsh Office for undue timidity and lack of grip in setting in train the Notice of Complaint procedure. Some blame must be attached also to the placement authorities but the history underlines the difficulties facing such authorities in monitoring adequately distant residential establishments.

39.25   We echo the comment of SWSO J K Fletcher on Dôl Rhyd School, following a visit in October 1983:

> "The final question remains, irrespective of the nature and quality of the regime what relevance has a medium term residential unit in rural Wales to the needs of inner city boys especially if, as now appears to be the case, they are sought from among the "healthy" and not seriously delinquent."

ALLEGED ABUSE OF CHILDREN IN FOSTER HOMES IN GWYNEDD BETWEEN 1974 AND 1996 (Chapters 40 to 43)

This part of the report is similar in form to Part V of the report, which deals with foster homes in Clwyd. We give an account in this part of the general fostering arrangements in Gwynedd and then deal with 8 foster homes in respect of which there are known to have been complaints. The complaints in 4 of these homes were of sexual abuse, of which the gravest was the case of Malcolm Scrugham. One of the other 4 cases, the case of M, led to a prosecution and to an independent inquiry by a three member team, who presented a report extending to 98 pages in the autumn of 1995. This case is dealt with, therefore, in a separate chapter in the report.

The overall provision of foster care in Gwynedd, 1974 to 1996 (Chapter 40)

40.01 On 1 April 1974 there were 122 children in foster care and the number rose to a peak of 181 by 31 March 1986. There was then a progressive decline to 137 by 31 March 1994.

40.02 The total number of children in care in Gwynedd remained fairly steady, around 300, for the first 10 years of this period, but then began to fall quite steeply with the result that there were only 159 "looked after children" by 31 March 1994.

40.03 The picture for the whole of Wales was broadly similar, except that Gwynedd began the period with a higher percentage of children in foster care. As the total number of children in care declined, the percentage in foster care in all the Welsh counties rose to 81.3 per cent by 31 March 1994, but the actual number of children in foster care was then about 1,600, as it had been 18 years earlier.

40.04 During the first part of the period under review Area teams in Gwynedd were responsible for the recruitment, selection and preparation of foster parents as well as the placement and supervision of foster children. There was little guidance available to social workers involved in fostering, however, apart from supervision from senior staff, and there were considerable variations in practice.

40.05 Increasing recognition of the complexity and specialist nature of foster care service led to the establishment in 1984 of a fostering unit at Cartref Bontnewydd[1]. Under a partnership arrangement with Gwynedd County Council the unit assumed responsibility for the recruitment, selection, preparation, review and support of fosterparents whilst the Areas retained responsibility for the placement and supervision of children in foster homes.

---

[1] See paras 37.02 and 37.03 of this Summary.

40.06 In the report of the Examination Team on Child Care Procedures and Practice in North Wales[2], Adrianne Jones commented that Cartref Bontnewydd was a relatively small unit to bear responsibility for so many carers, spread over wide and difficult terrain, as well as the responsibility for recruitment and reviewing activity. It had been argued in 1991, when the Children Act 1989 was implemented, that additional resources were required and that a family placement officer ought to be established in each of the county's 5 areas, but that argument had not prevailed. Moreover, a report in March 1994[3], commissioned by SSIW, concluded that "The structure of the fostering service in Gwynedd. . . has evident weaknesses that flow largely from the level of investment in staffing and the under developed management information system".

The case of M (Chapter 41)

41.01 M, who was born on 7 March 1974, was the youngest of 5 children admitted into care on 11 January 1978, pursuant to a care order made in matrimonial proceedings. He was placed successively in 2 community homes initially but was then boarded out with foster parents from 5 October 1979 until 11 April 1986, after which he returned to live with his natural mother. He was discharged from care on 10 June 1988, at the age of 14 years.

41.02 M's first placement with foster parents from 5 October 1979 to 11 November 1980 was unsuccessful but he made no complaints about his treatment by them.

41.03 M's second placement with Norman and Evelyn Roberts at Gwalchmai in Anglesey lasted from 11 November 1980 to 11 April 1986. Norman Roberts was a quarryman with a smallholding, who also ran a mobile grocery business, and his wife was a former nurse. They had 2 sons and a daughter of their own; and they fostered another boy and 2 girls as well as M, whilst the latter was with them. M's placement was initially intended to be for 9 to 12 months but he then remained with the Roberts family on a long term basis from early 1982.

41.04 In statements to the police in 1992 M made wide-ranging allegations against Norman and Evelyn Roberts and their elder son, Ian (aged 21 years in 1980). He complained of being treated like a slave and required to feed the animals daily at 6 am; and he alleged that he had been undernourished throughout his stay. He complained also of being punished unjustly with a cane and a horsewhip and by being forced to eat dog biscuits.

41.05 Whilst he was placed with Norman and Evelyn Roberts, M attended 2 local schools successively and he claimed to the police that friends at school had seen marks on him caused by the whipping. He said also that he had shown such marks to teachers at his senior school, although he had been too scared to tell them what had happened. They had reported the matter to his social worker and he had been taken to hospital, where a doctor had photographed his injuries. Later, when his social worker and the Area Officer had visited the

---

[2] Presented to Parliament on 17 June 1996.
[3] By a Children Act Research Group of the University of Wales, Cardiff.

foster home he had said at first, in the presence of the foster parents, that a schoolboy was to blame; but he claimed to have told his social worker just before she left that it was his foster parents. The social worker had replied that "it was a bit too late to say that now". The result was that nothing else happened then and he continued to be ill-treated until his mother managed to have him back home.

41.06 On the basis of M's statements, Norman, Evelyn and Ian Roberts were charged with various offences and stood trial in June 1993 in the Crown Court at Mold. The 2 foster parents were charged with cruelty to M. **Norman Roberts** was charged also with assault occasioning actual bodily harm in relation to the incident in September 1985 that had led to the hospital visit; and **Ian Roberts** was charged with common assault on the footing that he had assisted his father in roping M up and suspending him for whipping.

41.07 Both foster parents were acquitted by the jury of cruelty but Norman and Ian Roberts were convicted of the separate assault charges against them. On 2 July 1993 the trial judge ordered that the 2 men should be conditionally discharged for a period of 2 years and that both should pay £1,000 towards the costs of the prosecution. The judge expressed the view that an inquiry should follow the trial and that it should cover not only the events in 1985 but also the preceding period from 1980.

41.08 Very full evidence was put before the court in the 1993 trial, as we explain in paragraph 41.18 of the Tribunal's report, and it has been neither necessary nor appropriate for that exercise to be repeated before the Tribunal. We received written evidence, however, from all 3 defendants in which they repeated the substance of what they had said at the trial in response to M's allegations.

41.09 We have not received any evidence to cast doubt upon the correctness of the jury's verdicts. It is right to say, however, that the trial judge inferred, from a question posed by the jury after they had retired to consider their verdicts, that they were not satisfied that Ian Roberts had played any part in whipping M, although they accepted that he had assaulted M by suspending him.

41.10 An independent inquiry was set in train in response to the judge's suggestion and the activities of Gwynedd SSD in relation to M between 1978 and 1988 were subjected to minute scrutiny by the inquiry team. The report of the team (the Walton report as it is called) was severely critical of many aspects of the handling of M and his complaints by Gwynedd SSD and the main heads of criticism are summarised in paragraph 41.56 of our own report. It is sufficient here to mention some of the major points that have a bearing on our overall conclusions and recommendations.

41.11 Between November 1981 and August 1985 3 different field workers were allocated to M in succession. In September 1985 a fourth social worker was about to take over his case but she was on leave when the bruising was reported. In February 1983 the Area Officer had complained that only three-quarters of all child care cases were receiving the attention that they should because the team establishment had been reduced.

41.12 There was evidence of earlier visible signs of injury to M and complaints or suspicion that he was being physically abused. A retired school canteen lady, for example, alleged that she had reported finding red marks on M's buttocks to his headmaster via the school cook. M's social worker also heard in 1983 from the police school liaison officer that M was telling his friends that his foster parents were hitting him.

41.13 There were no records on file of any 6 monthly reviews of M for 2 years between August 1984 and August 1986 and the reviews held before that appeared to have been carried out in a routine manner without any reappraisal of M's long term future. There was little evidence that when M had been seen, his feelings and wishes on such matters as his long term future had been discussed.

41.14 It was the Deputy Headmistress of Bodedern School who reported on 11 September 1985 that M had disclosed bruises on his body to his school fellows, claiming that he had been hit on the bottom by his foster father.

41.15 The Area Officer was the only available member of staff with knowledge of the case and he visited the foster home, where he saw M in the presence of his foster parents with predictably unsatisfactory results. He did not examine the bruises.

41.16 The Area Officer did take M to see a consultant paediatrician the following evening at the nearest major hospital. Two doctors examined the injuries and took photographs of the injuries, which they regarded as "classic", for teaching purposes. In their view the injuries had been inflicted deliberately, probably 7 or 8 days earlier. M gave conflicting accounts of how they had occurred.

41.17 On the return of M with the Area Officer to the foster home, Norman Roberts admitted slapping M with a soft slipper but did not offer any other explanation of M's injuries.

41.18 The Area Officer sent a Notice of Accident form to the Director of Social Services on 17 September 1985 in which the injuries were described as:

> "2 or 3 strap marks about 6 inches across both buttocks. Confirmed by Consultant Paediatrician as 3 successive blows to the buttocks with a hard object. Photographs have been taken."

41.19 Senior Officers of the SSD blame each other for the subsequent inaction by that department. What is clear is that, whatever errors had occurred prior to 17 September 1985, there was a lamentable failure to take appropriate action from then on, for which several senior officers must bear some of the blame. There were also, in our judgment, deliberate failures to inform the police and to report the facts fairly and accurately to the Chairman and members of the County Council's Children's Sub-Committee.

41.20 In paragraphs 41.38 to 41.52 of our report we trace the subsequent relevant history leading to M's return home on trial on 11 April 1986 and the roles played, in particular, by **Larry King**, the Principal Officer responsible for child protection, and **Gethin Evans**, initially a Principal Officer also but who became Assistant Director (Children) from 30 September 1985.

41.21 We comment that it would not be profitable to spend time trying to weigh precisely the apportionment of blame amongst the senior officers for the 15 items of criticism listed in paragraph 41.56 of our report. A continuous thread emerges of pre-occupation with preservation of the placements of all 4 foster children rather than rigorous investigation of the foster parents and the true cause of the marks on M's buttocks. There was also considerable confusion about the authority of individuals. Having reviewed the evidence of all the senior officers, including that of the Director and the Deputy Director of Social Services, our clear conclusion is that a major share of the blame for Gwynedd's failures must rest upon Gethin Evans, although King must also bear some of the blame in view of his responsibilities for child protection.

Alleged sexual abuse of children in foster homes in Gwynedd (Chapter 42)

42.01 We discuss in this chapter 4 cases of alleged sexual abuse in Gwynedd but, in the first 2 discussed, Clwyd was the placement authority. Whilst Gwynedd agreed to undertake the supervision in both cases, the statutory responsibility for the care of the 2 children remained with Clwyd throughout.

42.02 The Tribunal received in evidence statements from only 2 of the complainants but we have had access to the social services files, complainants' statements and court records in respect of the other cases.

42.03 The most serious was that of A, who was born in Clwyd on 29 July 1975 of a single mother and placed in care at a very early age. A was first fostered in Clwyd from August 1976 to October 1984. In August 1984, however, the foster parents announced their intention to emigrate to South Africa without her and proposed that she should be placed with their friends, Malcolm and Maria Scrugham, who had 2 young children of their own and who had moved to Bala in 1982.

42.04 A was placed with the Scrughams by her first foster parents, without authority, on 20 October 1984 and she remained in their household until April 1993. She was well known to them before the placement, because she had spent holidays with them during the preceding 2 years, but neither Scrugham was a registered foster parent and, as far as the Tribunal is aware, the placement was never formally approved by Clwyd.

42.05 A's complaint of sexual abuse by **Malcolm Ian Scrugham** became known to a Clwyd family placement worker on 5 June 1992. The complaint was reported to the police and a full investigation ensued.

42.06 A alleged that Scrugham had begun to assault her sexually from about January 1987 and that she had been subjected to full sexual intercourse on a regular basis until she was 14 years old. She had then begun crying and resisting and there had been no sexual contact between them since. Additional allegations were that Scrugham had forced her to perform oral sex with him and that he had encouraged her to have sexual intercourse with 2 boy friends.

42.07 On 23 April 1993, in the Crown Court at Caernarvon, Scrugham was convicted of 2 representative charges of raping A (between the ages of 11 and 14 years), indecently assaulting her and aiding and abetting a boy friend of A to have unlawful sexual intercourse with her. He was convicted also of an indecent assault on the boy friend. Scrugham was then sentenced to a total of 10 years' imprisonment.

42.08 Although neither Clwyd or Gwynedd social workers had any reason to suspect before June 1992 that A was being sexually abused, there are grounds for substantial criticism of Clwyd SSD and to, a much lesser extent, of their counterparts in Gwynedd.

42.09 There was a regrettable failure by Clwyd SSD to grasp hold of A's case and to make effective long term plans for her. Despite the fact that Clwyd purported to be "monitoring the situation closely", they took no effective steps for nearly 8 years to rationalise and secure the status of A, who was ostensibly in voluntary care, or to regularise or terminate the placement with the Scrughams. It seems that adoption was being mooted in 1985 and again from 1989 but no action was taken to resolve the problem.

42.10 There was also a failure to ensure that the placement was properly supervised. This was undertaken by Gwynedd SSD after A had been transferred to the Scrughams but it seems to have faltered in 1987 (the year when the sexual abuse began). In December 1988 Gwynedd wrote formally to Clwyd confirming an earlier intimation that it was unable to continue supervising A because the responsible social worker was leaving and the child care team was fully stretched; and this followed immediately upon a letter to Clwyd from the social worker reporting concerns expressed by a general practitioner about conditions in the foster home and the presence there of a homeless young man.

42.11 It cannot be said with confidence that the sexual abuse would not have occurred if the Boarding Out Regulations had been strictly complied with but the possibility of disclosure would have been greatly increased by such compliance.

42.12 The second Clwyd placement in Gwynedd was of the girl E, born on 27 December 1974, whose escapade at Butlins Holiday Camp on 2 September 1988 led to the Park House inquiry that year[4]. Her complaint against her foster parent pre-dated this because she was placed with **Mr and Mrs B** at Conwy between 1986 and 1987. E's allegation, apparently first made to the police in 1987, was that she left the Bs after a year as a result of being sexually abused by Mr B. The latter denied her allegations, however, and referred to E's persistent demands to return to Park House, where she had a particular friend.

42.13 Detective Superintendent Ackerley told the Tribunal, on the basis of the sparse surviving documentation, that E's complaint was investigated by the police in 1987 but that no prosecution followed, in the absence of any corroboration.

42.14 There is no sufficient evidence before us to support a finding that Mr B did abuse E and we have no evidence to justify any criticism of either Clwyd SSD or Gwynedd SSD in relation to this placement.

---

[4] See paras 17.23 and 17.24 of this Summary.

42.15 The other 2 cases discussed in this chapter were placements by Gwynedd SSD.

42.16 C1 was the only girl of 4 children who were made the subject of care orders in matrimonial proceedings on 24 April 1980 and who were fostered with **Mr and Mrs C** at Caernarvon from 22 October 1979. C1, who was born on 19 May 1970, remained with the Cs for 4 years until 14 October 1983.

42.17 Mr and Mrs C had 4 other children living at their home during this period and C1 alleged that the eldest of these other children, X, who was a teenager, forced her to have sexual intercourse with him on 3 occasions. C1 told friends at school after the third occasion and they encouraged her to tell a teacher. She did not return to the foster home after reporting the matter to the teacher. The eventual result was that, on 11 May 1984, X pleaded guilty to unlawful sexual intercourse with C1 and was fined £100.

42.18 There were complaints also about a girl in the household (Y). C1 and her older 2 brothers alleged sexual assaults, indecent behaviour and persistent bullying and cruelty by Y. Both brothers allege that they complained to their social worker about Y's bullying but only the complaint of the elder is recalled. According to his social worker, the complaint was made after the boy had run away to Y Gwyngyll on 3 December 1980 but it was not confirmed by C1 or his younger brother and was denied by Y. Mr and Mrs C said that the boy's complaint was "the last straw" and he was moved to Tŷ'r Felin shortly afterwards.

42.19 The Tribunal were unable to trace Mr and Mrs C or X and Y and we are unable to reach any satisfactory conclusions about the extent of any abuse by Y, although it seems likely that all 3 complainants were subjected to some bullying by her.

42.20 The surviving documentary evidence is insufficient to enable us to assess the quality of care provided by the SSD during the placements but C1's file suggests that it was poor: it is difficult to determine from that file the frequency of visits to the foster home but recorded visits when C1 was reported to have been seen were at very irregular intervals. Moreover, there were complaints on the file from Alison Taylor about the lack of basic information provided to Tŷ Newydd on C1's admission following her complaint about X and later, by an SRCCO at Tŷ'r Felin, about the unprofessional manner of her admission there without any proper introduction by the social worker. C1 was the subject of 8 placements in all but she was adopted by her last foster mother just before her 18th birthday.

42.21 **Foster child D**, who was born on 8 February 1974, was received into care on 3 January 1979. Between 26 June 1980 and 6 September 1991 she was placed successively with 4 pairs of foster parents, the placements being interrupted only by a stay of about 2 years from December 1984 at Tŷ Newydd.

42.22 D alleged that she was sexually abused in the first and last of these foster homes. Her allegation about the first home, to the effect that she had been abused by the eldest son of the family, came to light through her second foster mother in December 1982. It was investigated by the police but no prosecution was instituted.

42.23 There was another complaint by D of indecent assault or gross indecency in December 1984 but D subsequently admitted that it was false and withdrew it formally. A case conference decided that she was in need of expert guidance and advice in a controlled environment, which was the reason for her admission to Tŷ Newydd.

42.24 D's fourth placement was from 10 August 1988 to 6 September 1991. In the course of it she appears to have made allegations against the foster father as early as 4 months after her arrival but she retracted them on that occasion. Her later allegation in September 1991 was that the foster father had had full sexual intercourse with her for a period of years, having begun to abuse her sexually within a few months of her placement with him and his wife.

42.25 D was moved to lodgings and did not return to the foster home after this last complaint. The foster father was arrested but denied all the allegations, pointing out that D had made false allegations earlier. In the event there was no corroboration of the allegations and the foster father was not prosecuted.

42.26 D did not provide any evidence to the Tribunal and we see no reason to criticise the response by the relevant authorities to her successive complaints.

42.27 In our conclusions in this chapter of the report we comment that the case of foster child A demonstrated a very alarming series of shortcomings in child care practice with dire results, albeit unforeseen; and, if good practice had been followed, the abuse might have been avoided or halted earlier. We underline 3 additional points: firstly, that a long series of short term or medium term foster placements may be even more damaging than frequent changes of residential home; secondly, the importance of school teachers and other members of a school staff as potential recipients of information or complaints from abused children and the need for clear guidance to schools about how to respond; and, thirdly, the need for vigilance by social workers about the danger of abuse within a foster home by persons other than the foster parents.

Other allegations of abuse in Gwynedd foster homes (Chapter 43)

43.01 We discuss 3 foster homes in this chapter but the third is of marginal relevance only because we received little evidence about it. In the first fostering case discussed the placement authority was the City of Manchester but Gwynedd SSD undertook to supervise the placement.

43.02 **Mr and Mrs A** responded to advertisements for foster parents that appeared in the local press in Manchester shortly before they moved, with their own 3 children, from Manchester to Rhosneigr in Anglesey in 1975. Then, on 1 December 1975, Manchester SSD placed with them 4 foster children (3 boys and a girl) of one family, whose mother had died in June 1974, shortly after care orders had been made in respect of each of the children.

43.03 At the time of this placement, the oldest child was aged 8 years and the youngest, a boy, was $3\frac{1}{2}$ years old, having been born on 2 June 1972. The latter, A1, was the only one of the 4 to complain subsequently of abuse by the foster parents; and he remained with them for 11 years until 13 February 1987. The other 3 children remained with the As until each reached the age of 17 years, but the middle son attended Ysgol Talfryn[5] from the age of 14 years, returning to the foster home for his holidays.

43.04 During the period of A1's placement with them, Mr and Mrs A moved the household from Rhosneigr to a large bungalow at Llanfaelog, also in Anglesey. On 13 February 1987, however, A1 started a serious fire at the foster home: he was convicted of arson on 8 July 1987 and ordered to be detained for 5 years under the provisions of section 53(2) of the Children and Young Persons Act 1933. Under that order he was admitted 3 months later to the special unit at Red Bank School near Warrington.

43.05 A1 told the Tribunal in his oral evidence that he was well looked after by Mr and Mrs A but that things changed for him after about 5 years, when the younger of his brothers began stealing. According to A1, Mr and Mrs A, who were active members of the Evangelical Free Church, began to "take it out on him" to try to ensure that he did not behave similarly as he grew older. His major complaint was that Mr A began to hit him with a buckled belt: he referred to 2 specific occasions when this occurred and added that he was beaten in this way on more than one occasion also for swearing or for just having fun with other children.

43.06 A1's main allegations against Mrs A were that she was aware of the beatings and that she herself smacked him across the face on a couple of occasions. She had also thrown a golf club at him after he had been cautioned by the police for stealing.

43.07 A1 said that his arson offence was not triggered by any specific incident: his feelings had built up over the years that he had been with the As and he was intending to pay them back for what they had done.

43.08 The documentary evidence before us indicates that suspected abuse of A1 was investigated in 1978 when bruising and weal marks were observed on his back; and A1 alleged that his first beating left him with quite a few cuts, which he showed to his schoolteacher. The evidence is that the headteacher of A1's school telephoned the foster home on 28 June 1978 and spoke to Mrs A about the marks; and A1's social worker called at the foster home twice that day. The records show that the incident was followed up and that A1 told the social worker that he had toppled backwards on to a Tonka toy. There were references also by others to A1 falling off a bicycle. A1 disputed these records and said in evidence that he told a teacher that Mr A had hit him with a belt.

43.09 In his written statements to the Tribunal Mr A denied ever hitting A with a belt. He said that the middle boy and A1 had been the naughtiest of the 4 children, stealing money from the As, a church and teachers, and that he had used a slipper to them from time to time as a reminder to them that the As would not put up with dishonesty. Apart from that, the children had been smacked but all had been treated equally. He and his wife would have liked to adopt all the children but could not afford to do so.

---

[5] See paras 19.01 to 19.07 of this Summary.

43.10   A1 was seen by a consultant psychiatrist, on the advice of a Gwynedd social worker, in preparation for his appearance in Court in July 1987. In the course of the consultation it emerged that A1 had stolen money from the foster home and had been asked to recover it shortly before he started the fire: his resentment then was directed against Mrs A rather than Mr A. However, he showed the psychiatrist "extensive old scarring", which he claimed was the result of being "belted" at the age of about 8 years, and he referred also to the alleged golf club incident.

43.11   The allegations made by A1 to the psychiatrist were investigated by Gwynedd SSD and 2 social workers visited the As but their investigation did not reveal any new information. On 16 June 1987 the local Review Committee did not accept that abuse had occurred.

43.12   The Welsh Office then intervened by asking Gwynedd to investigate the matter because a social services inspector had learned of A1's allegations on a routine visit to Red Bank School. In response to this, Larry King saw A1's sister, who said that she knew of no abuse taking place in the foster home, apart from her eldest brother having to wash his mouth out with soap after lying. A further Case Conference was held on 26 April 1988 and it concluded that there was no evidence that A1 had been physically abused in the As' household and that medical and other evidence did not support the contention.

43.13   A letter to this effect was sent by the Director of Social Services (Lucille Hughes) to the Welsh Office on 28 April 1988. In that letter the Director accepted that a case conference should have been held in 1978/1979. She said, however, that the A family should be complimented for the efforts that they had made over many years with the 3 difficult boys whom they had fostered. The Director was critical of the original placement by Manchester because of lack of preparation of the foster parents and the emotional and psychological disturbance that it caused to all the children in the household. She said that Gwynedd would not in future agree to supervise on any other authority's behalf without a full contractual visiting arrangement by that authority.

43.14   It is impossible for us now, 11 years after the final Case Conference, to reach any different conclusion about the alleged physical abuse of A1. The As' regime was probably too strict and they may have resorted to inappropriate physical chastisement on occasions by the standards of many at the time but it would be wrong for us to hold that they were guilty of abuse. It is to be noted also that A1 told the police in September 1992 that, although he did not agree with the punishment that he had received at the hands of Mr A, he did not wish to make a formal complaint about it and did not wish the police to investigate the matter.

43.15   We endorse the criticisms of the placement made by Lucille Hughes in her April 1988 letter (which involved, in effect, setting up a small group home without adequate resources) and add that it was much too far from Manchester for any meaningful supervision to be carried out from there. Manchester SSD played little or no part in the supervision once the placement had been made, despite its continuing statutory responsibility; and it was not even represented at the regular reviews that were held.

43.16 **Mr and Mrs B**, who were approved by Gwynedd County Council in 1977 as foster parents for both short and long term placements, lived in a detached bungalow on the edge of an industrial estate just outside Caernarvon. They were then about 40 years old and there were 5 children of their own in the household (3 by Mrs B's first marriage), ranging from about 20 years to 11 years old.

43.17 In the following years the Bs fostered a large number of children and we heard evidence about the complaints of 3 of them. The main complainants were 2 sisters, B1 and B2, who were placed with Mr and Mrs B from 9 September 1985, when they were aged 9 and 8 years respectively, to 20 August 1986. At that time there were 8 in the household, including 2 of the Bs' own children, a former foster son aged 21 years and a foster son aged nearly 11 years.

43.18 Both B1 and B2, who had had a disrupted life with their mother previously, made stringent criticisms of the Bs' home in their oral evidence to the Tribunal. A major complaint was that B2 had to share a bed at weekends with Mrs B's daughter, who was then 23 years old and unstable. B1 and B2 shared a bedroom, which was damp and cold, and the bedding was inadequate. They complained also about their food and clothing, of having their hair washed and cut by Mrs B, and of bathing only once a week with insufficient hot water.

43.19 It is clear from the documentary evidence before us that some of these complaints were made at the time by B1 and B2 to their social worker and to their aunt and a grandmother and they were even seen at headquarters with the aunt and grandmother by Larry King[6] within a month or so of the placement. The girls' social worker told the police in July 1992 that she was responsible for supervising the placement until May 1986: she visited them at least once a month and spoke to them alone. Her recollection was that the girls were unhappy because they wanted to be with their mother but she did not recall them ever complaining about conditions at the foster home. Nevertheless, the social worker was not satisfied with the state of cleanliness of the premises and was disgusted on one occasion by the dirtiness of the lavatory.

43.20 The social worker did not recall visiting the girls' bedroom, despite the fact that the statutory review form contained a question about it. She said that oversight of the foster homes was dealt with by Cartref Bontnewydd, which had the responsibility for examining them, and that the SSD had limited influence over the Fostering Unit.

43.21 Statutory reviews took place on 25 November 1985 and 3 April 1986 and referred to complaints made by the girls' extended family. The complaints were, however, rejected. In the second of these reviews it was said that the girls' mother had made no complaints whatsoever.

43.22 The third complainant was fostered with the Bs for 2 short periods before B1 and B2, that is, from 2 July to 30 September 1984 and from 13 November 1984 to 10 April 1985, the latter period spanning his 15th birthday. He is the complainant referred to in paragraph 36.05 of this Summary, who was

---

[6] Principal Officer (Children).

subsequently placed at Queens Park. This witness said that the Bs were not suitable foster parents for anyone: the house was dirty and there was never any food in by the end of the week. He complained also of being bullied by the former foster son who was still living there. He left the first time because of this bullying and, on the second occasion, because of being required to wear unsuitable second-hand trousers when he needed correct school uniform.

43.23 This witness' social worker told the police that she thought that the foster home was untidy but that it was a suitable placement for him.

43.24 In their joint statements to the Tribunal Mr and Mrs B denied that the foster home was dirty and untidy but said that considerable alterations were being carried out so that there were occasions when it was more like a building site than a family home. There was never any shortage of money or food and the bungalow was centrally heated. They denied also that B2 had had to share a bed with Mrs B's daughter.

43.25 Our conclusion is that, although there was probably some exaggeration by the complainants in their description of conditions in this foster home after the lapse of many years, those conditions were far from satisfactory in the period from 1984 to 1986. In favour of the Bs, it must be said that they had a successful fostering record before this but, in our judgment, they were taking upon themselves excessive responsibilities by the mid 1980s, when (apparently) extensive work was being carried out at the foster home. General conditions were low: a placement there may have been just about adequate for a robust teenage boy but the foster home was unsuitable for 2 very young girls who had just been taken away from their mother in distressing circumstances.

43.26 A troubling aspect of the case is that the available records do not contain any account by a social worker of the position of Mrs B's daughter at this time or of the relevant bedroom accommodation. There appears to have been some confusion of responsibility between the Cartref Bontnewydd Fostering Unit and the SSD; and there were discrepancies in the accounts by different social workers of the number of bedrooms and persons resident. We have no reason to doubt that B2 did have to share her bed, as she alleges, from time to time but social workers seem to have been unaware of this and it should not have been countenanced.

43.27 Mr and Mrs C were foster parents who lived at Llangefni in Anglesey and no complaint is made against either of them. C1, who was born on 11 April 1980, was placed with them, together with her elder sister, for about 4 months from September 1983, after they had been admitted to care because of alleged excessive chastisement of the older girl by their father.

43.28 In a written statement to the Tribunal, C1 complained of being shouted at and slapped by a baby-sitter, in the absence of Mr and Mrs C, after C1 had soiled herself through no fault of her own. C1 was unable to say whether Mr or Mrs C was told about this incident. The allegation is that C1's father saw the outline of a hand mark on her bottom when she returned to her home at the weekend and that he made an official complaint to a Gwynedd social worker.

43.29 C1's father said that, following this complaint, he spoke to someone he believed to be a supervisor and was told that, if he pursued his complaint, it would be a retrograde step, if he wished to get his children back with him. He did not pursue the matter but remains embittered about the disparity between the way in which he was treated for chastising a child and the response to the baby-sitter's behaviour.

43.30 We have not been able to see any social services record of this matter and cannot, therefore, reach any satisfactory conclusion about it. The complaint is that of the father rather than C1, whose own recollection of the matter must be questionable.

43.31 To sum up, the evidence before us has not revealed any widespread physical abuse by foster parents in Gwynedd. On the contrary, the complaints that we have heard have been limited in scope and there have been some positive aspects of the fostering, particularly in the case of Mr and Mrs A. Nevertheless, both cases that we have considered in detail have revealed serious defects in the management of fostering by Gwynedd SSD and important lessons should be learned from them.

THE RESPONSIBILITY OF HIGHER MANAGEMENT IN GWYNEDD
(Chapters 44 to 46)

Management structures and responsibility for Gwynedd Social Services from 1974 to 1996 (Chapter 44)

44.01 As in Clwyd, there were 3 successive Directors of Social Services in Gwynedd during the period under review, namely:

Thomas Edward (T E) Jones, the former Director for Caernarvonshire, from 1 April 1974 to September 1982, but who was absent on sick leave from May 1982.

Lynn Ebsworth, the Chief Personnel Officer and Management Services Officer for Gwynedd, who took over from T E Jones in an acting capacity in May 1982 and then served as Director from September 1982 until 30 September 1983.

Lucille (Margaret) Hughes, a former Children's Officer for Caernarvonshire and Anglesey and then Deputy Director for Caernarvonshire, from 1 October 1983 until her retirement on 31 March 1996.

44.02 It will be seen that Ebsworth's period was only a short interregnum. He had been recruited from industry by Gwynedd in 1975 and had no training or experience in any aspect of social services. However, it was during his period as Director that the emerging roles of Gethin Evans and Nefyn Dodd were defined.

44.03 T E Jones was appointed as Director on 1 July 1973, in advance of reorganisation, when he was 51 years old. His experience was almost wholly as a County Welfare Officer before he became Director of Social Services for Caernarvonshire in 1971 and he had no professional qualification.

44.04 For most of T E Jones' period as Director, the senior officer responsible for children's services in Gwynedd was the Deputy Director, **David Alan Parry**, who had been Director of Social Services for Anglesey for the preceding 3 years. Parry, who is 10 years younger than T E Jones, had been an applicant for the post of Director in Gwynedd and his major earlier experience had been as Deputy Children's Officer and then Children's Officer for Anglesey. He was also the possessor of several professional qualifications. In the event, he retained his responsibility for children until July 1981 but was then sidelined. He remained Deputy Director whilst absent from work following a car accident, but he became Assistant Director (Special Duties) on his return in May 1983 until he accepted voluntary redundancy, with an enhanced pension, on 31 March 1987.

44.05 Parry did not assume responsibility for children's services immediately. He began with wider roles, including preparation of the social services budget, but

T E Jones was dissatisfied with his performance and placed him in charge of the Children's Section from February 1976. Under him, Parry had a Senior (later Principal) Officer (Children) and also, for a time, a Senior Assistant (Children). Parry's evidence was that there were also on the staff of the Children's Section a Homes Officer and a Fostering/Adoptions Senior Officer.

44.06 The Senior Officer (Children) was redesignated as a Principal Officer from 1 June 1979. The holder of this post from 1 August 1975 was **Larry King**, then nearly 50 years, who had a background in the colonial police but who had been employed in social services from 1969 and had obtained the Home Office Letter of Recognition in Child Care. King was to remain prominent in the management structure in relation to children until he retired on 14 May 1988.

44.07 Parry was said to be a regular visitor to children's homes, and particularly to Tŷ'r Felin, between 1976 and 1981. The Homes Officer with immediate responsibility for them was Elizabeth Hughes but she, like too many others from time to time, was absent on prolonged sick leave in 1978 and it was her absence that led to the progressive enlargement of Nefyn Dodd's duties and advancement of his status[1].

44.08 It is clear that Parry became an uncritical admirer of Dodd and that it was he who initiated these developments in Dodd's career. To that extent Parry was guilty of a considerable error of judgment but he cannot be blamed for the consolidation of Dodd's position in 1982 and his later promotion, which took place despite cogent criticisms in the Dyfed team's report[2].

44.09 The effective demotion of Parry occurred in July 1981, when responsibility for the Children's Section was transferred to **Lucille Hughes**, who had been Principal Assistant Director since February 1976, with responsibilities for the elderly and mental health. This change coincided with the commissioning by the Chief Executive of the inquiry by the Dyfed team into Y Gwyngyll.

44.10 The report of the Dyfed team contained criticisms of T E Jones as well as many other criticisms and recommendations. The authors commented, for example, that T E Jones took "little or no interest in the work of the Children's Section" and they expressed the view that there was a "complete lack of rapport and working relationship between the Director and the Deputy Director". In his written evidence to the Tribunal T E Jones repudiated the criticisms and said that they had not been put to him by the Dyfed team. In his view, it was commendable that Gwynedd had provided the level of service that had been achieved, notwithstanding the financial constraints, with comparatively few complaints of abuse.

44.11 Another report presented at about the same time (in March 1982) was by consultants who had been asked by the District Auditor to carry out an investigation into the Social Services Department, excluding the Children's Section. The report found, amongst other things, that the Director and Principal Assistant Director were overloaded with work and that the issue of

---

[1] See paras 33.11 and 33.12 of this Summary.
[2] Ibid, paras 35.04 and 35.05.

accountability in individual cases was confused. They said that the structure failed to provide effective line control between headquarters, area and establishment administration officers and staff.

44.12 When these reports were presented, T E Jones, who was well liked, was on the eve of retirement and unwell. A protective veil was thrown around him and only a very small number of persons saw the Dyfed report. Attention was focussed on D A Parry and a disciplinary panel was appointed to consider his position but there is no evidence of any discussion of broader issues and it is not even clear that the report was seen by the panel.

44.13 By this time a new senior figure in the Children's Section had emerged. This was **(Owain) Gethin Evans**, a professionally qualified social worker, who had moved to headquarters in 1978, on his appointment as Senior Officer (General). He had then become Principal Officer (Children) with responsibility for fostering and adoption but, on the transfer of responsibility for children to Lucille Hughes, he was asked to assist her. His wider responsibilities were formally recognised in June 1982, when he became Head of Children's Services, and he remained with Gwynedd until August 1995, when he was appointed Director of Social Services for the nascent Ceredigion County Council. Evans was de facto Head of Children's Services in Gwynedd, under the Director, from 1982 to 1995, apart from a period between 1987 and 1992, when he was Assistant Director (Resources and Support); but he had not been involved with children in residential homes before this.

44.14 Thus it was under Ebsworth as Acting Director that Evans was appointed to the senior post in the Children's Section; and one of Evans' early actions in this period was to write a memorandum, on 10 August 1982, emphasising that Dodd had full responsibility for all community homes. It appears that neither Lucille Hughes nor Evans had been shown a copy of the Dyfed team's report. Evans did not see that report until 2 months before he gave evidence to the Tribunal.

44.15 Evans' explanation of his action in writing the memorandum is that he simply accepted Dodd's role as it had already become but that does not explain adequately his long term acceptance of Dodd's dual position. He submitted a report to committee dated 6 August 1982 in which he spelt out the functions of a Supervisor/Co-ordinator in some detail. The report was intended to provide an overall strategy for residential care in Gwynedd based on the 4 existing units, each with specific roles, and it was agreed with Ebsworth, Lucille Hughes and Dodd before it was presented to (and accepted by) committee. Some of its detailed recommendations were implemented but, as a blue print for differing functions for the community homes, it was largely ignored.

44.16 The vacant post of Deputy Director of Social Services was filled by the appointment of an outsider, **(David) Glanville Owen**, who was nevertheless a native of Pwllheli, from 2 April 1984. The other short-listed candidate for the post was Gethin Evans. Owen himself was professionally qualified and had wide experience of fieldwork with children, although he had never managed nor worked within any community home for children.

44.17 Under Lucille Hughes and Glanville Owen, the management structure of the SSD provided for 5 Assistant Directors, including Parry. However, the post of Assistant Director (Children) was unfilled until Gethin Evans was appointed to it from 30 September 1985. His position as Head of Children's Services was thus formally recognised. Prior to that, he and King had both been Principal Officers in the Children's Section, with King the senior by date of appointment but not in terms of responsibilities.

44.18 On Evans' appointment as Assistant Director (Children), Dodd's wide responsibilities were recognised by his appointment as a Principal Officer in Evans' place but with the different title of Principal Officer (Residential Care - Children) from 1 October 1985.

44.19 Like Clwyd, Gwynedd adopted a form of devolution to divisions towards the end of the period under review. One of Glanville Owen's early tasks as Deputy Director was to formulate proposals for reorganisation of the SSD and a new structure was eventually operated from April 1987 but it was abandoned in April 1992.

44.20 Some details of this new structure are given in paragraphs 44.30 to 44.34 of the Tribunal's report but only a bare outline is necessary here. The county was divided into 2 operational divisions: Menai division comprised the areas of Arfon and Anglesey; Llyn/Eryri comprised Aberconwy, Dwyfor and Meirionydd. Each division was headed by an Assistant Director and there were 2 other Assistant Directors, one responsible for Development and the other (Gethin Evans) for Resources and Support, at headquarters. In relation to Children's Services, the Assistant Director (Menai) was the line manager accountable for the work of 2 headquarters based Principal Officers responsible respectively for Children's Residential Services, including residential and day care establishments, and Children's Other Services, including adoption.

44.21 The new Assistant Director (Menai) with responsibility for the Children's Section was **Robert Evans**, who had been Area Officer for Aberconwy from 1984 and who was professionally qualified, with over 10 years experience of social work. The 2 Principal Officers accountable to him initially were Larry King, who was designated Principal Officer (Child Protection) and Nefyn Dodd.

44.22 On King's retirement on 14 May 1988, he was replaced by **Peter James Hibbs**, a professionally qualified social worker who had been with Gwynedd since 1979. Then, on Dodd's retirement on 23 May 1990, Hibbs succeeded him and the post was redesignated as Principal Officer (Adolescent Services) with responsibility for residential services, youth justice and leaving care. Unfortunately, however, Hibbs was greatly affected by his wife's death in November 1990 and he was only able to work intermittently after that until his own retirement on health grounds on 8 January 1993.

44.23 Although Robert Evans bore line management responsibility for the Children's Section during this period, his actual involvement in the work was comparatively slight because of the pressure of other work upon him. The new structure does not appear to have clarified and tightened line management. Hibbs, for example, told the Tribunal that, on becoming a Principal Officer, he worked more directly to Gethin Evans than to Robert Evans and he had little contact with either the Director or the Deputy Director. Hibbs saw Robert Evans about once a week whereas he saw Gethin Evans daily. In 1988 Welsh Office SWSOs commented that the distribution of duties between these 2 Assistant Directors was not formally defined; and only one of the relevant 3 Principal Officer posts was filled at the time of their inspection.

44.24 The final major reorganisation of the SSD, implemented in 1992, involved abandonment of line management arrangements based upon 2 divisions. The Area Officers became accountable again to the Deputy Director of Social Services and there was a headquarters team of 5 Assistant Directors responsible for the "specialist" fields. Gethin Evans, who had been responsible for the development of children's services as part of his remit between 1987 and 1992, resumed direct line management responsibility for these services as Assistant Director (Children).

44.25 From April 1992 there was a headquarters team of 5 (later 4) working under Gethin Evans, including Hibbs (Adolescent Services) and an officer responsible for Child Protection. Hibbs was replaced in March 1993 by **Dafydd Ifans**, who became the line manager responsible for the 3 remaining community homes. He found that there were still line management problems involving the Area Managers (as they had become), the specialist Assistant Directors and the Deputy Director, which remained unresolved despite an attempt by the Director to clarify them.

44.26 In the Tribunal's report we give an account also of the role of the 3 successive Chief Executives of Gwynedd during the period under review. They were:

(David) Alun Jones, the former Clerk of Denbighshire County Council, who was Chief Executive from 1974 to 1980 and then became the Commissioner for Local Administration in Wales until 1985.

Ioan Bowen Rees, who was County Secretary and Solicitor of Gwynedd County Council from 1974 before serving as Chief Executive from 1980 to 1991 and who died in May 1999.

Huw Vaughan Thomas, a former civil servant, who was Director of the Training Agency, Wales, before becoming Chief Executive of Gwynedd on 24 April 1991. He has held the same office in Denbighshire since the further reorganisation of local government.

44.27 Three important points about the organisation of the County Council emerged from the evidence of Bowen Rees, whose knowledge of it covered the widest span, from 1974 to 1991.

44.28 The first of these is that the Council was composed mainly of Independents, with no political party in power. There was no Leader of the Council and, although there was a Policy and Resources Committee, it was not until a late stage in the 1980s that there was a Chairman of that Committee who was prepared to take a corporate lead.

44.29 Secondly, the departmental committees were the main committees, with Chairmen tending to respect one another's fiefdom. Bowen Rees' own terms of appointment referred to him as head of the Council's paid service, having "authority over all other Officers so far as this is necessary for the efficient management and execution of the Council's functions". But, in his oral evidence, Bowen Rees agreed that Chief Officers were allowed their heads to run their own departments. He had no choice in the matter because it was the Council's choice: the Chairmen and Chief Officers, in combination, ran their departments. It was a federation, even a confederation, rather than a unified state.

44.30 Thirdly, it was not until 1986 that a Priorities Sub-Committee of the Policy and Resources Committee was set up. By 1989 a Policy Unit under the Chief Executive had been established also but the financial situation throughout the 1980s caused a feeling of helplessness.

44.31 Despite these constraints, it seems that Bowen Rees was more interventionist than his predecessor in SSD matters. For example, it was he who initiated the Dyfed team's investigation of Y Gwyngyll and he was actively involved in the decision making about Parry after that team's report was received, although his advice was not followed. Later on, he issued much criticised statements to the press early in November 1986 to the effect that the police report had completely vindicated the decision by the County Council not to suspend any officer. Bowen Rees was also involved in the discussions about re-structuring the SSD into divisions: he said that he opposed the proposal and was disappointed when the Council backed the Social Services Committee and not him.

44.32 Both Alun Jones and Bowen Rees were very conscious of the restrictions on local government spending for almost the whole of the period up to 1991 but neither recalls that children's services were claimed to be in special need. Bowen Rees was aware in 1983/1984 of comments by the County Treasurer on the low funding of children's services but he said that he satisfied himself that this was largely attributable to the Council's policy of boarding out children whenever it was possible to do so.

44.33 Vaughan Thomas effected a number of structural improvements in the last phase of the Council, despite imminent reorganisation. He restructured his own department to provide broader strategic planning and gave priority to introducing more modern management techniques. He succeeded also in establishing a standing Audit Sub-Committee to vet departmental/committee proposals and to encourage re-distribution of resources alongside necessary budget reductions. Thomas found that, within the SSD, there was an initial lack of readiness to consider whether changes were necessary to current procedures and practices and repeated approaches were often needed before a response was received.

44.34 It follows from what we say in this chapter that, despite the quite frequent organisational changes that were made during the period under review, a very small headquarters team took active responsibility for child care matters on a day to day basis throughout. From 1976 to 1981 Parry was the Head of the

Children's Section, with King as the main person under him, and it was during this period that Dodd began to emerge with added responsibilities. Then, from 1982 until the late 1980s, Gethin Evans was the Head of Children's Services, with King and Dodd under him; but Dodd was given a largely free hand in relation to the community homes. The re-structuring from 1987 to 1992 was unsuccessful and Gethin Evans remained influential in relation to children's services, although Robert Evans was the titular head. King and Dodd retired during this phase and Gethin Evans resumed, in effect, his former position as Assistant Director (Children's Services) in 1992, with very limited Principal Officer support, mainly from Ifans.

44.35 In our judgment, the Children's Section was seriously undermanned for most of the period under review and there was no adequate supervision or monitoring of its performance. Lack of resources and prolonged illnesses do not excuse the SSD's failure to institute and maintain a clear system of line management for its community homes and effective arrangements for the care and protection of children. Dodd was wrongly permitted to dominate residential homes for children and placements for a decade, during which the county had no comprehensible strategy for residential services for children. Councillors and successive Directors of Social Services appear to have been pre-occupied with services for the elderly and the mentally handicapped at the expense of those for children in care; and it was only in the late stages that coherent attempts were being made to put children's services on a sound footing.

The failure to eliminate abuse (Chapter 45)

45.01 An important distinction between Gwynedd and Clwyd is that the evidence before the Tribunal has not disclosed the presence of any persistent sexual abuser in any of the community homes within Gwynedd or in any of the private residential establishments; and the 2 proved sexual abusers in foster homes in Gwynedd were prosecuted promptly after complaints had been made. In general, however, the lessons to be learned from Clwyd's experience of sexual abuse are equally relevant to local authorities within the former Gwynedd for the future.

45.02 We do not suggest that there were particular failures by the Gwynedd SSD in relation to sexual abuse, as distinct from other forms of abuse, in the period under review. In this chapter in the report, therefore, we deal generally with Gwynedd's failure to eliminate abuse. Not surprisingly, the underlying reasons for this failure were broadly similar to those that we have found in Clwyd but the pattern of abuse and the relevant line management in Clwyd were different.

45.03 About two thirds of the known Gwynedd complainants were former residents of Tŷ'r Felin during the period when Nefyn Dodd was Officer-in-Charge; and from about 1981 to 1989 he was also the line manager for all the community homes in Gwynedd. Much of the discussion in this chapter hinges, therefore, upon his dominant role and authoritarian personality.

45.04 It is questionable whether Dodd was a suitable person to appoint as head of an Observation and Assessment Centre, bearing in mind his limited credentials and even lesser experience. We accept, however, that those responsible for his appointment could not have been expected to foresee how his personality and practices would develop. The strongest criticism is that he was permitted to develop them, without any restraining influence, and then encouraged to extend his methods and authority, without any close supervision or monitoring. The initial responsibility for these errors must rest upon the Deputy Director at the time, Parry, who had ample opportunity to observe Dodd.

45.05 The responsibility for Dodd's later advancement does not rest upon Parry. Lucille Hughes and Gethin Evans were plainly at fault and must bear the primary blame, but, in partial mitigation, neither was shown the Dyfed team's report. More senior officers such as Bowen Rees and Ebsworth must bear the blame for the limited circulation of that report with the result that the broad issues that it raised were not discussed.

45.06 The inappropriate delegation of important headquarters responsibilities reflected a penny-pinching attitude to child care matters in Gwynedd and Dodd's position became even more anomalous when he was advanced to Principal Officer, whilst remaining Officer-in-Charge at Tŷ'r Felin. The pattern of delegation without effective accountability in return was a feature of the SSD throughout the period under review with the result that the interests of children in care were neglected at the highest level.

45.07 In practical terms, the effect of these arrangements was that there was no meaningful channel of complaint, even for members of the residential care staff, as the experiences of Alison Taylor illustrate. The denial of access to headquarters was not confined to residential care staff but extended to Area Officers and thence to field workers in respect of children in community homes. This was spelt out expressly in a memorandum dated 15 October 1984, which was drafted by Gethin Evans but signed by Lucille Hughes.

45.08 The blame for these misconceived arrangements rests squarely upon Lucille Hughes and, under her, upon Gethin Evans and they are not excused by lack of knowledge of the Dyfed team's strictures over 2 years earlier. The arrangements were bad structurally and, by 1983/1984, Hughes and Evans had had full opportunity to acquaint themselves with Dodd's weaknesses and limitations. Unhappily, however, they provide strong evidence of Lucille Hughes' failure to involve herself actively in the management of children's services, despite her pre-1971 experience, and of Gethin Evans' disinclination to involve himself in the practical aspects of his responsibilities for community homes.

45.09 It is difficult to see how any conventional complaints procedure could have been effective in the face of these arrangements but the reality was that there was no such procedure until the latest stages of the period under review. Moreover, such documents as there were dealing with residential care practice were largely out of date and were not readily available to residential care staff.

45.10 A pamphlet called "Handbook for Children in Residential Care"[3], drafted by Dodd and approved by Evans in 1988, contained a section on complaints but it was already obsolescent when it was distributed to heads of homes on or about 28 October 1988, in view of the impending Children Act.

45.11 If any additional discouragement was needed for potential complainants, it was provided by the actual response of higher management to the few contemporaneous complaints that were pursued, which we have illustrated in Chapters 33 and 34 of the report. The response to them was symptomatic of a pervasive intention amongst senior officials from Nefyn Dodd upwards to suppress complaints when they were made, however serious they might be. Notable examples were the response to the complaint of A at Queens Park[4] and the case of M, in which a prosecution was delayed in consequence for 7 years[5].

45.12 In this climate any "whistleblower" was likely to receive short shrift and so events proved. Quite apart from Alison Taylor's experiences, a former member of the staff at Tŷ'r Felin wrote to the Deputy Director of Social Services, Glanville Owen, in January 1985 listing a series of criticisms of Dodd's management of the home. We give details of the response to this in paragraph 33.122 of the report: it is sufficient to comment here that Owen, in his oral evidence, looking at the matter 12 years on, said that he was quite appalled by the allegations and the way in which they were not investigated by him.

45.13 Any suggestion that Alison Taylor was a lone disaffected employee in her complaints about Dodd is rebutted by the fact that the representative of social workers and child care officers in the Children's Section wrote a letter to Lucille Hughes on 24 January 1986 complaining about the conditions under which they were working and of the way in which they were being treated by Dodd. It concluded "We are all being hoodwinked, manoeuvred, and degraded, we ask for your help in putting these matters right before it is too late".

45.14 To sum up, the organisation and management of community homes in Gwynedd were such that a degree of child abuse was almost bound to occur and the only cause for relief is that it did not occur on a greater scale than has been disclosed by the evidence. Residential care staff were largely untrained and opportunities for in-service training were very limited. There were no clear guidelines for staff and children with widely varying needs were placed in community homes without reference to any overall care strategy or individual care planning. Access to field workers was limited and, for most of the period, control of the community homes was vested in a single individual, without any adequate provision for monitoring and supervision by higher management. There was no recognised complaints procedure, direct contact with headquarters was discouraged and such complaints as did penetrate the system were treated dismissively.

---

[3] Ibid, para 33.39(a).
[4] Ibid, para 36.05.
[5] Ibid, paras 41.01 to 41.21.

45.15 For these failings the 2 main Directors of Social Services must bear major responsibility, together with the headquarters staff responsible for child care matters, to the extent that we have indicated. Members of Gwynedd County Council and, in particular, the Social Services Children's Sub-Committee must also, however, bear a share of the responsibility for their failure to acquaint themselves with conditions in the community homes and to monitor and control the operation of the Children's Section of the SSD.

Basic failings in the quality of care (Chapter 46)

46.01 We revert to a number of the matters discussed in the preceding 2 paragraphs of this Summary in Chapter 46 of the report. In that chapter we identify the same major failings in Gwynedd in the provision of an acceptable standard of care as those that we found in Clwyd. They are:

    (a) The lack of adequate planning of each child's period in care.

    (b) The absence of any strategic framework for the placement of children in residential care.

    (c) Ineffective reviewing processes and lack of consultation with the child.

    (d) Intermittent and inadequate surveillance by field social workers.

    (e) Failure to establish any co-ordinated system for preparing residents for their discharge from care.

46.02 Each of these failings is discussed in Chapter 46 of the report in the context of what happened in Gwynedd. Amongst our findings are that there was little evidence of detailed assessment prior to care and that the object of admission into care was often stated to be for assessment without any indication as to what was to be assessed or the purpose of the assessment.

46.03 In relation to placements, Dodd was the supreme arbiter in respect of the community homes in the county. In many cases they were determined by availability rather than the particular needs of the child and the failure to implement any coherent strategy accentuated the risk of drift in care. Moreover, SWSOs who visited Gwynedd in the autumn of 1988 summarised their views on the boarding out arrangements as follows:

> "The evidence was of a placement policy and practice in need of major overhaul. We found hasty or ill-conceived introduction; poor preparation of foster home and child; an absence of agreed objectives and targets; long delays between solution and conclusion; little or no choice of family placement and placement at long distance and/or inappropriate locations."

46.04 The same inspectors reported favourably on some aspects of the reviewing process in 1988 but they found 2 inescapable problems: the first was that it was very difficult to review in the absence of a foundation assessment and care plan; and, secondly, there was a lack of available resources to follow plans through. There were wider criticisms, in relation to the period before 1988, by witnesses such as Larry King, that statutory reviews were not being carried out. There were freezes on recruitment and periods of industrial action on several occasions that aggravated the situation and resulted in files being stacked. Later, King's successor, Hibbs, found that there was difficulty about the allocation of field social workers to children: up to 60 children were allocated to a single social worker; there were delays in allocation; and some children in residential care did not have a social worker allocated to them.

46.05 A separate, but central, criticism of the reviewing process during the period of almost 10 years to 1988 was that Dodd's views almost invariably prevailed when they were in conflict with those of field workers. There were also inhibitions about the sharing of information about children; and, even after King left, Hibbs found that field workers were not being afforded access to records in the home, having to rely instead on a "skeletal" report from the head of the home.

46.06 In this climate Area staff understandably felt that they were being deliberately distanced from the children for whom they were responsible by a combination of organisational and procedural decisions and the overall attitude of Dodd. The result has been that few of the former residents of community homes and foster homes in Gwynedd have spoken of a meaningful relationship with their field workers.

46.07 Headquarters staff were well aware of unrest amongst Area Officers and their staff about the arrangements in place from 1982 onwards and they were aware also that field workers were not visiting children in the homes as frequently as they should; but no effective action was taken to remedy the position.

46.08 The loosening of the tie between field social workers and the children in residential care was likely to have particularly adverse consequences when the time came for a child to be discharged from care.

46.09 In Gethin Evans' 1982 strategy document[6] it was envisaged that the community home that would prepare adolescents for independent living would be Y Gwyngyll. This was to be the main focus of the unit: Evans had in mind that social links were to be forged with the careers' service, local employers and the private and public housing sectors, with the assistance of field workers; and other Area staff were to be involved in group work with adolescents. Thus, Y Gwyngyll was to take over and expand, in effect, the earlier role of Tŷ Newydd when it was a hostel[7].

46.10 This description of Y Gwyngyll's role was not in accord with the Regional Plan, which was already obsolescent. More importantly, however, Y Gwyngyll never fulfilled the role envisaged by Evans. Its design included bed-sitting accommodation for 2 school leavers, but not even this was used for the purpose.

---

[6] Ibid, para 44.15.
[7] Ibid, para 34.02.

46.11 We have found no evidence of a continuing strategy for adolescents leaving care in the 1980s. It was not until nearly the end of the period under review that Gwynedd's Departmental Manual No 2 included detailed guidance on the preparation of children for leaving care, drafted by Ifans in the light of the requirements of section 24 of the Children Act 1989 and the SSIW's report on its Inspection of Outcomes for Children Leaving Care.

46.12 A disquieting aspect of the history that we have related was the failure of Gwynedd SSD to take appropriate remedial action in response to adverse reports. The most striking example of this was their failure to act upon, or even to discuss broadly, the report of the Dyfed inquiry team into Y Gwyngyll[8] in late 1981 and it is unnecessary to expand upon that criticism here.

46.13 Another notable, but less startling, example was the failure of the SSD to respond adequately to criticisms made by SWSOs in their report on 12 children in residential care in Gwynedd on 19 September 1988. Part of the background to this was that there was still no effective strategy for residential child care in Gwynedd and the inspectors had found that the children in Tŷ'r Felin and Queens Park were "interchangeable with reference to their ages and the kind of problems they presented".

46.14 Gethin Evans eventually presented a response to this report to the Social Services Committee on 5 September 1989. This 8 page document failed to address the problem of the use of the children's homes and other major problems highlighted in the report: it was superficial and dismissive. The committee were told that the overall tenor of the report was generally positive and a tribute to the hard work done within the homes and the Area Offices; and the detailed criticisms were buried in defensive comment. Glanville Owen conceded in cross-examination that Gethin Evans' response did not reflect the content of the report and he said that he did not agree with the response. However, both he and Lucille Hughes left Evans to deal with the matter.

46.15 All the senior officers who gave evidence to the Tribunal stressed that children's services were handicapped by lack of financial resources but this can only be a comparatively minor explanation of Gwynedd's failure to make adequate provision for children in care for 2 main reasons. The first is that many of the failings stemmed from defects in the organisation of children's services and failures by the staff responsible for those services. The second is that it was Gwynedd County Council and, in particular, its Social Services Committee, that was responsible for the low priority given to children's services in the allocation of resources.

46.16 The evidence before us indicates that the allocation of expenditure to individual departments within the overall county budget remained substantially unchanged until the early 1990s, when the Chief Executive introduced by stages the Audit Sub-Committee[9]. Before that there was no effective mechanism to enable the Council to re-consider priorities on a global basis and there was no will on the part of councillors to achieve that objective.

---

[8] Ibid, paras 44.10 to 44.12.
[9] Ibid, para 44.33.

Allocations between committees followed broadly the pattern established by the 3 predecessor county councils.

46.17 It is questionable whether any substantial attempt was made at any time by the Social Services Committee to obtain a significant additional share of the overall county expenditure. The recollection of the most prominent Chairman of that Committee (from 1977 to 1981) was that there were 2 occasions in 1979 when increased allocations to the SSD were obtained to improve the pay of residential care staff.

46.18 We do not have sufficient statistical information to enable us to express a firm view about the level of expenditure by Gwynedd on social services but we do have strong evidence to support Lucille Hughes' implicit opinion that the expenditure on children's services was inadequate. She said that this imbalance was councillor driven and her view about this was supported by a member of the Social Services Committee and the Children's Sub-Committee. Gwynedd had an unusually high proportion of elderly residents and their needs were given priority. The rigidity of the budgeting system and the commitment of councillors to other services were such that Lucille Hughes "did not make a huge fuss about it" during her long tenure as Director of Social Services.

46.19 In a report to the County Council on the 1993/1994 accounts the District Audit Service drew attention to the fact that Gwynedd was spending only £29 per child under the age of 18 years compared with an average for similar councils of £40 (a difference of £600,000 in budgeted expenditure for the year). This under-funding had serious effects on the quality of care provided in many ways, some of which were reflected in contemporary reports.

46.20 The low priority given by councillors to children's services was part of a wider insensitivity to the needs of children in care. Two criticisms that we heard repeatedly were that attendances at meetings of the Children's Sub-Committee were almost invariably poor and that councillors persistently failed to fulfil their obligations to visit the community homes under a rota system, despite repeated reminders and exhortations.

46.21 The few councillors who did on occasions carry out their rota duties were uneasy about their roles and, particularly, about actual contact with the children in care; and their reports, usually mentioning only complaints by staff about housekeeping and maintenance matters, reflected their unease. By the late 1980s officers of the SSD appear to have abandoned their fruitless attempts to persuade councillors to visit the homes but no alternative arrangement was found until an independent inspection unit was established in the 1990s.

46.22 Apart from these specific individual failures by councillors to fulfil their obligations, there was a collective failure by the Children's Sub-Committee particularly to monitor and oversee adequately the provision of children's services. As the Dyfed team noted in 1981, the Sub-Committee relied far too often upon oral reports from attending officers; and its minutes disclose few examples of any thorough discussion of either principles or practice.

46.23 We have been compelled to the conclusion that the County Council as a whole and its senior officers consigned children's services to a low place in its scale of priorities. A consequence was that these services were chronically under-funded but this was not the sole cause of serious blemishes in the provision of child care. Another major factor was the authority's failure, over many years, to establish a fully effective senior management team with the result that control rested in very few hands without adequate monitoring or accountability.

THE ROLE OF THE WELSH OFFICE
(Chapters 47 to 49)

In this part of the report we give an account of the role of the Welsh Office in relation to children's services during the period under review, mainly as the Welsh Office itself perceived it in accordance with the existing legislation and central government guidance from time to time. But we comment on the continuing and over-riding responsibility of central government for the welfare of children who are placed in care under statutory provisions ordained by central government itself through Parliament.

The position of the Welsh Office in the structure and its child care objectives (Chapter 47)

47.01 Responsibility for child care at central government level was not transferred to the Secretary of State for Wales until 1 January 1971. Until then, the Home Secretary had borne the responsibility, giving general guidance with the assistance of an Advisory Council on Child Care. The transfer to the Welsh Office included responsibility for the work of voluntary bodies in the field of child care but it did not include responsibility for approved schools and remand homes, which was transferred on the same date to the Secretary of State for Social Services. The latter took over also, in relation to England only, the child care functions and ancillary matters that, in Wales, were transferred to the Welsh Office.

47.02 The former Children's Department of the Home Office was disbanded on 1 January 1971, although the Home Office itself retained some responsibilities in relation to children and young persons.

47.03 Responsibility for the former approved schools and remand homes passed to the Welsh Office in 1973, by which time they had been assimilated into the community home system. The Secretary of State for Wales took over responsibility also for adoption services that year.

47.04 Unlike the English Departments of State exercising parallel functions, the Welsh Office had a very wide range of responsibilities, covering almost the full spectrum of local authority services and some others. It was inevitable, therefore, that the Welsh Office would look, in particular, to the Department of Health and Social Security and the Department of Education and Science for leads in their respective fields of expertise.

47.05 In order to deal with its new responsibilities the Welsh Office set up a Community Health and Social Work Division, headed by an Assistant Secretary, within a larger Health and Social Work Group, led by an Under Secretary.

47.06 At the same time an integrated professional social work service, known as the Social Work Service, directed by the Principal SWSO, was established. It comprised the former Home Office Children's Inspectors who had served in Wales and the former Welsh Office Social Work Officers, forming a single group, SWSOs.

47.07 The remit of the Social Work Service was not, however, restricted to services for children. It was said to be "available to assist the Welsh Office, local authorities, hospital authorities and voluntary bodies in Wales in all social work aspects of their functions".

47.08 According to the detailed record produced to us, there was a swift increase in the number of SWSOs from a low of 8 in 1974, of whom 4 were involved directly in services for children, to a peak of 18 in 1978 (including a Chief and 2 Deputies). But the number then reduced and the usual establishment from 1982 onwards was 10 or 11.

47.09 In 1985 the Social Work Service in England was re-designated as the Social Services Inspectorate and the Welsh Office followed suit, but not apparently until 1989, by re-naming its service the Social Services Inspectorate Wales (SSIW). This was said to be part of a policy of quality assurance and was intended, amongst other things, to play an important part in the Welsh Office's appraisal of authorities' social care plans. It was proposed also that it should advise and monitor the operation of the new registration and inspection units of the local authorities.

47.10 Within the Welsh Office there was no separate Policy Division devoted solely to children's services. In the Tribunal's report we trace the various changes that occurred. In the first half of the period under review there was relative stability whilst children's services were part of the responsibility of the Local Authority (latterly Personal) Social Services Division. But there was considerable upheaval in the second half of the period, with major changes in 1987, 1991 and 1994/1995.

47.11 The Welsh Office was unable to give us accurate numbers of staff dealing with issues relating to children over the period, partly because, even at the time, work on children's matters was not separately quantified. However, **John Lloyd**, who was Director, Social Policy and Local Government Affairs from 1988, told the Tribunal that from 1987 there was a separate branch dealing with children in the Health and Social Services Policy Division. At first, the branch comprised a part-time Grade 7 civil servant with 4 support staff but this was increased progressively to what he described as the current complement of 2 Grade 7s and 11 support staff.

47.12 Devolution to Wales in education has a long history from 1882 and in 1970 responsibility for the oversight of almost all educational matters in Wales was transferred to the Secretary of State for Wales. The Welsh Office Education Department (WOED) was established at the same time and the Inspectorate in Wales became part of it, although technically on loan to it until September 1992, when the Office of Her Majesty's Chief Inspector of Schools in Wales (OHMCI(Wales)) came into being as an independent, non-ministerial government department under powers conferred by the Education (Schools) Act 1992.

47.13 The responsibilities of the WOED were extended to higher and further education in 1979 but its responsibilities for the education of children remained largely unchanged from 1970. From 1979 it had 3 divisions, one of which dealt with schools, but this Schools Division was itself split in 1989 into a Schools Curriculum Division and a Schools Administration Division. In 1997/1998 the latter division had a staff of 30, of whom the equivalent of 3 full time staff had responsibility for SEN and independent schools.

47.14 The latest statistics provided for us by OHMCI(Wales) show that in Wales there are about 2,000 LEA-maintained schools of which 54 are special schools (40 per cent of which have residential provision). There are 17 grant-maintained schools and 62 independent schools. Ten of the independent schools cater wholly or mainly for SEN pupils and all but one of these are residential.

47.15 During the period under review the number of HMIs rose from about 47 to 59 in 1992. Following the establishment of the OHMCI(Wales), there was a rapid decline to 43 in 1996; and the establishment from 1997 was 35. Since 1993, however, OHMCI(Wales) has been funded to contract the inspection of individual schools to independent inspectors, whom it recruits and trains.

47.16 According to John Lloyd, the Welsh Office's main task in relation to children's services was to ensure effective implementation of legislation and develop good practice, jointly with developments in England. The statutory framework had placed the duty for caring for children on local authorities within a system subject to overall regulation and supervision by the Secretary of State. The emphasis of central government policy throughout the period was upon giving local authority social services departments as wide a discretion as possible in the discharge of their functions.

47.17 In the 1970s, central government still intended to be involved in the planning and development of social services and to ensure that they were closely co-ordinated with health services. Thus, before local government reorganisation took effect, the Secretary of State for Wales called upon local authorities to submit 10 year development plans for social services.

47.18 In the event, it was found that drawing up plans on a 10 year basis was unrealistic. From 1978 the requirement was for 3 year plans, to be reviewed annually. In the meantime, however, a standstill in local authority current expenditure had been called for by the Government in 1975. Then, in 1979, the new Government announced its intention to reduce substantially the number of bureaucratic controls in order to give local authorities more choice and flexibility.

47.19 According to Lloyd, a new "climate of disengagement" was thus created. An illustration of this was that Welsh Office circulars on the forward planning of social services were discontinued; the last circular on the subject of 3 year plans was issued on 11 March 1987.

47.20 During the 1970s, one particularly relevant aspect of forward planning, namely, for the provision of accommodation of children in care and for the equipment and maintenance of the accommodation was undertaken by children's regional planning committees established under Part II of the Children and Young Persons Act 1969. For this purpose Wales was designated as one region. The CRPC for Wales was established by the Welsh local authorities in 1970 and then re-constructed on 31 May 1974, following reorganisation. Welsh Office assessors attended its meetings as did an HMI, and the SWSW was also invited to attend.

47.21 The CRPC for Wales employed no staff itself. It was serviced by appropriate chief officers of the local authorities and staff engaged full time on CRPC functions from 1974 were formally employed by Mid Glamorgan County Council. It set up a Placement Information Liaison Service from 1 October 1975 to provide a "clearing house" for vacancies and the officer of this service (PILO) was John Llewellyn Thomas[1]. There was a procedure also for monitoring placements outside Wales.

47.22 The first regional plan (the 1971 Plan) for Wales had to be submitted for approval to the Secretary of State by 31 December 1971 and came into effect on 1 April 1973. A revised plan (the 1979 Plan) was later required to be submitted by 1 April 1979 and this came into operation on 1 April 1980.

47.23 The demise of CRPCs appears to have been part of the development of the policy of reduction of controls outlined in the 1979 White Paper[2]. It was being asserted also that local authorities had become self-sufficient in meeting the residential needs of children in their care or nearly so. There was also increased emphasis on placing children in community homes near their own homes and the use of boarding out/fostering instead of residential care had grown substantially.

47.24 Section 4 of the Health and Social Services and Social Security Adjudications Act 1983 abolished the statutory requirement for children's regional planning and substituted a permissive power for local authorities to combine with others to meet their joint needs for community homes. In the absence of a statutory requirement for its activities the CRPC for Wales did not survive beyond the early months of 1984 and the PILO left in February 1984.

47.25 Following the announcement of the standstill in local government current expenditure in 1975, local authorities' sources of revenues and their freedom to exploit them were increasingly constrained. A regime of penalties was introduced in 1980 and strengthened in 1982; and "capping" was applied from 1985.

47.26 Figures produced by John Lloyd in his written evidence suggest that (at constant 1995/1996 prices) local authority expenditure in Wales on all local authority services remained very approximately level in the 1980s but rose by 13.5 per cent in the following 5 years (in terms of expenditure per 1,000 relevant

---

[1] See para 28.10 of this Summary.
[2] Department of the Environment: Central Government Controls over Local Authorities, Cmnd 7634, September 1979, HMSO.

population). Expenditure on personal social services in the 1980s on the same basis rose gradually by about 19 per cent. A very substantial increase then occurred, largely due to the progressive transfer of funds to local government to support its new responsibilities for the purchase of community care for the elderly and adults under the National Health Service and Community Care Act 1990.

47.27 Expenditure in Wales in the 1980s on all children in residential care or boarded out dipped in the mid-1980s but was about the same at the end of the decade as it had been at the beginning; and it rose by only 5 per cent in the following 5 years. On residential care alone, however, it dropped in real terms by about a third over the full 15 years, the steepest fall occurring in the early 1980s. Expenditure on boarding out/fostering in Wales, per 1,000 relevant population, almost quadrupled between 1979/1980 and 1994/1995, but the total cost of residential care for children still exceeded it in the latter year by over 25 per cent.

47.28 The figures for Clwyd in the same period, calculated on the same basis, showed a substantial decline in expenditure on all local authority services in the 1980s (18.4 per cent); and by 1994/1995 less than half of this "loss" had been recovered. The percentage of this expenditure directed to personal social services rose from 7 to 20 but the major part of this increase (10 per cent) occurred in the 5 years to 1994/1995, reflecting the progressive transfer of community care funding to local government. Expenditure on residential care for children and boarding out/fostering rose by almost 30 per cent in the 1980s, despite dropping in the middle of the decade, and the rate was the same as for the whole of Wales in 1989/1990; but it then fell by 7.5 per cent in the following 5 years.

47.29 In Gwynedd expenditure on all local authority services per 1,000 population was appreciably higher (886 : 719) in 1979/1980 than the average for the whole of Wales; but it fell to a similar figure in the mid-1980s and ended the decade about 3 per cent above the Welsh average. A major increase then occurred, raising it almost to its 1979/1980 level. Expenditure on personal social services increased slightly in the 1980s but doubled in the following 5 years, as a result of the community care changes. Expenditure on residential care for children and boarding out/fostering was lower in Gwynedd, however, per 1,000 population, than in Clwyd and the whole of Wales throughout the whole period of 15 years. At its low point in 1984/1985 it was only half the average for the whole of Wales. In 1989/1990 it was £24 against £40 for Clwyd and for the whole of Wales; and, in 1994/1995, the comparable figures were £29 for Gwynedd, £37 for Clwyd and £43 for the whole of Wales.

47.30 We do not place great emphasis on these unanalysed figures because their reliability has not been tested and conditions across Wales varied considerably, but the general pattern is of interest and the figures do confirm that there was reason for concern about under-spending on children's services in Gwynedd over a long period.

47.31 Major criticisms advanced to this Tribunal of the role played by the Welsh Office are that:

(a) it failed throughout the period under review to play a sufficiently interventionist part in the management and operation of county social services departments to ensure that appropriate standards were observed;

(b) as part of (a), it failed to plan the development of social services by setting clear aims and objectives and ensuring that they were understood;

(c) it failed to collect and disseminate adequate information about the services that were being provided on the one hand and the needs that ought to be met on the other;

(d) it failed to monitor adequately the performance of county social services departments in such a way as to promote the achievement of aims and the maintenance of standards;

(e) it failed to provide sufficient practical guidance to social services departments in a readily accessible form;

(f) it failed to provide adequate resources to enable those responsible in the Welsh Office itself and the county councils to discharge efficiently their respective wide and onerous duties in respect of children's services and, in particular, the protection of children in care.

47.32 Lady Scotland QC on behalf of the Welsh Office and Sir Louis Blom-Cooper QC representing Voices from Care[3] submitted from their different standpoints that detailed criticisms of this kind are "fundamentally unsound" because they misinterpret the statutory functions of central government in the child care field. According to this argument, the Children Act 1948, with its emphasis on "localism", foreshadowed the future of child care. It placed the duty on local authorities to provide a comprehensive service for the care of children deprived of the benefit of normal home life; a duty was imposed on local authorities to take into care those children who needed care; a statutory preference for boarding out was declared; and local authorities were required to promote the best interests of the child. The duty imposed by the Act of 1948 on central government, on the other hand, was to give general guidance only and it exercised control only indirectly, by financing local authorities and by its ability to influence policy and practice. This remained the approach decreed by Parliament as expressed in section 7(1) of the Local Authority Social Services Act 1970; and it was not until 1 April 1991 that the Secretary of State was given power to give directions to local authorities as to the exercise of their social services functions[4].

---

[3] Formerly NAYPIC Cymru, an organisation for young people in Wales who are in care or who have left care but remain under local authority supervision.
[4] By section 50 of the National Health Service and Community Care Act 1990.

47.33 We accept, in general terms, the account of the legislative history very briefly summarised in the preceding paragraph but, in our judgment, it does not provide a complete answer to the suggested criticisms of the Welsh Office. The Welsh Office forms part of central government and the latter cannot absolve itself of ultimate responsibility for the fate of children in care by referring to legislation that successive governments initiated from time to time, with or without expert advice. Central government must bear responsibility for the arrangements that it makes, by legislation or otherwise, for a vulnerable section of the population placed in care under statutory provisions. It may be said also that this residual responsibility is particularly grave in respect of children, who are unlikely to be fully aware of their basic rights, within a system under which the High Court has only a very limited power to intervene because decision making has been vested by statute in local authorities, without any right of appeal[5].

47.34 It follows from what we have said that, in our judgment, central government could not shed or deny its responsibility for the general framework of arrangements for the care of the former children in North Wales with whom we are concerned, for the overall strategic planning of those arrangements, for monitoring them effectively and for informing itself about what was happening in practice.

47.35 In considering the role played by the Welsh Office itself from 1974 onwards we have had very much in mind that it was new to child care responsibilities and that it did not have the ultimate authority to decide what financial resources were allocated to it. Moreover, the evidence indicates that, to a very large extent, it followed the lead of the Department of Health and Social Security (later the Department of Health) in child care matters. These considerations cannot inhibit us from identifying what went wrong but we do not attempt to pin responsibility upon individuals for specific acts and omissions because it would be inappropriate to do so on the evidence before us, bearing in mind the very frequent changes in personnel and duties that occurred within the Welsh Office.

47.36 Three other general considerations are of importance, namely:

(a) Almost the whole of the abuse with which we have been concerned occurred between 1974 and 1990, before the Children Act 1989 came into operation.

(b) Central government and local authorities did not have in mind that there was a significant possibility that children in residential care generally were being abused by staff until the second half of the 1980s.

(c) The evidence of the Inspectorates is that inspections are not a means by which either sexual or physical abuse is likely to be detected and the investigation of such abuse is not a purpose of inspections.

---

[5] See A v Liverpool City Council (1982) AC 363.

It was not until September 1986 that the Welsh Office became aware, through an anonymous letter to the Prime Minister, that there were allegations of mistreatment in social service establishments in Gwynedd; and it was in August 1990 that the Welsh Office was first told of alleged sexual abuse at Cartrefle in Clwyd, having heard before that of only an isolated case at Little Acton in March 1978.

47.37 An inescapable conclusion must be that the scale of reorganisation at the beginning of the 1970s was too great in too short a time span. Important consequences were that the Children's Department of the Home Office ceased to exist and that it was not replaced by any equivalent specialist section in the Welsh Office. At the same time local authority Children's Departments headed by a Children's Officer disappeared and the specialists within them were dispersed. The emphasis was on "generic" social work and the continuing need for specialists in the field of children's services was either overlooked or, at best, insufficiently heeded.

47.38 The effect of these changes was aggravated by the radical reorganisation of local government administrative areas and the many changes in responsibility for the residential care of children introduced by the Children and Young Persons Act 1969.

47.39 In this context we have been particularly dismayed by the absence of any clear guidance to either the old or the new county councils in relation to the conduct and management of the former approved schools. None of the relevant county councillors or officers in Clwyd (or Denbighshire before that) had any experience of approved schools and the need for clear guidance and active development work to support Clwyd ought clearly to have been foreseen.

47.40 A further compelling conclusion is that for over half the period under review children's services were given insufficient priority by central government and the Welsh Office: it would not be an exaggeration to say that they were neglected. There was an overall failure on the part of the Welsh Office to give an effective lead in the implementation of existing legislation and to inform itself adequately of what was happening on the ground, that is, in the individual county social services departments, in field social work practice and in the residential homes. An illustration of the lack of leadership is the way in which forward planning was allowed to wither and die, in particular, in relation to residential care, without any audit by the Welsh Office to establish whether the overall provision of residential care was both adequate and available. A result was that Gwynedd ended up with 4 homes that appeared to be indistinguishable in terms of their residents and purposes.

47.41 Another striking omission was the failure of central government to take any effective action before the Children Act 1989 to regulate private children's homes. Public concern led to the Private Members Bill that became the Children's Homes Act 1982 but the relevant provisions were not brought into force until they were re-enacted with some modifications in the Children Act 1989, in contrast to the provisions of the Registered Homes Act 1984, governing private homes mainly for adults and elderly people, which were nearly all brought into effect on 1 January 1985.

47.42 Even more striking was the failure of central government to take steps to ensure that adequate facilities were made available for the training of residential care workers. As long ago as 1967, the Williams report[6] recorded that the overwhelming majority of residential care staff were untrained (98 per cent in old people's homes and 82 per cent in children's homes). In 1991 SSIW reported[7] that only three quarters of heads of children's homes and just over half of second tier managers had relevant social work qualifications, whilst only a fifth of the other care staff were qualified (a broadly similar picture to that given for England by Sir William Utting[8]).

47.43 A number of explanations have been advanced for the limited monitoring activities of the Welsh Office during the period under review. One given by the former Chief SWSO/SSIW, **David Evans**, was that frequent inspection of individual homes was thought to be inconsistent with the policy of the Local Authority Social Services Act 1970. Another explanation was limited resources within the Inspectorates and other Welsh Office departments. "Disengagement" was referred to and yet another explanation was that emphasis was being placed on seeking alternatives to reception into care. These explanations do not, however, excuse the failure of the Welsh Office to acquaint itself adequately with the state of children's services in North Wales in order to ensure that children in care there were safe from harm in a wide sense.

47.44 To sum up, in our judgment there were serious failings by the Welsh Office in providing the leadership, guidance and monitoring to ensure effective implementation of the new legislation relating to children that came into force at the beginning of the 1970s and the development of good practice. At least some of those failings were attributable, in part, to wider government policies; and there were other aspects of personal social services policy in which the Welsh Office gave a positive lead. For the future, however, the lesson must be that special attention will need to be given to the welfare of children in care in Wales by the Welsh Office and the Welsh Assembly[9] in the wake of further government reorganisation; and the limited size and resources of the 22 new authorities will be important factors to be considered when a child care strategy is formulated.

The effectiveness of Welsh Office inspections (Chapter 48)

48.01 In this chapter we deal with the work of the 2 separate Inspectorates, namely:

(a) the Social Work Service for Wales (SWSW) employing SWSOs until it became the Social Services Inspectorate Wales (SSIW) staffed by SSIWs, in or about 1989;

(b) HMIs employed by the Welsh Office Education Department (WOED) until September 1992, when they became an independent body, OHMCI(Wales), under a Chief Inspector (HMCI).

---

[6] Caring for People - Staffing Residential Homes, 1967, National Council for Social Services.
[7] Accommodating Children, November 1991.
[8] Children in the Public Care, 1991, HMSO.
[9] References to the Welsh Office (in the future) and to the Welsh Assembly are made in this form for convenience.

48.02 The former Chief SWSO/SSIW said that the majority of the Service's time was spent in dealing with queries about individual cases brought to the attention of the Welsh Office, studying reports on the role of local authorities and, in consultation with administrative colleagues, dealing with day to day work and longer term policy questions. He stressed that SWSOs had no executive responsibilities for children's services, either for policy or for practice.

48.03 The functions of the Service appear to have become more sharply focused after it was re-designated as the SSIW. The latter's Inspection Guide in 1995 defined its objectives as:

"● To provide Ministers and the Welsh Office with information about social services in Wales.

● To provide advice to enable the Welsh Office to develop policies which will lead to improvements in the quality, effectiveness and efficiency of the services and to enable the Department to carry out its statutory and other responsibilities relating to social services.

● To evaluate the effectiveness of social services in Wales and how well they work with other services.

● To promote improvements in the quality, effectiveness and efficiency of services amongst the agencies who provide services."

48.04 Part XI of the Children Act 1989 codified and extended a number of provisions governing the Secretary of State's functions and responsibilities. Section 80 dealt with inspection of children's homes and extended the power to inspect the placements for children under general health and welfare legislation and in independent schools. However, local authorities were directed by the Secretary of State to establish their own inspection units by April 1991, exercising powers conferred upon him by section 50 of the National Health Service and Community Care Act 1970.

48.05 The following table indicates the allocation of manpower resources within the SWSW/SSIW during the last 9 years of the period under review (the asterisk insertion is ours).

Allocation of Resources (SSI Equivalents)

Year	Children's Services	Services for adults	General Training/ Finance/ Research	Inspection*	All
1987/88	2.4	3.6	1.3	0.7	8
1988/89	2.5	6.0	1.0	1.5	11
1989/90	2.2	3.6	1.6	3.6	11
1990/91	2.4	4.1	2.3	2.2	11
1991/92	4.0	3.2	2.5	1.3	11
1992/93	3.0	4.0	1.6	2.4	11
1993/94	3.0	4.0	1.5	2.5	11
1994/95	1.7	2.2	1.5	4.4	11(sic)
1995/96	1.9	1.7	1.7	4.4	10

Note: Staffing figures include Chief Inspector & Deputies

*all services

48.06 Prior to 1992 the statutory basis for inspections of educational establishments was contained in section 77 of the Education Act 1944, which required the Secretary of State to cause inspections to be made of schools, including special and independent schools, and certain other educational establishments. The inspections were to be at such intervals as appeared to the Minister to be appropriate and special inspections were to be made when the Minister considered them to be desirable.

48.07 HMIs did not have any right to enter community homes, whether or not they provided education, because they were not within the definition of schools for the purposes of the Education Act 1944. However, on occasions, HMIs did join SWSOs/SSIWs, at the latter's invitation, in inspecting community homes such as Bryn Estyn; and the reverse happened in relation to some inspections of schools.

48.08 Up to 1992, HMCI had no powers apart from the inspection of schools by HMIs. The Education (Schools) Act 1992 gave HMCI power to advise the Secretary of State on any matter connected with schools in Wales and to cause any school inspection by registered inspectors and their teams to be monitored by HMIs. Section 6 (1) required HMCI to keep the Secretary of State informed about various aspects of schools, including the adequacy of their financial resources. HMCI had the duty to ensure that every school in Wales within a wide range was inspected on a 5 year cycle.

48.09 The types of inspection have remained largely the same since the Act of 1992. The purposes of the inspections are said to be to assess quality and standards, to identify and disseminate good practice, to identify unsatisfactory/poor practice and bring it to the attention of those responsible, to improve overall quality and standards and to enable HMIs to advise the Secretary of State and others on the educational system.

48.10 At the beginning of the period under review the policy of SWSW was to make quite frequent inspections of community homes, particularly of former approved schools and assessment centres, but this changed by the end of the 1970s. According to the former Chief SWSO, the "culture" of inspections inherited from the Home Office appeared to be increasingly out of step with the relationship between SWSW and all other social services; and monitoring by inspection virtually ended in the early 1980s, except (again according to Evans) for community homes with education, secure accommodation and voluntary homes.

48.11 Professionals working in the children's services field were dissatisfied with this change of policy[10] and what eventually emerged was described as an "enhanced" inspection programme. This appears to have been started in or about 1987 and to have resulted in a doubling of the time devoted to inspection work (from 12 per cent to 25 per cent) by 1989/1990. The inspections from 1987 onwards, however, were of aspects of children's services in selected counties rather than of individual community homes; and from early 1987

---

[10] See the Barclay report, Social Workers: Their Role and Tasks published in May 1982 for the National Institute for Social Work.

SWSW/SSIW began to publish most of its reports. Before that there had been a division of opinion between those who regarded the reports as confidential and others who thought that there should be greater openness.

48.12 Inspections of particular relevance to our inquiry were of residential services in Gwynedd (1988/1990) and of children leaving care in Clwyd, Powys and South Glamorgan (1992/1993).

48.13 In relation to private establishments in Clwyd, the power to inspect was exercised almost wholly in relation to the Bryn Alyn Community and in conjunction with HMIs. Between 1975 and 1989 SWSOs visited the Community at approximately 3 year intervals but there were at least 3 other visits in between. There was one visit to Ystrad Hall School on 26 February 1975.

48.14 In Gwynedd the main focus of attention by SWSW/SSIW was upon Hengwrt Hall (later Aran Hall) School to which 9 visits were paid between January 1986 and February 1996.

48.15 In early 1994 SSIW was divided into separate inspection and policy groups. Lay people, including users and carers, were introduced into the process of inspection. A Deputy Chief Inspector was made responsible for inspection with 4 SSIWs as lead managers of inspection work; and thenceforth half of SSIWs time as a whole was to be dedicated to the inspection programme.

48.16 We have read a large number of the inspection reports prepared by SWSOs/SSIWs and, in general, we have been impressed by both the thoroughness and the high standard of these reports. However, it is clear that SWSW/SSIW did not at any stage of the period under review provide an effective monitoring or supervisory service for residential care establishments for children in North Wales; and it was unlikely to play any significant role in the detection or elimination of abuse.

48.17 We list 4 main reasons for this, namely:

(a) the establishment was insufficient to carry out regular inspections of the very many children's establishments requiring monitoring;

(b) the small core of officers with Home Office experience of inspections of these establishments dwindled rapidly;

(c) the need for monitoring and inspection was not recognised by the Welsh Office until the late 1980s and the programme of inspection formulated then was directed to wider children's service issues than the standard of care in individual homes;

(d) awareness by central government and by social services professionals of the possibility of serious child abuse occurring in residential care establishments for children was a late development in the period under review.

48.18 It was not until June 1990 that the Welsh Office issued a circular[11], to supplement advice and guidance in Working Together 1988[12], asking local authorities to review their policies relating to cases of actual or suspected abuse of a child within a residential school or other establishment accommodating children.

48.19 Even within the limited scope and purposes of the inspection system, there were noteworthy deficiencies, particularly before the inspectors' reports began to be published in 1987. Any follow up by SWSW to recommendations in the reports was, at best, sporadic. Circulation of the reports was very limited and there were no guidelines for informing councillors and relevant officers of their contents. Thus, the dissemination of information about good practice was very uncertain and wider re-consideration of procedures was unlikely.

48.20 Conversely, SWSW/SSIW was rarely, if ever, informed of the results of other investigations commissioned by county social services departments so that the (two- way) exchange of information between central and local government envisaged in the Seebohm report was seriously flawed[13].

48.21 In Clwyd, inspections by HMIs of local authority community homes and residential schools were confined to 3 at Bryn Estyn at approximately annual intervals between 1976 and 1978 and 3 visits to Ysgol Talfryn between 1988 and 1996. There were visits also, however, to the Bryn Alyn Community and 3 other private residential schools. Bryn Alyn was visited at least 17 times between 1975 and 1996 and there were 9 visits in all between 1974 and 1984 to Ystrad Hall School (4), Berwyn College for Girls (1), and Clwyd Hall School (4).

48.22 We have not been told of any visits by HMIs to local authority community homes in Gwynedd but they made numerous visits to Hengwrt Hall (later Aran Hall) School and to the Paul Hett establishments. There were not less than 15 visits to the former between 1976 and 1996 and we calculate that HMIs visited the latter on about 20 occasions between March 1974 and November 1991.

48.23 We have no criticism to make of the assiduity of HMI in visiting and reporting upon these establishments in Clwyd and Gwynedd. On the contrary, we have been impressed by the frequency with which the HMIs visited the private residential schools. The outcomes were less satisfactory but responsibility for this does not, in our view, rest with HMI. In the separate case of Bryn Estyn, a community home with education not within the definition of a school, Clwyd County Council was spurred to set up a working party to consider support by the Education Department, which made helpful recommendations, but few of them were implemented.

48.24 The 2 main defects in the administrative arrangements during the period under review were, firstly, the exclusion of community homes with education from the requirement of inspection by HMI and, secondly, the laxity of the

---

[11] Welsh Office Circular 37/90: Child Protection.

[12] DHSS and Welsh Office, July 1988, HMSO.

[13] Report of The Committee on Local Authority and Allied Personal Social Services, Cmnd 3703, 1968, para 647(c).

arrangements for enforcing school closures (de-registration) on failure to remedy defects.

48.25 We recognise fully the practical difficulties attendant upon the summary closure of a private residential school but the delays in meeting their needs were crucial for the individual pupils affected, occurring as they did at times in the pupils' lives when opportunities lost were unlikely to recur. For them, there was no time for prevarication or for vain hopes that adequate standards would be achieved eventually.

48.26 The opinion expressed by HMCI (Wales) is that considerable improvements have been effected since 1992 in the follow up to inspections of schools that are judged to be unsatisfactory. She attributes these improvements to the Education (Schools) Act 1992 and the Education Act 1993. Nevertheless, in our judgment, the time scale of remedial action is all important and steely resolve on the part of WOED is necessary if paramount consideration is to be given to the best interests of the child.

48.27 Major lessons to be learned are:

> (a) the need for tighter and more continuous liaison between the 2 Inspectorates, particularly in relation to both private and local authority residential schools and community homes with education;
>
> (b) the need to strengthen procedures for the follow up and discussion of inspectors' reports and recommendations and to monitor the implementation of those procedures; and
>
> (c) the importance of regular audits of field work practice to ensure compliance with statutory regulations.

In relation to (b), we regard it as very important that councillors and a wide range of relevant staff should be informed not only of the contents of the reports but also of the steps taken to implement recommendations.

Other relevant activities of the Welsh Office (Chapter 49)

49.01 The evidence submitted to the Tribunal by the Welsh Office extends to several thousand pages and it covers a wide range of the Welsh Office's activities over the period of a quarter of a century on which it is neither necessary nor appropriate for us to comment. Within the field of children's services a high proportion of the material deals with recent activities in connection with the Children Act 1989 and since then.

49.02 The Tribunal itself is concerned essentially with the question "what went wrong in the period between 1974 and 1990, when the major abuse occurred?" Although sub-paragraph (d) of the terms of reference of our inquiry requires us to consider whether the relevant "caring agencies" are discharging their functions appropriately now, we take this to refer primarily (but not exclusively) to the successor local authorities. A review of national developments in law, procedure and practice since the abuse in North Wales occurred would be wholly impracticable for a Tribunal constituted, as we have been, with the major purpose of establishing disputed facts: neither our composition nor our method of investigation would be appropriate for a comprehensive audit of current practice and procedure and proposals for change that have been made since the Tribunal was appointed.

49.03 Before this inquiry was decided upon, Adrianne Jones had been appointed by the Secretary of State for Wales to examine child care and other procedures related to the care and protection of children and the employment and management of staff in the SSDs of Clwyd and Gwynedd and to assess the proposals for procedures and practice in the 6 successor authorities. She submitted the report of her examination team in May 1996 and we do not propose to traverse the same ground.

49.04 In their evidence to the Tribunal, the 2 senior Welsh Office witnesses highlighted 9 areas of its activities, apart from regulation, registration and inspection, and we deal with these in some detail in Chapter 49 of our report. They were recruitment and staff management; control and discipline; training; visiting; complaints procedures; fostering; the Welsh Office responses to Alison Taylor; other relevant information communicated to the Welsh Office; and the responses to the Adrianne Jones report. For the purposes of this Summary, however, it is only necessary to refer to a few of these in brief outline because the impact of most of them upon the events in North Wales with which we are concerned was only marginal.

49.05 The guidance given by the Welsh Office to local authorities on the subject of control and discipline prior to the coming into force of the Children Act 1989 was contained in Welsh Office Circulars issued in 1972, 1988 and 1990. The 1972 Circular[14] said that for all practical purposes the use of corporal punishment would be confined to measures and conditions approved in advance for each home by the local authority so that the latter would be publicly accountable both for the measures approved and for the conditions of their use. It was hoped that local authorities would authorise the use of corporal punishment sparingly and as a last resort and would consider at each annual review, in the light of experience, whether it was still needed.

49.06 When corporal punishment was proscribed in community homes and voluntary children's homes by the Children's Homes (Control and Discipline) Regulations 1990, Welsh Office Circular 5/90 advised that corporal punishment (not defined in the regulations) included "any intentional application of force as punishment, including slapping, throwing missiles and rough handling". The guidance continued "It does not prevent a person taking necessary physical action, where any other course of action would be likely to fail, to avert an immediate danger or personal injury to the child or another person or to avoid immediate danger to property".

49.07 Finally, on this subject, further guidance on permissible forms of control in children's residential care was given in Welsh Office Circular 38/93 in 11 sections, covering such matters as the restriction of liberty, physical restraint and other methods of care and control falling short of such action. On physical

---

[14] Welsh Office Circular 64/72.

restraint, it was said that the minimum force necessary to prevent injury or damage should be applied and that every effort should be made to secure the presence of other staff before applying it because they could act as assistants or witnesses.

49.08 In or about 1991, the Parliamentary Under Secretary for Wales, Nicholas Bennett MP, instructed the SSIW to carry out a review of residential care in Wales, in the form of an audit of the quality of care being provided in Welsh children's homes. The report of the review, entitled "Accommodating Children" was published by the Welsh Office in November 1991. The authors of the report said that the review had not revealed examples of the causes of concern (abuse) that had given rise to it. Their conclusion was that there was no evidence to suggest that sexual or systematic physical or emotional abuse occurred frequently in children's homes in Wales. In their view, the risk of such abuse would be minimised by careful vetting of appointments, including the usual checks, and by encouraging children and staff to talk to other staff, to line managers and other professionals inside and outside the home.

49.09 The report, did, however, make many critical findings and helpful recommendations. According to John Lloyd, the Welsh Office accepted these recommendations and also the recommendations made in 1992 by the Warner Committee in relation to the selection, development and management of children's homes[15]. Welsh Office Circular 34/93 set out a 3 year action plan for implementation of the SSIW's recommendations: a key element was the need for local authorities to establish an integrated plan for children's services, including the defined role of each children's home. A further circular, 11/94, required this plan to be produced by 31 March 1995.

49.10 We have not heard any evidence about implementation of the provisions enabling independent visitors to children in care to be appointed. The only comment made in Accommodating Children about the actual practice of appointing such visitors in Wales was that "one authority had plans for an enhanced role for the independent visitor". Our firm impression is that little use was made of them. It is desirable, in our view, that the practice under the latest statutory provisions[16] should be assessed and that consideration should be given to revising the pre-conditions for appointing independent visitors.

49.11 The account given by David Evans, the former Chief SWSO/SSIW, of Alison Taylor's representations to central government and other relevant persons and bodies between 1986 and 1996 extends to 44 pages. The Welsh Office first became aware of allegations of mistreatment of children in social services establishments in Gwynedd in September 1986 when an article appeared in the *Daily Mail*[17] referring to a police investigation into such allegations and an anonymous letter from "concerned parents and residents in Gwynedd" addressed to the Prime Minister was forwarded to the Welsh Office. The first communication from Alison Taylor, also addressed to the Prime Minister and forwarded to the Welsh Office, was dated 2 December 1986.

---

[15] Choosing with Care, 1992, HMSO.
[16] Schedule 2, para 17 to the Children Act 1989 and the Definition of Independent Visitors (Children) Regulations 1991.
[17] On 11 September 1986.

49.12 Our comment on the protracted correspondence that followed is that it underlines the need for an independent agency to investigate complaints of the kind made by Taylor. However widely she spread her net, it was left to the Welsh Office to reply and the Welsh Office's response was invariably to the same effect, even though the mode of expressing it changed. It was unwilling to act in respect of "old" complaints that had been investigated and fresh complaints had to be addressed to Gwynedd County Council, despite the allegedly unsatisfactory manner in which the latter had dealt with the "old" complaints.

49.13 It will no doubt be said that experience shows that a high percentage of persistent complainants who address their allegations to a range of government departments are eccentrics or persons with worn out axes to grind, but not all are so and severe recriminations are inevitable when it emerges in the end that the persistent complaints were well founded.

49.14 Our criticism of the Welsh Office's responses in the correspondence is not simply directed to the "stonewalling" that we have cited. We do not accept that it was right for the Welsh Office to accept as readily as it did, without any independent investigation of the background or circumstances, that Alison Taylor was a troublemaker. An enquiry of the police might have been fruitful, despite the views of the senior police officer conducting the investigation. It is perturbing also that Gwynedd alleged that it had conducted its own inquiry into the allegations but we have not received evidence of any process that merits that description. It is also very unsatisfactory also that it was wrongly suggested to Taylor that the 1988 inspection by SWSOs covered the allegations that she had made because it is clear beyond argument that it did not do so.

49.15 This last point was taken up in 1993 by solicitors on Taylor's behalf and the answer drafted for the Secretary of State was to the effect that the inspectors had not held an investigation but had had discussions with the youngsters in private in which the latter had been given an opportunity to raise and discuss any issue in relation to the regimes and practices of the homes: no reference to abuse had emerged from those talks and, if it had, it would have been taken up "in the most appropriate manner with the relevant agency".

49.16 It appears from the evidence presented by the Welsh Office that they received only 2 relevant "complaints" in the first 12 years of the period under review. The first related to the employment in 1976 at Tŷ'r Felin of a gardener/handyman with a previous conviction for indecent exposure, who had received a reference, from a charitable foundation that had employed him, which made no reference to the conviction. The second related to the conviction of Leslie Wilson referred to in paragraph 12.07 of this Summary.

49.17 The first of these matters came to light when an SWSO visited Tŷ'r Felin and the Deputy Director of Social Services for Clwyd visited the Welsh Office in order to disclose the second matter and to give an account of the difficulties that had arisen at Little Acton Assessment Centre. The response of the Welsh Office in each case was appropriate.

49.18 As we have said earlier, it was not until August 1990 that the Welsh Office first heard of more widespread sexual abuse at Cartrefle; and its response then was much less satisfactory. The account by David Evans of the correspondence between SSIW and Clwyd (mainly with the Director of Social Services) on this subject extends to 66 paragraphs and it makes dispiriting reading.

49.19 The Director of Social Services, with the agreement of Clwyd County Council, invited SSIW to carry out a full inspection of Cartrefle. In response, the Chief Inspector (incorrectly, in our view) pressed for "an internal management and ACPC review as under Part 9 of Working Together 1988". The correspondence continued for 5 years. SSIW refused to conduct an inspection and the Chief Inspector continued to urge a Part 9 review. The Director pointed out that there were 4 other matters that merited consideration in a review of child care quality standards in Clwyd but the Chief Inspector recommended that the review should be confined to incidents at Cartrefle.

49.20 The result was an initial review by 3 independent professionals, whose reports were presented in June 1991 and were then considered by an independent panel of 5 senior professionals, whose report was presented in February 1992, 20 months after Norris' arrest. By that time, the major police investigation had been underway for several months and the chairman of the panel had suggested that, in view of recent events, it might be better to "ditch the report on Cartrefle".

49.21 In the event, the report could not be published for reasons that we have explained earlier in paragraphs 32.14 and 32.15 of this Summary. The Chief Inspector did, however, receive a copy of the panel's report for his personal attention only in September 1992, 3 days before the Parliamentary Secretary announced that a public inquiry into allegations of abuse in North Wales would take place when the North Wales Police had completed their inquiries.

49.22 On 6 January 1995 the Chief Inspector and the SSIW responsible for children and family matters met the Director of Social Services for Clwyd and members of the management team to discuss the issues raised by the panel's report. Matters needing further attention were then spelt out in a confirmatory letter from the Chief Inspector to the Director dated 26 January 1995.

49.23 We describe the procedure that was followed in the Cartrefle "review", on the Chief Inspector's insistence, as incorrect because it was an attempt to bring it within the procedure recommended in Part 9 of the 1988 edition of Working Together for very different circumstances. The latter procedure was designed to deal with the case of an individual child who had been abused in a domestic setting and this remains true, even though the 1991 edition did refer for the first time to a child accommodated by a local authority in a residential setting or with foster parents. The need for urgent action is stressed and the procedure is not appropriate for the investigation of wide ranging abuse in a children's home. As it developed, the procedure adopted by Clwyd was cumbersome, long drawn out and repetitive; and, although the analysis and recommendations, particularly those of John Banham, were excellent, the report was of limited benefit because it could not be published.

49.24 These events and the similar experience in relation to publication of the Jillings report[18] underline the need for clear guidelines to government departments and local authorities on the procedure to be followed when inquiries are deemed to be necessary into matters of public concern of this kind.

49.25 Adrianne Jones made 41 recommendations in all for improvements in 11 areas of procedure and practice. Her terms of reference related to North Wales but the decision of the Welsh Office was to implement her recommendations throughout Wales. For this purpose a central development fund of £500,000 was allocated for the years 1996 to 1998, of which £440,000 was made available to local authorities by means of a grant scheme. Plans were invited for expenditure of up to £20,000 by each authority on one or more of 6 "themes".

49.26 Those themes are:

(1) Reviews of inherited policies and procedures: defining and clarifying roles and responsibilities; and the development of new procedures, practice guidance and child care manuals.

(2) The implementation of the Warner recommendations[19].

(3) Department of Health "Looking after Children" materials.

(4) Planning, in particular, comprehensive placement strategies.

(5) Children's Rights.

(6) Complaints procedures.

49.27 An internal Welsh Office group, the Adrianne Jones Report Implementation Group, has been formed to spur, co-ordinate and monitor progress. According to John Lloyd, a key feature of the process is continuing dialogue with each local authority about its implementation of each recommendation.

49.28 The material summarised in this chapter of the Tribunal's report confirms that, prior to the lead up to the Children Act 1989, the Welsh Office did not take any initiative of its own that was relevant to the possible occurrence generally of child abuse in either children's residential homes or foster homes.

49.29 It can fairly be said that, by the end of 1986, most of the major abuse that we have investigated had already occurred so that action by the Welsh Office then could not have prevented it. It is a matter for concern, however, that the response of the Welsh Office to Alison Taylor was so negative for at least 5 years and that the response generally to information available by the end of 1986 was lethargic, despite the gravity of the risk. Thus, the possibility of abuse in children's homes was not discussed in the Welsh Office's guidance about control and discipline in 1990 and 1993; action to establish complaints procedures was belated; and decisive action is still awaited in relation to the provision of residential child care training.

---

[18] See paras 32.16 to 32.29 of this Summary.

[19] Choosing with Care: The report of the Committee of Inquiry into the Selection, Development and Management of Staff in Children's Homes, 1992, HMSO.

49.30 Despite the increased attention given to children's services with the enactment of the Children Act 1989 and more recently in response to the Adrianne Jones report, further positive and firm leadership will be required from the Welsh Office and the Welsh Assembly if the safety of children in care in Wales is to be safeguarded adequately and the quality of care provided is to be improved.

THE POLICE INVESTIGATIONS IN CLWYD AND GWYNEDD (Chapters 50 to 52)

The general history of the police investigations and the nature of the criticisms (Chapter 50)

50.01 The police force for the 5 predecessor counties of North Wales from 1 October 1967 was Gwynedd Police, which was re-named as the North Wales Police from 1 April 1974.

50.02 The first Chief Constable of the North Wales Police was **Sir Philip Myers** OBE, QPM, DL, who retired in 1982 and then became one of HM Inspectors of Constabulary. Sir Philip's successor was **David Owen** CBE, QPM, who had been Chief Constable of Dorset from 1980 and who remained head of the North Wales Police until his retirement on 31 March 1994. He served as President of the Association of Chief Police Officers in 1990/1991. Finally, Owen's successor, **Michael Argent**, remains in post and has a similar background of wide police experience to his predecessors. His last post before his North Wales appointment was that of Deputy Chief Constable of Suffolk from 1992.

50.03 At the time of Owen's retirement, there were 1,384 officers in the North Wales Police, of whom 120 were then in the CID.

50.04 Between 1974 and 1980 there were 10 relevant investigations by the police, all in Clwyd, and 6 persons were convicted. The first 5 convicted were **Anthony David Taylor** (Bryn Alyn, 1976); **Leslie Wilson** (Little Acton, 1977); **Bryan Davies** (Ystrad Hall, 1978); **Gary Cooke** and **(Arthur) Graham Stevens** (1980). The sixth was **Albert Frederick Tom Dyson**, then aged 40 years, who was convicted in 1980 of 3 offences of indecency against a boy resident of Bryn Estyn, for which he was sentenced to 18 months' imprisonment. Dyson, who had befriended the boy's family, was the owner at the time of a club in Rhyl; and he admitted to the Tribunal that the boy was in care and placed at Bryn Estyn when the offences were committed.

50.05 The other persons investigated by the police in this period but not prosecuted were the gardener/driver at Upper Downing (1976); Carl Evans (Little Acton, 1977); Paul Bicker Wilson (Bryn Estyn, 1977) and Huw Meurig Jones (1980).

50.06 We have not received any general criticism of these investigations by the police but it has been submitted that there was a paedophile ring in existence and that the investigations of Cooke, Stephens and Dyson in 1980 should have gone further than they did. We deal with this subject in Chapter 52 of the report.

50.07 It has not been suggested that these 10 investigations were sufficient to trigger a wider investigation by the police of possible abuse of children in care in the county in the absence of other complaints brought to their attention. The allegations ought, however, to have given rise at least to anxiety in the SSD and a corresponding determination to be vigilant. Unhappily, the climate of suppression was such that there was no general awareness of the potential problem and even co-operation with the police in cases such as that of Wilson seems to have been faint-hearted.

50.08 The pattern of investigations in Clwyd between 1981 and 1989 was similar. There were 11 investigations by the police and 5 persons were convicted of sexual offences against relevant children. They were **Iain Muir** (Bryn Alyn, 1986); **Jacqueline Elizabeth Thomas** (Chevet Hey, 1986); **David John Gillison** (1987, a social worker who was not then employed in residential care); **William Gerry** (1987, a former resident of Bryn Estyn); and **Gary Cooke** (1987, for further offences). Only the first 2 of these were employed in children's residential establishments at the time when their offences were committed and Thomas' conviction was for an offence against a 15 years old boy who was not in care at the time.

50.09 One other relevant person, **Huw Meurig Jones**, was charged in 1981 with alleged sexual offences against a boy in care in Clwyd. Meurig Jones was then an unqualified social worker for Clwyd County Council but had not been employed in residential care (as far as we are aware) since March 1976. He resigned on 28 July 1981 and the charges against him were not proceeded with.

50.10 The other 5 persons investigated in this period were all involved in residential child care work. They were Frederick Rutter (Bryn Estyn, 1983); Paul Bicker Wilson (Chevet Hey, 1985); Kenneth White junior (Bryn Alyn, 1988); Y (Ysgol Talfryn, 1989); and David Evans (Park House, 1989). Only the latter, however, was alleged to have committed sexual abuse (by touching 2 girls) and the CPS advised that there was insufficient evidence to justify a prosecution. The other 4 persons were all alleged to have committed physical assaults against boys in care but none was prosecuted.

50.11 Again, the only criticism of the police investigations in this period is that there should have been a wider inquiry into the possible existence of a paedophile ring, to which we revert later, but it will be noted that Gary Cooke was again convicted (receiving 7 years' imprisonment in 1987, following 5 years' imprisonment in 1980).

50.12 The facts of the linked cases of Thomas, Gillison and Gerry were very perturbing but the response of the County Council to the trial judge's call for an internal limited investigation was both perfunctory and dilatory[1].

50.13 The first relevant police investigation in Gwynedd was into the alleged incident at Tŷ'r Felin on 24 May 1984, referred to in paragraph 33.29 of this Summary, in which a boy resident at Tŷ Newydd who attended classes at Tŷ'r Felin alleged that he had been assaulted by John Roberts. According to the former head of the North Wales CID, the incident was not reported to the police until September 1984. There was then "an investigation by experienced officers, who, after consideration, decided that there should be no prosecution".

[1] See para 14.23 of this Summary.

50.14 It was in February 1986 that the first major investigation into Alison Taylor's complaints began, following a meeting between the head of the CID (Det Ch Supt Gwynne Owen), Councillor Marshall and Alison Taylor. The first phase of this investigation ended in October 1986, when the initial decision not to prosecute anyone was taken. It was then re-opened because of fresh allegations against Dodd by a former girl resident at Tŷ'r Felin; and the second phase was not completed until April 1988, shortly before Gwynne Owen retired in July 1988. No prosecution followed.

50.15 This Gwynedd investigation has been heavily criticised and we discuss it further in the next chapter. The decision to suspend Alison Taylor was made shortly after the end of the first phase. In the meantime the Chief Executive of Gwynedd had made an ill-considered statement to the press to the effect that the police report had "completely vindicated" the County Council's decision not to suspend any officer whilst the investigation took place.

50.16 Investigations by the police in Clwyd and Gwynedd were much wider ranging in the remaining 6 years or so before reorganisation. They began with separate investigations into **Frederick Rutter** (April 1990) and **Stephen Norris** (June 1990) and the major investigation covering the whole of Clwyd, at the request of the County Council, began about a year later. This was extended to the whole of Gwynedd towards the end of 1991, again at the request of the County Council. The intense part of that investigation was completed in 1993 but further cases have continued to emerge with the result that there were at least 2 (Leake and Groome) awaiting trial when the Tribunal's report was signed.

50.17 In this last part of the period under review, that is, between 1990 and 1996, 10 persons were prosecuted for offences against children in care, of whom 8 were convicted. Those convicted were **Stephen Norris** (1990, Cartrefle and 1993, Bryn Estyn); **Frederick Rutter** (1991, as foster parent in Clwyd and Hostel Warden); **Malcolm Ian Scrugham** (1993, Clwyd foster parent in Gwynedd); **Norman and Ian Roberts** (1993, Gwynedd foster parent and son); **Peter Norman Howarth** (1994, Bryn Estyn); **Paul Bicker Wilson** (1994, Bryn Estyn); and **John Ernest Allen** (1995, Bryn Alyn). Evelyn Roberts, the wife of Norman Roberts and mother of Ian, was acquitted, as was David Gwyn Birch (of Bryn Estyn and Chevet Hey).

50.18 We do not have a comprehensive list of other investigations by the police during this last period but it is clear that there was at least one complaint of physical abuse at Gatewen Hall (Bryn Alyn Community) in 1990. They were involved also on many occasions towards the end of that year in resolving or investigating incidents arising at or stemming from Ysgol Hengwrt (a Paul Hett establishment).

50.19 Since the hearings by the Tribunal began there have been further investigations and prosecutions, some originating with communications to the Tribunal. In order to avoid prejudicing continuing investigations, we adopted the general policy that we would not hear evidence in support of complaints that were still under investigation by the police at the time when the evidence would otherwise have been heard by us. To that extent, our investigation has been necessarily incomplete but we have been kept informed of the progress and outcome of the police investigations.

50.20 The best information that we have to date is that allegations by 9 complainants in statements to the Tribunal have been under investigation and that some other complaints not contained in Tribunal statements have been investigated. Altogether over a dozen former members of staff of residential homes have been named in the allegations, including one who died in the course of the investigations.

50.21 We refer in our report to 9 relevant prosecutions that have occurred since our hearings began. They are as follows:

> (1) 17 March 1997, **Roger Platres Saint** (Clwyd foster parent), 6½ years' imprisonment[2].
>
> (2) 14 March 1997, **Robert Martin Williams** (Gwynfa), 6 years' imprisonment[3].
>
> (3) 4 July 1997, **Noel Ryan** (Clwyd Hall), 12 years' imprisonment[4].
>
> (4) 9 September 1998, **Mr B** (Clwyd foster parent), 3 years' imprisonment.
>
> (5) 23 June 1999, Richard Dafydd Vevar (Bryn Alyn Community), acquitted.
>
> (6) 4 August 1999, **Roger Owen Griffiths** (Gatewen Hall proprietor before Bryn Alyn Community), 8 years' imprisonment.
> **Anthea Beatrice Roberts** (his former wife), 2 years' imprisonment.
>
> (7) 22 November 1999, **Derek Brushett** (SSIW, formerly Headmaster, Bryn-y-Don Community Home, Dinas Powis, South Glamorgan), 14 years' imprisonment.
>
> (8) 24 November 1999, **Richard Ernest Leake** (Bersham Hall and Ystrad Hall School).
>
> (9) 2000, **Richard Francis Groome** (Tanllwyfan and Clwyd Hall School), awaits trial early in 2000.

50.22 **Roger Griffiths** and his former wife **Anthea Roberts** were the proprietors of 'Gatewen Hall School from 1977 to 1982 before selling the premises to the Bryn Alyn Community. The Tribunal did not receive evidence from any complainant in respect of this period but Roger Griffiths was convicted in the Crown Court at Chester on 3 and 4 August 1999 of offences of buggery (1), attempted buggery (1), indecent assault (1) and cruelty (4), all committed between 1977 and 1982 at the school. His former wife was convicted of 2 indecent assaults on boy residents aged under 16 years.

---

2 Ibid, paras 25.01 to 25.28.
3 Ibid, para 20.05.
4 Ibid, paras 23.07 to 23.11.
5 Ibid, paras 27.02 to 27.05.

50.23 **Derek Brushett** was not the subject of investigation by the North Wales Police. As an SSIW, he took part in a few inspections in North Wales but there was no allegation of misconduct by him in that capacity, as far as we are aware. He was convicted at the Crown Court at Cardiff on 22 November 1999, after the Tribunal's report had been signed, of 27 offences (20 sexual) committed against boys aged 11 to 16 years whilst he was headmaster in the 1970s, from May 1974 onwards, of Bryn-y-Don Community Home.

50.24 **Richard Ernest Leake**[6] was convicted in the Crown Court at Chester on 24 November 1999 of 14 offences of indecent assault committed between 1972 and 1978 on boy residents at Bersham Hall and Ystrad Hall School. Sentencing was adjourned to 17 December 1999.

50.25 **Richard Francis Groome**[7] has been committed for trial early in 2000 on charges alleging sexual offences involving one former boy resident at Tanllwyfan, 4 at Clwyd Hall School and others at establishments in Shropshire between 1981 and 1989.

50.26 Comparatively few of the complainants alleged that they made a complaint to the police of physical or sexual abuse whilst they were still in care. Of those who said that they did, most claimed to have done so when apprehended by the police as absconders, saying that they told a police officer that the particular abuse had been the reason for their absconsion.

50.27 It is impossible for us to reach any confident conclusion about individual allegations of this kind in the absence of any supporting documentary evidence. It is likely, however, that there were a few complaints by children in care direct to the police.

50.28 According to Counsel for the North Wales Police, about 50 per cent (134) of the former residents of children's homes and foster children whose evidence is before us absconded at one time or another; and about 57 of them said that they came into contact with the police (not necessarily the North Wales Police) in the course of, or in connection with, absconding. We heard oral evidence from 49 of the 57 but only about 10 in all (including 3 whose evidence was read) criticised the way in which they were dealt with as absconders.

50.29 Only one of these critics alleged that he complained to the police of being sexually abused in care. As we explain in the report, however, contemporary records at Corwen Police Station, to which he was taken, cast some doubt on the accuracy of his recollection of the circumstances and we cannot be confident that he made the complaint.

50.30 Three others alleged that they told the police of being assaulted physically but were disbelieved; and others complained that they were not asked for their reasons for absconding, although they did not themselves volunteer the information. They were questioned, however, about any offences that they might have committed whilst "on the run" and one witness described being told off for absconding.

---

[6] Ibid, paras 22.07, 22.08.
[7] Ibid, paras 18.06 to 18.08 and 23.12.

50.31 This evidence does not provide a firm basis for severe strictures on the North Wales Police about their response to individual complaints, bearing in mind the general lack of awareness of the risk of abuse in care for a substantial part of the period under review. The limited complaints about this that we have heard do, however, underline the importance of both vigilance and sensitivity on the part of police officers when dealing with complaints by children in care, whether or not they are absconders and whether or not they have committed criminal offences or otherwise appear to be troublesome.

50.32 We deal in this chapter with one other criticism of the North Wales Police that was widely discussed in the press before our hearings began but about which very few questions were actually put to witnesses in the course of the inquiry. This was the suggestion that freemasonry had had an impact on the police investigations and had led to a "cover up" in favour of some individuals.

50.33 The reason why freemasonry soon became a non-issue in the inquiry is that there was no evidence whatsoever that it had had any impact on any of the investigations with which we have been concerned.

50.34 We have already dealt in paragraph 9.05 of this Summary with lack of any masonic influence on the conduct of the investigation and decision making in the case of Gordon Anglesea; but we repeat here that no relevant officer of the North Wales Police, other than Anglesea himself, was a freemason. Moreover, the Chief Constable issued a directive in September 1984 discouraging officers of the North Wales Police from becoming or continuing to be Masons on the ground that "openness must be seen by all"; and he refused to modify it when asked to do so by a leading Mason, Lord Kenyon, who was also a member of the North Wales Police Authority.

50.35 Anglesea did not take part in any of the relevant investigations (except as a person under scrutiny himself). The only other person of significance to this inquiry who is known to have been a Mason is John Ilton, who was for a time a member of the same lodge at Wrexham as Anglesea. His evidence to the Tribunal was that he knew Anglesea by sight and vaguely remembers him as a member of the same lodge, but that he had never approached Anglesea.

The three main police investigations (Chapter 51)

51.01 As we have said, the 3 main police investigations during the period under review were in Gwynedd from 1986 to 1988, at Cartrefle in 1990 and finally in both Clwyd and Gwynedd from 1991 onwards. Only the first of these attracted substantial criticism in the end but the criticisms led to anxieties about the last investigation, which persisted until the Tribunal's hearings.

51.02 Det Ch Supt Gwynne Owen was appointed to conduct the investigation in Gwynedd in 1986 after he had submitted a preliminary report on Alison Taylor's allegations, following his meeting with her and Councillor Marshall in February 1986. In view of the sensitivity of the matter, Owen decided to carry out the investigation himself with the assistance of only one woman detective constable. He decided also not to inform responsible officers of Gwynedd County Council that he was to conduct an investigation. It follows that Nefyn Dodd was not suspended from duty during the investigation: Owen said in his evidence to the Tribunal that he did not believe that his investigation would be hampered by the continued presence of Dodd at Tŷ'r Felin because none of the complainants was still resident there at the time.

51.03 We give an account in Chapter 51 of the investigation that Owen carried out between May and September 1986. According to Owen, 13 "cases" in all were considered but only about half of them could be investigated further. None of the cases was clear cut and Owen's own notes of the investigation were defective.

51.04 The report by Owen in September 1986 extended to 97 pages. In the course of this report he expressed hostile and critical opinions about most of the complainants and he was strongly critical also of informants such as Alison Taylor and Beryl Condra (of Queens Park), attributing demeaning motives to them. The general tenor of his comments was that the complainants had been manipulated by Taylor and that their complaints were not spontaneous.

51.05 Owen defended the opinions that he expressed in his report by saying that the Director of Public Prosecution's guidelines encouraged investigating officers to comment upon the reliability of particular witnesses, to refer to their previous convictions and to indicate, when evidence conflicted, which version was thought to be nearest the truth.

51.06 We do not dispute Owen's right to make observations on witnesses and issues in his report; and, in any event, we are not persuaded that his comments had any significant impact on the outcome of the investigation, bearing in mind the state of the evidence at that time. Nevertheless, we regard it as very regrettable that he expressed himself as he did. To an independent observer the report appears to have been very one-sided and gives the impression that he approached the investigation with a closed mind.

51.07 Another criticism of the investigation must be that there was no coherent liaison between Owen and the Gwynedd SSD. Co-operation from some employees of the Department was plainly necessary in the search for, and interviewing of, complainants and witnesses, many of whom were still in care; and examination of relevant records in an ordered way was equally necessary. In the event, police officers did talk to quite a wide range of employees and had (unexplained) access to some records but we can see no reason why the Chief Executive should not have been consulted at the outset and appropriate arrangements made for systematic scrutiny of the relevant documents, including personal files and logs.

51.08 The conclusion of the Senior Crown Prosecutor, based at Colwyn Bay, was that prosecution would not be justified in 12 of the 13 cases but that attempts should be made to trace 2 named potential supporting witnesses in the other case. They were subsequently found and made statements in February 1987 but the view of the Senior Crown Prosecutor then was that the evidence remained insufficient to justify prosecution.

51.09   There was a further investigation between January and October 1987 of fresh allegations by a woman who had been a resident at Tŷ'r Felin. She alleged assaults by Dodd on 5 other former residents that she had witnessed and she named 4 former members of the staff as potential supporting witnesses. A sixth complainant emerged during the investigation.

51.10   There were numerous difficulties about the statements provided by the complainants and potential witnesses in the course of this further investigation, as we explain in our report. One of them was that all the complainants had been discharged from care and 4 of them were living in England (2 as far away as Yorkshire). These 4 complainants were not interviewed by Owen or his assistant in the investigation: instead, they were interviewed by police officers local to their homes on the basis of instructions that Owen transmitted to them.

51.11   In his second report, dated 13 October 1987, Owen said that his view of Taylor remained unchanged and that there was every likelihood that she would manipulate others in the future; but he did not refer to any established link between her and the woman who had made the fresh allegations or any of the 6 new complainants.

51.12   In his response the Senior Crown Prosecutor again suggested that 2 other potential witnesses should be traced. Only one of them could be found and he denied seeing any assault with the result that the Senior Crown Prosecutor confirmed on 5 April 1988 that there was insufficient evidence to justify a prosecution of Dodd.

51.13   In his evidence to the Tribunal, Owen said that he saw the Director of Social Services, Lucille Hughes, on 3 occasions in connection with these investigations. At their first meeting, on 5 June 1986, he outlined the "thrust" of the allegations against Dodd. At the second, on 23 October 1986, he briefed Hughes about the outcome of the first investigation; and, at the third, on 22 May 1987, he told her of the further investigation, of which she was already aware.

51.14   There is conflict between Owen and Hughes about what was said at the second of these meetings. Owen told the Tribunal that he stressed to Hughes the difficulties of the investigation and that the decision not to prosecute Dodd did not mean that he was entirely innocent of the allegations but reflected the lack of evidence to support a successful prosecution. His written statement continued "I did in fact inform Miss Hughes of my belief that Mr Dodd had physically assaulted some of the children and I left her in no doubt of my opinion of Dodd, who I saw as a vain, immature individual who, in my view, was unsuited to his position". Owen's oral evidence was that he repeated this view at his third meeting with Hughes but he conceded in cross-examination that he could not be certain that he did tell her on either occasion that Dodd was unsuitable for his job.

51.15   Lucille Hughes told us that she had no recollection of Owen expressing the opinion that Dodd was unsuitable. What she had carried away from the second meeting was that Dodd had "overstepped the mark on occasion in terms of his behaviour towards children". She regarded it as serious enough for her to take action and she spoke to Dodd subsequently, reminding him of the Council's policy in relation to corporal punishment. She received many reassurances from him about the future but she warned him that he would be likely to lose his position if there was a recurrence.

51.16 We are satisfied that Owen did make some adverse comment about Dodd to Lucille Hughes at their second meeting, despite the absence of any such comment in his September 1986 report, but we are equally clear that he did not go as far as to suggest that Dodd was unfit for his job. Such a comment would have been remarkably inconsistent with the tone of that report.

51.17 Sir Ronald Hadfield, assessor to the Tribunal in respect of police matters, was critical of many aspects of the Gwynedd investigation from 1986 to 1988; and his views are set out in Appendix 11 to the Tribunal's report. In our judgment, all these criticisms are fully justified. Whether or not any criminal charge would have been brought if the defects referred to had not occurred is a matter of speculation; but a serious consequence of the way in which the investigation was conducted was that seeds of distrust of the North Wales Police were sown.

51.18 The investigation into events at Cartrefle began on 17 June 1990 and was completed, with the conviction of Stephen Norris, in less than 4 months. There was close co-operation with the SSD, through the latter's Area Office, and there were 4 social workers in the team provided by the SSD. The only major criticism of the investigation put to the Tribunal has been that it ought to have been widened to include Bryn Estyn because Norris had been employed there before moving to Cartrefle. The criticism is, however, somewhat academic because the main North Wales wide investigation began within about 10 months of Norris' conviction for his Cartrefle offences and he was convicted again in November 1993 in respect of his Bryn Estyn offences.

51.19 It is relevant to this criticism that the investigating officer, Det Insp Donald Cronin, and the detective officers under him did not have access to social services' headquarters files. Det Insp Cronin is satisfied that the social workers involved in the investigation worked with the police in good faith but they too did not have access to headquarters files. The police had to rely upon Geoffrey Wyatt for information because it was understood that he had assumed personal responsibility for examining the relevant files.

51.20 There were meetings of an SSD Internal Departmental Co-ordinating Group in August and September 1990 at which the question of widening the investigation was discussed but the police were not represented at these meetings. At the last of these meetings, on 7 September 1990, it was reported that the police had decided that they did not wish to extend their enquiries.

51.21 Sir Ronald Hadfield's view is that Det Insp Cronin took the investigation as far as could be expected at that time. A full indictment for serious offences had been preferred against Norris; there were no known complaints from Bryn Estyn; there was no indication from the SSD that Norris might have committed offences at Bryn Estyn; and the cost and delay involved in an extended inquiry had to be considered as well as the desirability of a speedy trial.

51.22 Sir Ronald's conclusions are persuasive. The weak link was that the police did not have access themselves to headquarters files and that Wyatt was disinclined to probe them further. But, on the evidence before us (contrary to what Det Insp Cronin was later told) the files would not, at that stage, have revealed sexual misconduct by Norris at Bryn Estyn or his practice of inviting young boys to his farm.

51.23 The investigation by the police from 1991 onwards was planned as a large scale investigation from the outset. It began in Clwyd in July 1991 in response to a written request by the County Secretary. A separate investigation began in Gwynedd in October 1991 following a request by the Director of Social Services, triggered by an HTV television broadcast on 26 September 1991. Then, from 2 December 1991 the 2 investigations were merged and put on the HOLMES computer system[8].

51.24 The merged investigation was managed by Det Supt Peter Ackerley as Senior Investigating Officer with Det Insp John Rowlands as his deputy. Ackerley had become Detective Superintendent (Crime Operations) from 23 August 1991.

51.25 By 19 December 1991 the broad outline of the inquiry had been established and the necessary resourcing decisions had been made, including the identification and posting of the officers necessary to carry it out. On 2 January 1992 a training and briefing meeting for the team members was held at Colwyn Bay.

51.26 The investigation continued on a full scale until August 1993, by which time about 3,500 statements had been taken; and Det Insp Rowlands took over the lead role from the beginning of the following month.

51.27 We are satisfied that this investigation was carried out both thoroughly and efficiently and that there was no "cover up". Confirmation of its reliability has been provided by the following facts:

> (a) almost all the complainants who provided statements to the Tribunal attested that the complaints made in their statements to the police were true;
>
> (b) few of them said that they had additional complaints to make against relevant individuals;
>
> (c) despite the publicity given to the Tribunal and the Tribunal's own "trawl" for additional witnesses, we received few fresh complaints from witnesses who had not been seen by the police in the course of their investigation.

51.28 It was decided by the police that, in general, potential complainants would be sought out and spoken to privately, without prior warning. The main reasons for this decision were that, in most cases, their personal circumstances were unknown to the police and that they were likely to be reluctant to talk about their experiences in care.

---

[8] Home Office Large Major Enquiry System.

51.29 There were some critics of this method of approach but most of the complainants who were asked about the matter said that they were dealt with sensitively and properly by the police. Those who were likely to be called to give evidence in criminal trials agreed that they were kept reasonably informed of the progress of the cases in which they were involved. An independent NSPCC telephone helpline was established in Wrexham from 4 December 1991.

51.30 Sir Ronald Hadfield's view is that he too would have chosen to arrive unannounced in the circumstances of this inquiry. His only qualification to this statement is that "there must always be the case for an exception".

51.31 The small number of complainants who did criticise the approach of individual police officers to them did so mainly to explain their failure to mention specific complaints. A more serious suggestion, made particularly on behalf of some members of the Bryn Estyn staff, was that police officers were aggressive towards witnesses, put pressure on them and, in some cases, suggested that compensation would be available or recoverable if they complained that they had been abused. Only about 3 witnesses, however, endorsed the suggestion that compensation had been mentioned and it was denied by the police officers to whom it was put.

51.32 By December 1996 it is estimated that 3,860 statements had been obtained by the police from 2,719 witnesses, of whom about 1,700 had formerly been resident in children's homes in North Wales as children in care. About 500 of them alleged that they had themselves been subjected to sexual or physical abuse whilst in residential care at the hands of care workers or social workers (156 alleged sexual abuse). Allegations of varying strength against 365 individuals were referred to the CPS for decision: some of them were the subject of more than one referral and police officers interviewed approximately 160 "suspects" under caution.

51.33 Scrutiny of decisions whether to prosecute named individuals is expressly excluded from the Tribunal's terms of reference. We should say, however, that in the course of the evidence presented by the North Wales Police to the Tribunal we were shown lists (covering the period of the investigation to the end of November 1993) of the individuals in respect of whom files were submitted to the Chief Prosecuting Solicitor. Those lists indicate the names of suspects in respect of whom recommendations to prosecute were made, those in respect of whom no recommendation either way was made, and those against whom the police recommended that no proceedings should be taken. It is sufficient for us to say that there is nothing in these lists to cast doubt upon the thoroughness of the investigation or the willingness of the police to prosecute.

51.34 One other issue raised in the course of the major police investigation was dealt with in evidence to the Tribunal. This was the question whether an outside police force should have been called in by the Chief Constable to carry out the investigation.

51.35 In paragraphs 51.60 to 51.78 of our report, we outline how this matter developed and the views expressed about it by the main persons involved. It was in the autumn of 1992 that the question was raised most prominently, following a series of articles in the *Observer* newspaper. By that time, however, the investigation under Ackerley was far advanced and criminal proceedings against a number of individuals were already in train. As the Tribunal's findings indicate, there was no reason for concern at that time about the actual conduct of the investigation (a view confirmed by HM Chief Inspector of Constabulary); and the Chief Constable, who was the person who had to make the decision, regarded it as both unnecessary and impracticable to call in an outside force to take over the investigation at that stage. He did, however, arrange meetings between senior police officers and Dr John Marek MP, Councillor Malcolm King and the County Solicitor for Clwyd in December 1992 and February 1993, at the suggestion of Earl Ferrers, in an effort to allay their anxieties.

51.36 Sir Ronald Hadfield's view is that there were many factors supporting the decision of the Chief Constable not to request that an outside force should take over the investigation and he does not criticise the way in which the Chief Constable exercised his discretion.

51.37 The Tribunal's conclusion is that the Chief Constable made the correct decision on the right grounds in difficult circumstances. By the autumn of 1992 he had substantial grounds for confidence that the investigation was being carried out with integrity and professional efficiency; and replacement of the investigating team, with all the attendant confusion, delay and expense, could not be justified. We should add that, in our judgment also, a review of the investigation by an independent senior officer at that stage would not have served any useful practical purpose in relation to the investigation itself but it is arguable that such a review would have helped to assuage public concern.

51.38 Although we do not think that any substantial criticism is justified of the later 2 investigations, there are important lessons to be learned from all 3 investigations. One is the importance of appropriate training in advance of a sizeable group of officers in each police force to equip them to carry out inquiries into abuse with appropriate sensitivity, however stale the allegations may be. Another is the need for close liaison between the police and other agencies, particularly social services departments. There will often be complications about this because allegations may impinge directly or indirectly on officers or staff of those agencies but a clear working relationship has to be established and access by the police to all relevant documents is of paramount importance.

51.39 There have now been widespread investigations into the alleged abuse of children in care in several parts of the country and it is strongly arguable that the time has arrived for a comprehensive inter-agency review of the conduct of such investigations, leading to the issue of appropriate guidelines.

Was there a paedophile ring? (Chapter 52)

52.01 This question was raised on 17 July 1991, at the outset of the major investigation, in the letter from the County Secretary to the Chief Constable, and it was the subject of quite frequent allegations subsequently by journalists and others such as Councillor Malcolm King.

52.02 Det Supt Ackerley gave evidence to the Tribunal that all these allegations were investigated by the police as they arose but that no evidence of any substance could be obtained to support them.

52.03 Ackerley dealt also in his evidence with the suggestion that there was a paedophile ring at Bryn Estyn, pointing out that the alleged victims of Howarth and Norris were clearly distinct types in terms of their ages and other circumstances. Our own analysis shows that no one alleged abuse by Howarth or Norris in the other's presence and only 5 out of 48 complainants of sexual abuse at Bryn Estyn alleged that they had been abused by both men. Ackerley concluded that the evidence obtained by the police did not establish that victims were being passed from one offender to another at Bryn Estyn.

52.04 The difficulty about dealing with the general question satisfactorily is that a paedophile ring may exist in many different forms and that the range of its possible activities is also wide. One cannot formulate easily, therefore, an umbrella definition that will withstand academic scrutiny; and lay persons are likely to have widely varying concepts of the meaning of the phrase.

52.05 We should say at once that no evidence has been presented to the Tribunal or to the North Wales Police to establish that there was a wide-ranging conspiracy involving prominent persons and others with the objective of sexual activity with children in care. Equally, we are unaware of any coherent organisation of men with that objective. What we discuss in Chapter 52 of the report is whether there were groups of men, known to each other and associating informally, who did prey on children in care together and individually for sexual purposes during the period under review.

52.06 In the light of the evidence that we have heard we consider this issue under 6 heads, namely:

  (a) Paedophile activity at and connected with Bryn Estyn and Cartrefle.

  (b) Recruitment generally.

  (c) Paedophile activity in and around Wrexham town.

  (d) The investigation of Gary Cooke in 1979.

  (e) The Campaign for Homosexual Equality.

  (f) Paedophile activity on the North Wales coast.

52.07 We have not heard any evidence of a significant association between Howarth and Norris at Bryn Estyn.

52.08 Only Wilson and Anglesea were named as persons who participated in paedophile activity with Howarth and the allegations against them were rejected by separate juries.

52.09 There has been no acceptable evidence that anyone else participated in or witnessed any of Norris' sexual offences.

52.10 We discuss in paragraphs 52.14 to 52.20 of the Tribunal's report a small number of allegations that Norris, Howarth and John Allen separately played a part in introducing boys to unidentified "outside" paedophiles but we are unable to accept these allegations as proved.

52.11 There is no evidence of the systematic recruitment of known paedophiles to the staff of children's residential establishments in North Wales; and no previously convicted paedophile was appointed to such a post during the period under review. The only foster parent approved after a relevant conviction was Roger Saint.

52.12 We have examined with particular care the circumstances in which Howarth and Norris were appointed to posts at Bryn Estyn and the part played by Arnold in those appointments but there is no sufficient evidence to justify a finding that Arnold or any other relevant person was aware of either man's proclivities when he was recruited.

52.13 Arnold met John Allen on a visit by the latter to Axwell Park Approved School before Arnold's appointment to Bryn Estyn but no adverse inference can be drawn from the fact that they met subsequently on 3 occasions for reasons that Allen has explained.

52.14 Gary Cooke was employed at Bersham Hall for 2 weeks before his services were dispensed with, probably shortly before the period under review began. He was later employed in 1976/1977 by the Bryn Alyn Community for over a year but this employment was in Cheshire and then Shropshire. We have no evidence that his 1963 conviction was either disclosed or known to those who appointed him then.

52.15 The main witness about paedophile activity in and around Wrexham was B, who gave evidence also about the investigation of Gary Cooke in 1979 and about the activities of the Campaign for Homosexual Equality.

52.16 According to B, paedophile activity in Wrexham centred mainly on King Street public lavatories and a cafe nearby, the Crest Hotel and various houses and flats, some associated with the Lift Project. He gave evidence of being sexually abused by Cooke on many occasions, beginning when he was an army cadet (before he was admitted to care) and Cooke was an instructor. Cooke subsequently introduced him to numerous other paedophiles: he was B's link with almost all the paedophiles whom B named, including men who frequented the Crest Hotel on Sunday evenings and persons associated with the Lift Project.

52.17 B's evidence was that he was sexually abused by no less than 20 men outside Bryn Estyn, including Cooke and Graham Stephens, and we received evidence from 16 of them (15 gave oral evidence). Of these 16 witnesses, 11 were admitted homosexuals but they all denied B's allegations vehemently.

52.18 Three other witnesses gave evidence of being sexually abused by Cooke, 2 at the age of 16 years and one at the age of 18 years; and the last mentioned was named in one of the 4 counts of buggery of which Cooke was convicted on 29 April 1987.

52.19 In Chapter 52 of the Tribunal's report we give accounts of the background and evidence of both Cooke and Stephens and their denials of the allegations against them. It is clear that there is now considerable antipathy between Cooke and B and he described B's allegations as "rubbish". Stephens, who is 22 years older than Cooke, said that he had fallen out with Cooke in the late 1970s and he made many allegations of paedophile activity by Cooke between 1974 and 1979.

52.20 In paragraphs 52.59 to 52.70 of our report we give an account of preliminary events that led ultimately to the convictions of Cooke and Stephens on 30 June 1980 for a number of sexual offences. In short, B was staying in Cooke's flat in Wrexham, in the absence of Cooke, at the end of July 1979 when he found some indecent photographs of boys taken by Cooke and possibly others. B himself was accused on 2 August 1979 of stealing a watch, a pair of jeans and some money from another man at the flat and the photographs were either handed to or found by the police in the course of the investigation. B was sentenced on 23 October 1979 to 3 months' detention for 2 offences of theft and extensive investigations continued meanwhile into the photographs. Both Cooke and Stephens made partial admissions leading to their convictions but only Cooke was convicted in respect of the photographs.

52.21 B criticised the police officer in the case on a number of grounds and made other criticisms of the conduct of the investigation. He suggested, in particular, that it should have been wider and that others should have been prosecuted for the activities disclosed in the photographs. He argued also that fresh inquiries should have been made into those activities in the course of the 1991 investigation, when additional evidence became available. It seems that B is particularly bitter that Cooke (and possibly Stephens) were not prosecuted for offences against him.

52.22 We have not been persuaded that any of these criticisms by B can be upheld. Cooke and Stephens were prosecuted in 1980 for a reasonably wide range of offences, for which they received substantial sentences of imprisonment. As for the 1991 investigation, Ackerley said in evidence that his team were unable to get hold of the file relating to the 1979 prosecution; and it was not until the end of October 1992 that it was realised that B was making fresh allegations. Ackerley did not then believe that it would be fruitful to question Cooke about B's later allegations because Cooke would not make any admissions and a prosecution could not be sustained on B's evidence alone. In the interim period, Cooke had been convicted in April 1987 of serious offences and a further investigation of his contemporary activities led to his conviction in December 1995 for 2 indecent assaults on a male aged 18 or 19 years, for which he received 2 years' imprisonment.

52.23 Sir Ronald Hadfield said in evidence that he did not detect any flaw in anything that Ackerley did in pursuing enquiries into these matters.

52.24 Some former officers and members of the Campaign for Homosexual Equality (CHE) were amongst the alleged abusers of B, some of whom were from the Wrexham area. It is a national organisation but we refer only to its Chester branch, which was set up in or about 1973 with an office in Bridge Street Rows, and nothing that we say in our report about CHE carries any imputation against the wider organisation. The evidence that we heard about CHE relates to the first 8 years or so of its existence in Chester and we were told by one founding member that the branch has not existed since the 1980s.

52.25 Former officers of CHE and some others closely involved with it said that the organisation, including its "helpline" telephone, was strictly controlled and that anyone who sought to use it as a means of "picking up" under-age boys was immediately proscribed. A small number of witnesses, however, were strongly critical of CHE. Cooke, for example, described it as "the most vile organisation ever thought of" and another Wrexham witness said that he walked away from it because it was being abused by those who wanted to have sexual relations with youngsters.

52.26 B's evidence was that he was taken along by Cooke to CHE and to homosexual clubs in Chester linked with it, where he was introduced to several paedophiles. This led in turn to invitations to "gay" parties and to invitations to stay in Cheshire.

52.27 It is clear from the evidence that B did stay for about 2 or 3 weeks in January 1980 at a bungalow in Mickle Trafford owned by a member of CHE. B alleged that this accommodation was arranged for him by his social worker, who (like others) assumed that he was "gay", but social services records suggest strongly that he went to stay at the bungalow on his own initiative. B claimed that he was sexually abused by 7 men (5 named) whilst staying at this bungalow and the records show that he was admitted to hospital on 26 January 1980, following an "overdose".

52.28 We have no difficulty in accepting that B was subjected to sexual abuse repeatedly by several persons during his stay at the bungalow, despite the denials of those whom he named as his abusers. It is clear also, in our view, that that abuse was, at least, a major cause of the overdose that he took.

52.29 The main focus of the small amount of evidence that we received about paedophile activity on the North Wales coast was upon the 15/20 Club in Rhyl, owned from about 1960 to 1980 by Albert Dyson. It was described by several witnesses as a "gay" club and Dyson himself told the Tribunal that it was "a gay venue" on Saturday night, organised by a Rhyl group, during the last 18 months to 2 years of his proprietorship.

52.30 As we have said earlier, Dyson was convicted in June 1980 of 3 offences of indecency with a boy, who was a member of a family that he had befriended and who was both in care and resident at Bryn Estyn at the time. Nevertheless, we have not received any evidence of actual paedophile activities in the Club.

52.31 Both Gillison and Cooke were questioned closely about their activities in the Rhyl area in more recent years but both denied associating with any persons in care.

52.32 To sum up, although much of the evidence that we have heard about the existence of a paedophile ring has been tarnished in one way or another and the evidence of B has been demonstrated to be incorrect in some respects, the cumulative effect of all the evidence has been to satisfy us that, during the period under review, a significant number of individual male persons in the Wrexham and Chester areas were engaged in paedophile activities of the kind described by B. Whilst we have no reason to doubt the evidence of some office holders of the Chester CHE that precautions had been taken to prevent abuse of the organisation, it is clear to us that some of its less reputable members or habitués saw it as a useful agency for identifying and contacting individuals.

52.33 These and other individuals were targeting young males in their middle teens and it was inevitable that some young persons in care should be caught in their web. The evidence does not establish that they were solely or mainly interested in persons in care but such youngsters were particularly vulnerable to their approaches for emotional and other reasons; and the abusers were quite prepared to prey on such victims, despite the risks involved.

52.34 Many, but not all, of these paedophiles were known to each other and some of them met together frequently, although there were strong antagonisms between individuals from time to time. Inevitably, some information about likely candidates for paedophile activities was shared, expressly and implicitly, and there were occasions when sexual activity occurred in a group.

52.35 We have concentrated our attention on evidence relating to children who were in care at the time, having regard to our terms of reference, but we have necessarily heard some evidence about others who were on the fringe of the care system, that is, children who were later committed to care and youths who had recently been discharged from care. In our judgment, the perils for such persons are as great in this respect as for those actually in care and our findings emphasise the importance of continuing support by social services for those who are discharged from care.

52.36 We draw the attention of Parliament also to the abuse suffered by B between the ages of 16 years and 18 years, in circumstances which appear to have made him question his own sexuality for a period. Much of the later abuse was not inflicted by persons in a position of trust in relation to him and there can be no doubt that he was significantly corrupted and damaged by what occurred.

52.37 To the extent that we have indicated, we accept that there was an active paedophile ring operating in the Chester and Wrexham areas for much of the period under review. We should add, however, that we are conscious of the difficulty of prosecuting individuals for specific paedophile offences alleged to have occurred many years ago on the testimony of one complainant alone or with the aid of only vulnerable corroborative evidence. It is for this reason that we have named only a small number of individuals in this chapter, but we are firm in our conclusions.

THE SUCCESSOR AUTHORITIES
(Chapters 53 and 54)

The new structures and resources (Chapter 53)

53.01 The relative approximate sizes and resources of the new areas and councils in April 1996 are summarised in the following table:

Council	Population	Area (hectares)	Size of Council	Total net budget (£000s)	Percentage expenditure on Social Services
Anglesey	68,500	71,500	40	62,580*	17.2
Conwy	110,700	113,000	60	79,000	20.4
Gwynedd	118,000	255,000	83	107,000	18.4
Denbighshire	89,000†	84,000	48	83,500	18.4
Flintshire	145,000	43,700	72	117,800	21.5
Wrexham	123,500	49,900	52	101,422	19.5

* This is the budget for 1997/1998 because we were not given the figures for the previous year.

† Denbighshire lost the area of Llangollen Rural (population about 1,800) in April 1997 to Wrexham. The population and area given exclude Llangollen Rural.

53.02 In Chapter 53 of the Tribunal's report we give an account of the organisation of the social services administration adopted by each of the 6 new councils but it is unnecessary to repeat the details for the purposes of this Summary. Instead, we draw attention only to particularly relevant facts.

53.03 The following table indicates how looked after children in North Wales were being accommodated on 15 January 1998:

County	Children looked after	Residential Care		Foster Care	
		In County	Out of County	In County	Out of County
Anglesey	61	4	0	51	6
Conwy	105	2 + 3	1	91	6
Gwynedd	67	5	0	51	9
Denbighshire	70	6	6	53	1
Flintshire	91	0	0	83	8
Wrexham	107	11	7	70	3
Totals	501	31	14	399	33

53.04 We cannot vouch for the accuracy of these figures but they give the clearest picture possible on the evidence available to us. They indicate that about 86 per cent of the children being looked after were being boarded out and that quite substantial use was being made of foster parents outside the placement authority's area. The figures for placements in residential homes out of county may well be understated as at 15 January 1998. Whether or not they are correct for that date, the evidence suggests that each of the North Wales authorities is likely to have to make out of county residential placements from time to time. Flintshire, for example, supplied us with a list of 14 out of county placements in 1997 and 1998. All but one of these were apparently boarding out placements but the exception was in secure accommodation as far away as County Durham. Three of the counties (Anglesey, Conwy and Gwynedd) have set aside contingency funds of £100,000 or £150,000 to meet the extra cost of residential placements outside the county.

53.05 The provision for children's residential care in North Wales is now very limited. **Anglesey** has Queens Park at Holyhead, with accommodation for up to 4 children in the age range of 13 to 16 years, but its future is under review. **Conwy** has one community home, Llwyn Onn at Rhos-on-Sea, with semi-independent accommodation for 3 adolescents; and it has a scheme providing accommodation for 3 others in separate houses with social services support. **Gwynedd** has Cartref Bontnewydd, with accommodation for 7 boys and girls aged 12 to 18 years. **Denbighshire** has accommodation at present for 6 children, of whom 4 of the same family are in one of its 2 homes temporarily, but it intends to have one community home only (run on their behalf by National Children's Homes), with accommodation for 4 children. **Flintshire** has no community home: it provides only 3 units, accommodating 6 children, for respite care and family support; and residential services are provided at these units by NCH Action for Children. Finally, **Wrexham** has 3 continuing community homes (Cherry Hill, 15 Norfolk Road and 21 Daleside Avenue) providing accommodation for 10 children. At present, there is one other temporary community home at Tan-y-Dre, which was opened in November 1997 to accommodate 3 young children from one family. Thus, the total provision in North Wales, excluding temporary arrangements, does not exceed about 30 places (6 per cent of the total number of children being looked after).

53.06 There are broad similarities between the administrative structures in 4 of the new authorities, namely, Anglesey, Conwy, Denbighshire and Flintshire. Each has a Social Services Committee and 2 of them (Conwy and Denbighshire) have Children and Families Sub-Committees composed of about half of the main committee. In Anglesey, the senior child care specialist is not a member of the Departmental Management Team but she is responsible to one of two Assistant Directors working immediately under the Director; and there are 2 dedicated children's teams working under her. In the 3 other counties the designated senior manager of services for children is a member of the Departmental Management Team. There is, however, cause for anxiety in Flintshire because, at the time of presentation of the County Council's evidence, the post of Director of Social Services and several senior posts in children's services were vacant and difficulty was being experienced in filling them appropriately.

53.07 The 2 authorities with different administrative structures are Gwynedd and Wrexham. Gwynedd has a Social Services Committee as one of 6 service committees but the County Council has adopted a structure based upon areas co-terminous with the old district boundaries of Arfon, Dwyfor and Meironydd; and there is no Children's Sub-Committee. The Area Director for Arfon, who is a member of the Departmental Management Team, has lead responsibility for children's services and there are now 4 Children's Services Managers (in response to Adrianne Jones' criticism of an earlier structure).

53.08 In Wrexham there is a Social Services Committee, without any Sub-Committee, presided over by Councillor Malcolm King, but the officer with the statutory role of Director of Social Services is the Director of Personal Services, who is responsible for 2 departments, each with a Chief Officer. The Chief Social Services Officer has a Management Team, which includes the Senior Manager (Children and Family Services). Delivery of social services has now been planned on the basis of 3 localities, each with a locality team.

53.09 Each of the 6 successor authorities claims to have increased its allocation of resources to children's services as a proportion of the social services budget since reorganisation. Wrexham said that 19.8 per cent was allocated to children and families in 1996/1997 and that specific additional provision has been made in subsequent years to strengthen children's services. In other areas, with a higher ratio of elderly residents, the proportionate allocation has been less, usually in the range of 12.5 to 14 per cent. The budget for children's services in Gwynedd in 1996/1997, however, was one of the lowest in Wales and only just over half the Welsh average. According to the figures presented to the Tribunal by the Director of Social Services, the social services budget was increased by £2,447K in 1997/1998, of which £446K was in respect of children's services, an increase of about 28 per cent in the latter.

53.10 A number of joint ventures or co-operative arrangements were agreed by some of the successor authorities in the interests of economy and efficiency. This has been accepted most generally in the field of inspection. Denbighshire, Flintshire and Wrexham have combined to form the North East Wales Registration and Inspection Unit, which serves the 3 administrative areas under a formal service delivery contract. Gwynedd, on the other hand, has provided a contracted inspection unit for Anglesey since 1 September 1997, absorbing the staff that previously served Anglesey's own inspection unit.

53.11 Other joint ventures are in fostering, under a joint agency agreement between Cartref Bontnewydd Fostering Services Unit, Gwynedd and Anglesey, and in an out-of-hours emergency service between those 2 counties and Conwy, in which the latter acts as lead authority. All 6 successor authorities participate in the North Wales Child Protection Forum and a shared guardian ad litem service.

Some continuing concerns (Chapter 54)

54.01 Sub-paragraph (d) of the Tribunal's terms of reference requires us "to consider whether the relevant caring and investigative agencies discharged their functions appropriately and, in the case of the caring agencies, whether they are doing so now". However, the format and composition of a Tribunal of Inquiry of this kind are not designed to enable it to carry out an audit of social work and that task was, in effect, assigned to Adrianne Jones' Examination Team on Child Care Procedures and Practice in North Wales shortly before we were appointed.

54.02 It is relevant also that the Welsh Office itself established the Adrianne Jones Report Implementation Group; and the SSIW carried out an inspection in October 1997 to assess the progress made in North Wales in implementing the recommendations of Adrianne Jones' team. The report on that inspection was issued in August 1998 and was based on the facts as they were over halfway through the Tribunal's hearings. We confine ourselves in this chapter to matters of specific continuing concern that are of particular relevance to the central purposes of our inquiry.

54.03 Adrianne Jones' report covered 11 areas of practice, namely, strategic planning, child protection, child care planning, residential care, foster care, management, personnel and employment, staff development and training, inspection, complaints and children's rights. Much of the written evidence submitted by the successor authorities to the Tribunal referred directly or indirectly to their responses to the team's 41 recommendations and Adrianne Jones herself assessed that evidence at our request: she told us that she approached her task primarily from the perspective of keeping children safe.

54.04 In their responses all the successor authorities referred to lack of financial resources and pressure on staff time: all of them spoke of identified needs that cannot be met in the current financial situation.

54.05 There have been some difficulties in recruiting staff, of which Flintshire's problems in relation to senior officers are the most striking. There is widespread difficulty in recruiting new residential care staff because of the poor pay structure and, possibly, the impact of this Tribunal's hearings. Anglesey referred to a shortage of bi-lingual staff and Gwynedd to a dearth of experienced social workers. Wrexham, on the other hand, has experienced a lack of quality in applicants for managerial positions and field social worker posts at level 3.

54.06 Each authority does now have a designated person with overall policy and service responsibility for children's services within each social services management team but Adrianne Jones' view is that not all of them have the structure that she would like to see. The issue is whether the children's service manager is sufficiently senior to take responsibility for and influence what is happening at the most senior level and to have responsibility "at the strategic level" for developing children's services and providing resources so as to ensure that they match needs.

54.07 Gwynedd has developed a structure of management not dissimilar to the earlier divisional structure adopted by the former Gwynedd between 1987 and 1992, which did not prove to be successful. The Arfon Area Director now carries lead responsibility for children's services but does not have line management responsibility for all those services and each Area Director carries responsibility for some of them. Moreover, Gwynedd acknowledges that the work load of the Arfon Area Director is such that "there is a need to strengthen the management structure to allow her to address children's services issues" appropriately.

54.08 Although combined action is being achieved in a number of fields, Adrianne Jones' view is that there is a need also for a North Wales forum "for residential care managers (including the independent sector) to share information about good practice and consider specialist issues affecting their day to day work". In her oral evidence, Adrianne Jones suggested that it should have a wider remit to encourage cross-boundary co-operation, such as the provision by one local authority of services to another, and to assist in the strategic planning of services; and part of the recommendation is that the forum should have the support of the SSIW.

54.09 There were varied reactions by the successor authorities to the idea of a national unit for inspection but the general view is that, whatever the overall structure may be, the actual inspection units should be locally based. There is wide support for 2 such units, covering North West and North East Wales respectively. There is general support also for the establishment of the inspection units as wholly independent entities from the local authorities whose services they inspect.

54.10 All the successor authorities are experiencing difficulties in recruiting foster carers, particularly for children with special needs, but these difficulties are occurring nationwide. The emergence of an increased number of private fostering agencies in competition with local authorities and willing to pay higher rates is one of the factors affecting the supply. The response to advertising tends to be poor and Adrianne Jones emphasises the need for local authorities to offer a "whole package" to prospective carers, involving training to enable them to develop the necessary skills and continuing support as well as remuneration reflecting the needs of the child.

54.11 Most children in foster care or residential care now receive information about the complaints procedures applicable to them when they are admitted. Less progress, however, has been made in relation to whistleblowing procedures, which we consider to be of at least equal importance. At the time when the evidence was submitted to us, only Flintshire had formally approved such a procedure.

54.12 In the closing stages of our hearings the Tribunal heard some disquieting evidence of dissatisfaction amongst professional staff in Flintshire about the response to staff complaints before the county's whistleblowing procedures were approved. Serious breaches of child protection procedures and record keeping in 5 separate cases were alleged and eventually 3 senior officers apologised for their respective roles in the events.

54.13 The evidence supplied by the successor authorities suggests that there is a continuing need for the appointment of independent visitors but that only one authority (Conwy) has appointed such visitors. Adrianne Jones commented that the authorities' responses raise the question whether all children who might be befriended by an independent visitor are being considered for such assistance and whether it would be available. The responses reinforce our own opinion that a wide review of the practice under paragraph 17(1) of Schedule 2 to the Children Act 1989 is desirable and that consideration should be given to revising the pre-conditions for appointing independent visitors.

54.14 In the concluding paragraphs of Chapter 54 we highlight 4 specific areas of concern for the future that have emerged from the evidence. They are:

    (a) the overall provision of residential care;

    (b) the monitoring of fostering placements;

    (c) the supervision of children leaving care;

    (d) financial provision generally.

54.15 In the light of the figures set out in the table in paragraph 53.03 of this Summary, we regard it as strongly arguable that the present provision for residential child care in North Wales as a whole is inadequate and that the extent of reliance upon out of North Wales placements (both actual and potential) is unacceptable. The range of needs of children for whom suitable foster placements are unavailable is certainly not met by the existing children's homes and it is likely that co-operative action, with Welsh Office/Welsh Assembly participation, will be necessary to find a solution.

54.16 It is important that any review should include the private and voluntary children's homes in North Wales (including unregistered homes) and similar private residential establishments for children, including schools that cater for special needs. Much dissatisfaction with the exclusion of children's homes accommodating fewer than 4 children from registration requirements has been expressed to us and, in our view, it should now be re-considered within the full framework of the provision of residential care.

54.17 The responsibility of monitoring the availability of placements and the quality of fostering services over a wide area is onerous and we are not persuaded that there is any effective mechanism for this in place. The need for it is closely linked with the problem of adequate residential care provision. Whilst the continuing bias in favour of foster care is understood and accepted, it does not provide a universal solution: the need for a range of alternative placements remains and the suitability of individual foster placements needs to be kept under continuous review, particularly in respect of children with special needs or who otherwise present special problems.

54.18 There is a particular need to keep under overall review the resort to multiple foster placements, which are likely to be highly damaging and may indicate a serious weakness in fostering practice. Comprehensive records of the success or failure of placements should be maintained and readily accessible.

54.19 The relatively low number of complaints against former foster parents received by the North Wales Police and this Tribunal does not justify complacency about the risk of abuse in foster care. Vigilance by everyone who has contact with the children is all important and it is particularly necessary that teachers, members of the medical profession, and police officers should be informed about and responsive to signs of abuse.

54.20 The requirements of section 24 of the Children Act 1989 and some recent SSIW inspections have done much to focus the attention of the successor authorities upon the needs of young persons leaving care. The problems facing former foster children may well be as severe as those for children leaving residential care and the successor authorities support Sir William Utting's recommendation that section 24 should be amended to extend the duties of local authorities to include helping foster carers to provide support to their former charges on leaving care.

54.21 The budget for social services for each new authority was derived from the budget of the former County Council for the area and did not take into account any additional expenditure that might be necessary to provide appropriately skilled higher management of those services. Moreover, subsequent imposed savings, enforced by capping, made it extremely difficult even to maintain the level of children's services.

54.22 There is a strong case, therefore, for a fresh assessment of the needs of children's services on an all-Wales basis. Such a re-assessment would be particularly timely following the implementation of the Children Act 1989 and the re-organisation of both central and local government in Wales. It would be able to take into account the special needs of the more numerous and smaller unitary authorities, including the opportunities for co-ordinated provision or action by them; and it would provide an opportunity for re-assessment of priorities in the social services, giving due weight to the parental responsibility of local authorities towards every child in care.

54.23 Amongst our recommendations is one identifying the need for management training of senior managers (first, second and third tier) in SSDs. One of many factors giving rise to this need is that re-organisation of the SSDs in North Wales was effected from within the former 2 counties at senior management level with the result that there has been little opportunity for cross-fertilisation of ideas and practice from outside. Moreover, the size of the authorities and the need for competence in Welsh speaking will inevitably limit to some extent the opportunities for recruitment from outside Wales in the future. The need to keep managers up to date with rapidly developing practices in many fields is, therefore, of special importance.

Conclusions (Chapter 55)

Introduction

55.01 A major benefit of this Inquiry has been that the evidence of 259 complainants, of whom 129 gave oral testimony, has been heard in public. For the vast majority of them this was the first opportunity for their accounts of their periods in care to be publicised and very many of them have expressed satisfaction that this has now been achieved. We are very conscious of the burden that giving evidence, in whichever form, imposed upon these witnesses; and that burden was generally most obvious when some of them were subjected to necessarily severe cross-examination by Counsel for those against whom they made specific allegations. We believe, however, that the satisfaction in their minds of knowing that they have been listened to will substantially outweigh the disadvantages of providing that evidence[1].

55.02 For the "Salmon letter" recipients the Inquiry has been a particularly anxious time: that has been unavoidable, given the nature of the allegations against them. The anxiety has been mitigated, as far as it was permissible for us to do so, by the Tribunal's anonymity ruling for the period of our hearings in respect of any person against whom an allegation of physical or sexual abuse had been or was likely to be made[2]. For reasons that we have explained in paragraph 6.14 of the report, that ruling could not properly be applied to the report itself but, we have exercised restraint in "naming names" and have done so only where we have considered it to be necessary in order to fulfil the purposes of this public inquiry.

55.03 Particular burdens upon the "Salmon letter" recipients (other than those against whom the allegations were limited to abuse) and Counsel who represented them were the wide range of matters with which they had to deal and the scale of the documentation involved. Whereas in conventional litigation between parties the issues are narrowed by statements of each party's case and there is ample time to study relevant documents, the ambit of our inquiry and the necessary timetable of our hearings did not permit these refinements. We acknowledge the additional strains that were imposed by the inquiry on those "Salmon letter" recipients and their Counsel and are grateful to them for their co-operation in accepting them. They are factors that we have borne in mind in reaching our conclusions.

55.04 We have outlined our approach to the evidence submitted to us in Chapter 6 of the report, in which we referred to the special difficulty of investigating a very

---

[1] See Appendix 5 to our report.
[2] See paras 1.04 to 1.05 of this Summary.

wide range of events, most of which occurred many years ago[3]. Although it may be obvious, it is necessary to stress also that an inquiry of this kind cannot emulate, for example, an investigation by the police. The resources of the Tribunal and its mechanisms inevitably limit its ability to seek out new witnesses and to interrogate them. Thus, in the course of probing the existence of an alleged paedophile ring, we have been unable to do more than hear what the relevant witnesses known to us have been prepared to say on the subject and there has been very little documentary evidence to assist us. These limitations, as well as the lapse of time, should be borne in mind when the report is read because they are reasons for the lack of specificity in some of our conclusions.

55.05 At the beginning of the period under review, 1 April 1974, there were 542 children in care in Clwyd and 290 children in care in Gwynedd. At that date, 203 of the Clwyd children were in residential care and 212 were boarded out whereas in Gwynedd about 80 were in residential care compared with 122 boarded out. The period under review ended on 31 March 1996 and the latest (1995) figures that we have show that the children in Clwyd now described as looked after children had been halved, to 244, of whom 190 were fostered. In Gwynedd the changes had also been substantial, if less dramatic, because by 31 July 1995 the number of children looked after was 157, of whom 18 were in residential care and all the rest were fostered.

55.06 Our inquiry has focussed upon the children's homes and foster placements that were the main subject of complaints by former residents. The comparatively few other complaints have not been investigated for a variety of reasons such as lack of identification of the abuser, the fact that the alleged abuse occurred outside the period under review, closure of the home early in that period and/or the fact that the complaint was an isolated one unsupported by any significant body of other complaints in relation to the same home.

55.07 The result has been that we have examined in detail the histories of nine local authority homes in Clwyd[4] (of 23 that existed from time to time) and one voluntary children's home[5] (of four). We have also investigated complaints emanating from a local authority residential school and a National Health Service residential clinic[6]. In the private sector we have examined residential homes/schools in Clwyd run by three organisations[7], namely, the Bryn Alyn Community, Care Concern International and Clwyd Hall for Child Welfare, embracing not less than eight establishments on different sites. Thus, the detailed Inquiry has covered 20 residential establishments in Clwyd over substantial periods as well as the investigation of complaints about seven foster homes[8].

---

[3] Ibid, paras 6.01 and 6.02.
[4] See Chapters 7 to 17.
[5] See Chapter 18.
[6] See Chapters 19 and 20.
[7] See Chapters 21 to 23.
[8] See Chapters 25 to 27.

55.08 On the same principle we have examined the histories of five local authority homes in Gwynedd[9] (of ten that existed from time to time). The only other establishments that required investigation in the light of the complaints were in the private sector and we examined particularly one that belonged to Care Concern International and three run by Paul Hett[10]. Thus, the Inquiry covered nine residential establishments in Gwynedd and eight foster homes[11].

55.09 It is our hope that, despite its length, the report will be read fully and widely by policy makers, members of the social services profession, administrators and all others who have responsibility for the welfare of looked after children. We draw attention specifically to the fact that many of the children in the residential establishments that we have discussed and in North Wales foster homes were placed there by English authorities. The accounts that we have given of the residential establishments reveal not only how sexual and physical abuse of children can arise and fester but also the extent to which many of these establishments have failed to provide an acceptable minimum standard of care for children in dire need of good quality parenting. The report discloses also widespread shortcomings in practice and administrative failings in the provision of children's services, including failure to apply basic safeguards provided for by regulation, which must be addressed if local authorities are to discharge adequately the parental responsibilities imposed upon them in respect of looked after children. The Children Act 1989 has provided a springboard for many improvements in children's services but the need for vigilance and further positive action remains if the ever present risk of abuse is to be minimised.

Summary of our conclusions

55.10 The following is a summary of the major conclusions that we have reached, as indicated in the report (the references here are to paragraphs of this Summary, unless otherwise stated):

Clwyd

Sexual abuse

(1) Widespread sexual abuse of boys occurred in children's residential establishments in Clwyd between 1974 and 1990. There were some incidents of sexual abuse of girl residents in these establishments but they were comparatively rare.

Local authority homes

(2) The local authority community homes most affected by this abuse were (a) Bryn Estyn, where two senior officers, Peter Norman Howarth[12] and Stephen Roderick Norris, sexually assaulted and buggered many boys persistently over a period of ten years from 1974 in the case of Howarth (paras 8.04 to 8.14) and about six years

---

[9] See Chapters 33 to 37.
[10] See Chapters 38 and 39.
[11] See Chapters 41 to 43.
[12] Sentenced to 10 years' imprisonment in July 1994 and died on 24 April 1997.

from 1978 in the case of Norris (paras 8.15 to 8.22) and (b) Cartrefle, where Norris[13] continued, as Officer-in-Charge, to abuse boys similarly from 1984 until he was arrested in June 1990 (paras 15.03 to 15.11).

(3) The Tribunal heard all the relevant and admissible evidence known to be available in respect of the allegation that Police Superintendent Gordon Anglesea committed serious sexual misconduct at Bryn Estyn but we were not persuaded by this evidence that the jury's verdict in his favour on this issue in his libel actions was wrong (para 2.04 and Chapter 9).

(4) In addition to the abuse referred to in (2) there were other grave incidents of sexual abuse of boy residents by male and female members of the residential care staff between 1973 and 1990 at five local authority homes in Clwyd, namely, Little Acton Assessment Centre (para 12.07), Bersham Hall (paras 13.09, 13.10), Chevet Hey (paras 14.17 to 14.23), Cartrefle (para 15.16) and Upper Downing (para 17.04).

Private establishments

(5) There was widespread sexual abuse, including buggery, of boy residents in private residential establishments for children in Clwyd throughout the period under review. Sexual abuse of girl residents also occurred to an alarming extent.

(6) The most persistent offender in the Bryn Alyn Community was the original proprietor himself, John Ernest Allen, who was the subject of complaint by 28 former male residents and who was sentenced to six years' imprisonment in February 1995 for indecent assault on six former residents (paras 21.08 to 21.13). One other member of the staff was convicted in 1976 of sexual assaults on boys (para 21.17) and another was under police investigation for alleged sexual abuse during the Tribunal's hearings and until his death in August 1998 (paras 21.16, 21.19). The Deputy Headteacher of the Community's school was also convicted in July 1986 of unlawful sexual intercourse with a girl resident under 16 years and sentenced to 6 months' imprisonment (para 21.18).

(7) Richard Ernest Leake, formerly of Bersham Hall, who was the first Principal of Care Concern's Ystrad Hall School from 1 July 1974 and later Director of the organisation, is awaiting trial on 8 November 1999 on charges of indecent assault on boys between 1972 and 1978 (paras 22.07, 22.08 and 50.24). The Tribunal is aware of 16 male former residents of Ystrad Hall School who have complained of sexual abuse by members of the staff (six have been named). The Deputy Principal, Bryan Davies, was convicted in September 1978 of three offences of indecent assault against two

---

[13] Sentenced to $3\frac{1}{2}$ years' imprisonment in June 1990 for indecent assaults at Cartrefle and to 7 years' imprisonment in November 1993 for buggery and lesser offences at Bryn Estyn.

boys and placed on probation[14] (paras 22.09 to 22.11). We were unable to hear the evidence in respect of Leake because of the continuing police investigation and the evidence that we heard in respect of other members of the staff was insufficient to justify a finding, except in respect of Davies (para 22.12).

(8) There was persistent sexual abuse, including buggery, of not less than 17 boy residents at Clwyd Hall School between 1970 and 1981 by a houseparent, Noel Ryan, for which he was sentenced in July 1997 to 12 years' imprisonment (paras 23.07 to 23.11). Richard Francis Groome, the former Officer-in-Charge of Tanllwyfan, who was Head of Care and then Principal at Clwyd Hall School between November 1982 and July 1984, has been committed for trial on charges of sexual offences against boys, some of which relate to former boy residents at these establishments. His trial will take place early in 2000.

(9) There was yet again persistent sexual abuse of boy residents of Gatewen Hall, which was a private residential school prior to its sale to the Bryn Alyn Community in 1982[15]. The abusers were the two proprietors from 1977 to 1982, Roger Owen Griffiths and his then wife, now Anthea Beatrice Roberts, who were convicted on 4 and 5 August 1999 in the Crown Court at Chester. Griffiths was sentenced to eight years' imprisonment and Roberts to two years' imprisonment[16].

Voluntary homes

(10) There were complaints of sexual abuse from six former boy residents of the only voluntary home that we investigated, namely, Tanllwyfan. They were directed against a former care assistant at the home, Kenneth Scott, who was there from 1974 to 1976 and who was sentenced in February 1986 to eight years' imprisonment for buggery and other offences against boys committed in Leicestershire between 1982 and 1985. We have no reason to doubt the accuracy of the two complainants who gave evidence of indecent assaults on them by Scott during his period at Tanllwyfan (paras 18.03 to 18.05). There is one charge against Richard Francis Groome in respect of his period as Officer-in-Charge of Tanllwyfan.

Gwynfa

(11) Allegations of sexual abuse during the period under review at Gwynfa Residential Unit or Clinic, an NHS psychiatric hospital for children, were made by ten former residents to the police and involved four members of the staff. One former member of staff was convicted in March 1997 of two offences of rape of a girl aged 16 years committed in 1991, when she was a resident but not in care (para 20.05). Allegations against another member of staff, Z, were being investigated by the police in the course of the Tribunal's

---

[14] See para 22.10 of this Summary for the full order of the Court.
[15] See para 21.05(d) of the report.
[16] See para 50.22 of this Summary.

hearings and some of them were made by former children in care but the decision has now been taken that Z should not be prosecuted (para 20.06). We have not attempted to reach detailed conclusions in relation to Gwynfa for reasons that we explain (para 20.09).

Physical abuse

(12) Physical abuse in the sense of the unacceptable use of force in disciplining and excessive force in restraining residents occurred at not less than six of the local authority community homes in Clwyd, despite the fact that it was the policy of Clwyd County Council throughout the period under review that no member of staff should inflict corporal punishment on any child or young person in any circumstances (para 30.02). It occurred also at most of the other residential establishments for children that we have examined.

Local authority homes

(13) Such abuse was most oppressive at Bryn Estyn, where Paul Bicker Wilson was the worst offender. There was a climate of violence at the home in which other members of the staff resorted to the use of impermissible force from time to time without being disciplined for it. Bullying of residents by their peers was condoned and even encouraged on occasions as a means of exercising control (Chapter 10).

(14) Physical abuse was less prominent in the five other community homes referred to in (12), namely, Little Acton, Bersham Hall, Chevet Hey, Cartrefle and South Meadow, but was sufficiently frequent to affect a significant number of residents adversely. The use of force was often condoned and its effects were aggravated by the fact that some Officers-in-Charge from time to time, such as Peter Bird, Frederick Marshall Jones and Joan Glover, were themselves the perpetrators (Chapters 12 to 15 and paras 17.07 to 17.15).

Ysgol Talfryn and Gwynfa

(15) Physical abuse occurred also from time to time at a local authority residential school, Ysgol Talfryn, and at the NHS residential clinic for children, Gwynfa (paras 19.04, 19.05; 20.08, 20.09).

Private establishments

(16) Physical abuse was prevalent in the residential schools/homes of the Bryn Alyn Community in its early years and to a lesser extent at Care Concern's Ystrad Hall School. John Ernest Allen himself was a prominent offender in this respect at the former but impermissible force was used by other members of the staff quite frequently (paras 21.23 to 21.30, 21.34; 22.13 to 22.15).

Abuse in foster homes

(17) There were comparatively few complaints of abuse in foster homes in Clwyd but the evidence before the Tribunal disclosed major sexual abuse in five such homes, in respect of which there were convictions in four of the cases (the fifth offender hanged himself before his trial) (Chapters 25 and 26, paras 27.02 to 27.14).

Failings in practice etc

Complaints etc

(18) It was a serious defect nationally that complaints procedures were not introduced generally until the late 1980s. In Clwyd, there were no complaints procedures in any of the residential establishments that we have examined in detail between 1974 and 1991 when the major incidents of abuse occurred (para 29.19).

(19) Few resident children made complaints of abuse (except at Park House, where long term residents felt freer to do so). Those who did complain were generally discouraged from pursuing complaints and recording of complaints was grossly defective (paras 30.11, 30.19, 30.20). It was, however, the complaint of a boy resident at Cartrefle to a sensitive member of staff that led to the first convictions of Stephen Roderick Norris (para 15.05).

(20) There were no procedures in any of the establishments to enable members of staff to voice matters of concern and, in many of them, complaints by staff were strongly discouraged.

(21) The worst exemplar of the "cult of silence" on the part of staff was Bryn Estyn, where there were grounds for suspicion and gossip about Howarth's "flat list" activities for many years but the Principal, Arnold, threatened staff with dismissal if they gave currency to the rumours. Arnold was responsible also for covering up the true circumstances in which a resident had been injured and both he and Howarth were seriously at fault in failing to deal with Wilson's oppressive conduct (paras 8.10 to 8.13, 10.11, 11.03, 29.22).

The quality of care

(22) The quality of care provided in all the local authority homes and private residential establishments examined was below an acceptable standard throughout the period under review and in most cases far below the required standard. Those well below the standard were Bryn Estyn (paras 11.16 to 11.20), Little Acton (para 12.17), Bersham Hall (para 13.25), Chevet Hey (para 14.28), Cartrefle (para 15.19), Park House (para 17.30), the Bryn Alyn Community (para 21.40) and Clwyd Hall School (paras 23.14, 23.15). The quality of care was also well below standard at Ysgol Talfryn by 1993 (para 19.07).

Secure units

(23) There was misuse of the secure units provided (but not approved for use as such) at Bryn Estyn (paras 11.04 to 11.08) and Bersham Hall (paras 13.61 to 13.65 of our report).

Education

(24) The provision of education was inadequate in all the local authority community homes with educational facilities (paras 11.09 to 11.15, 12.18 and para 13.67 of our report) and in the private residential schools at Bryn Alyn (para 21.37) and Clwyd Hall (para 23.14).

Recruitment

(25) There were many breaches of approved practice in the appointment of residential care staff, most notably at Bryn Estyn, where several members of the staff were recruited informally without references

and without any adequate investigation of their past records (paras 30.06, 30.07).

(26) Manifestly unsuitable residential care staff were appointed to some vacant senior posts in community homes without any adequate assessment of their suitability for those posts. This was most blatant at Cartrefle with the successive appointments of Stephen Roderick Norris and Frederick Marshall Jones (paras 29.07, 14.10, 15.12, 30.18).

Police checks

(27) Checks upon the records of potential employees and foster parents held by the police, the Department of Health and the Department of Education were not made routinely before appointments were confirmed. In the particular case of the foster parent Roger Saint the North Wales Police were at fault in failing to explain to the Social Services Department the narrow limits of their check on Roger Saint's record of convictions in August 1978; and the Department itself was at fault subsequently in failing to make a further check in 1982 at the request of Tower Hamlets and in failing to take any appropriate action when informed of his conviction in 1988 (paras 11.13, 11.14, 25.10 to 25.13, 25.17 to 25.25, 30.06, 30.07).

Training

(28) Training opportunities and practice guidance for residential care staff were grossly inadequate and no instruction was given to them in proper measures of physical restraint (paras 30.04, 30.21, 30.22).

Recording

(29) The recording of events within residential establishments was frequently of poor quality and on occasions knowingly false (para 30.20).

Visiting

(30) Visiting by field social workers was in too many cases both irregular and infrequent and recording standards were very variable; in general, the quality of contact was poor (paras 29.23 to 29.26, 31.08).

Care planning

(31) There were deficiencies in care planning and in the statutory review process for each child on a similar scale. Too often reviews were paper exercises carried out without the involvement of the child and much later than they should have been (paras 31.03 to 31.07).

Leaving care

(32) There were no adequate arrangements for preparing children for leaving care (paras 31.09 to 31.12).

Supervision by other authorities

(33) The supervision of children from outside Clwyd by the placing authorities, whether in a residential establishment or in a foster home, was generally inadequate.

Management

(34) The arrangements for the oversight of the operation of the Social Services Department at the most senior levels in the County Council were inadequate (paras 28.22, 28.23).

| | (35) | The Social Services Department failed to provide at the most senior level effective and positive leadership to ensure that, in relation to decisions affecting each child in their care, first consideration was given to the welfare of the child and to foster a climate in which that principle was followed (paras 28.18, 28.19, 31.13). |

Leadership (35) The Social Services Department failed to provide at the most senior level effective and positive leadership to ensure that, in relation to decisions affecting each child in their care, first consideration was given to the welfare of the child and to foster a climate in which that principle was followed (paras 28.18, 28.19, 31.13).

Structure (36) The senior management of the Social Services Department in relation to children's services was subjected to frequent changes and remained confused and defective without adequate expertise at the highest level and clear lines of responsibility and accountability (paras 28.18, 28.19).

Planning (37) The Social Services Department failed to establish any strategic plan for the provision of residential placements following the demise of the Regional Plan for Wales (paras 31.02 to 31.04).

Inspection and monitoring (38) There were no coherent arrangements by Clwyd Social Services Department for the management, support and monitoring of the authority's community homes and for supervision and performance appraisal of residential care staff for most of the period under review. This grave defect had its most serious impact on Bryn Estyn where, despite the existence of a management committee charged with responsibility for it and two other Wrexham community homes, the Principal was left to run the home without any effective supervision or guidance (paras 29.27 to 29.30).

Complaints and discipline (39) The response by senior management, particularly by Geoffrey Wyatt, to complaints was discouraging and frequently inappropriate; and the implementation of disciplinary procedures was fundamentally flawed (paras 30.11 to 30.19).

Response to reports (40) The Social Services Department failed to respond positively to successive adverse reports on individual community homes, most of which were of county-wide relevance in relation to the management of the residential sector and the state of the community homes (paras 32.04 to 32.15).

Information to the SSC (41) The information supplied to members of the Social Services Committee by officers, including the contents of reports on inquiries, was inadequate and, on occasions, positively misleading (paras 32.05, 32.06, 32.10, 32.12, 32.14, 32.15).

The role of councillors (42) Members of the Social Services Committee prior to 1990 failed to discharge their parental responsibilities to the children in their care by informing themselves adequately about the state of children's services in the county and insisting that officers supplied appropriate information to them about matters of concern (paras 32.01, 32.02 and Chapters 29 to 32 generally).

Visits by councillors etc (43) Visits to community homes by councillors and headquarters' officers were grossly inadequate for most of the period under review (paras 29.27 to 29.30).

(44)
*The Cartrefle and
Jillings reports*
Clwyd County Council cannot fairly be blamed for failing to publish the Cartrefle and Jillings reports before it ceased to exist, having regard to the continuing police investigation at that time and its contractual duty to its insurers; but it is desirable that the Law Commission should consider the legal issues that arise in relation to the conduct of inquiries of a similar kind initiated by local authorities or other public bodies and publication of the reports of such inquiries (paras 32.17 to 32.29).

Gwynedd

The reason for the inquiry

(45) Without Alison Taylor's complaints about Nefyn Dodd there would not have been any public inquiry into the alleged abuse of children in care in Gwynedd (paras 34.11 to 34.19 and 49.11 to 49.15). In general terms, she has been vindicated.

Complaints generally

(46) Of about 120 complainants to the police who were former residents of one or more of the five local authority community homes in Gwynedd that we have investigated, about half (58) made complaints that they had been abused by Nefyn Dodd; and all but six of the latter alleged abuse by him at Tŷ'r Felin.

Sexual abuse

(47)
*Local authority
homes*
We have not received acceptable evidence of any persistent sexual abuse in any of the local authority homes in Gwynedd (paras 33.22, 34.06, 35.08 to 35.10, 36.04 to 36.09 and 37.05). We did, however, hear perturbing evidence of incidents of alleged sexual abuse at different times by two women members of the staff (X and Y) at Queens Park community home involving one (different) resident only in respect of each. The allegations against X were inadequately and inappropriately investigated and, in effect, suppressed. The allegations against Y were not made until 1996. In the absence now of any supporting evidence in respect of either set of allegations we are unable to find that they have been proved (paras 36.05 to 36.09).

(48)
*Private
establishments*
There were some isolated incidents of sexual abuse at two of Paul Hett's establishments, namely, Dôl Rhyd School and Ysgol Hengwrt. The five alleged abusers were all male members of the staff involved with one victim each; three of the victims were boys and two were girls. Four of the abusers left the staff shortly after complaints had been made but the fifth was not the subject of complaint until 1993, over four years after the victim had run away (paras 39.13 to 39.18).

Physical abuse

Local authority homes

(49) Physical abuse in the sense that we have defined it in (12) occurred frequently at Tŷ'r Felin during the regime of Nefyn Dodd as Officer-in-Charge between 1978 and 1990 but was less frequent in the last three or four years of that period. There were 75 complainants to the police who alleged physical abuse there. The worst offenders were Nefyn Dodd himself (paras 33.23, 33.24) and John Roberts (paras 33.28 to 33.33). We have not been persuaded that either June Dodd or Mari Thomas was guilty of physically abusing residents (paras 33.26, 33.27, 33.34, 33.35).

(50) There was no persistent physical abuse at any of the four other local authority community homes in Gwynedd that we have investigated and comparatively few complaints of such abuse were made to the police about Tŷ Newydd (paras 34.07 to 34.09), Queens Park (paras 36.12 to 36.14) and Cartref Bontnewydd (paras 37.06 to 37.08). There were more (11) complainants to the police who alleged that they had been physically abused by a named abuser at Y Gwyngyll and four of them named Nefyn Dodd; but any incidents of physical abuse that occurred were isolated and were not the subject of complaint until many years afterwards. We accept, however, that Nefyn Dodd did use excessive force to residents at Y Gwyngyll on a limited number of occasions (paras 35.09 to 35.12).

Private establishments

(51) We did not receive any complaint of physical abuse at Hengwrt Hall School but there were complaints by the Spastics Society in 1988 and by a Senior RCCO in 1990 of incidents of alleged abuse, which gave rise to concern (paras 38.07 to 38.12).

(52) 15 former residents of Paul Hett's establishments complained of physical abuse by identified members of the staff but most of their complaints related to Ysgol Hengwrt between 1986 and 1990. We have no doubt that excessive force was used to residents quite frequently by largely untrained staff in the absence of any clear guidelines (para 39.23).

Other abuse

Nefyn Dodd

(53) The regime imposed by Nefyn Dodd and, to a lesser extent, John Roberts upon staff and children at Tŷ'r Felin was autocratic, oppressive and contrary to the best interests of the residents (paras 33.17 to 33.21 and 33.33).

Abuse in foster homes

(54) Both sexual and physical abuse of children in care occurred in a small number of foster homes in Gwynedd during the period under review.

(55) Complaints of sexual abuse were made by four foster children placed in Gwynedd, but two of them were placed there by Clwyd Social Services Department. One of the foster parents of a Clwyd child

(Malcolm Ian Scrugham) was sentenced to ten years' imprisonment in April 1993 for rape and other offences against the foster child (paras 42.03 to 42.11). Gwynedd foster child C1 was sexually abused by the eldest other child in her foster home, for which he was fined in 1984 (paras 42.16, 42.17). We are not satisfied that the two other foster children were sexually abused (paras 42.18, 42.19).

(56) Two foster children placed by Gwynedd were subjected to physical abuse in their foster homes. In the case of M, the foster father and one of his two sons were eventually convicted in July 1993 of assaults many years after they occurred; but there were many breaches of good practice by the Social Services Department earlier in dealing with M's complaints (paras 41.04 to 41.21). It is likely also that C1 and her two brothers were subjected to bullying in the foster home (paras 42.18, 42.19).

Failings in practice etc

Similarities to Clwyd

(57) Although the extent of abuse of children in care in Gwynedd was much less than it was in Clwyd the failings in practice were of a similar order or degree.

(58) The following failings in practice mirrored those in Clwyd:

Complaints

    (i) There were no complaints procedures in any of the residential establishments between 1974 and 1991 (paras 45.09, 45.10).

    (ii) The few residents who complained were discouraged and their complaints generally suppressed (paras 41.12 to 41.21 and 45.11).

    (iii) There were no procedures for staff to voice matters of concern and complaints by staff were strongly discouraged (paras 45.07, 45.08, 45.12, 45.13).

The quality of care

    (iv) Quite apart from the oppressive nature of Nefyn Dodd's regime at Tŷ'r Felin referred to in conclusion (53), the quality of care provided in all the local authority community homes was below an acceptable standard (paras 33.36 to 33.39, 34.02, 35.13 to 35.15, 36.10, 36.15, 37.09).

Education

    (v) The provision of education at Tŷ'r Felin was inadequate (para 33.38).

Visiting

    (vi) Visiting by field social workers was in too many cases both irregular and infrequent and the quality of contact was poor (paras 46.06 to 46.08).

Care planning

    (vii) There were serious and persistent deficiencies in care planning and in the statutory review process (paras 46.03 to 46.05).

Leaving care

(viii) There were no adequate arrangements for preparing children for leaving care (paras 46.09 to 46.11).

Supervision by other authorities

(ix) The supervision of children from outside Gwynedd by the placing authorities, whether in a residential establishment or in a foster home, was generally inadequate (paras 38.14, 38.15, 39.24, 39.25, 42.08 to 42.10 and 43.15).

(59) Monitoring by social workers of the quality of individual boarding out placements was inadequate and there was confusion of responsibility for this (paras 43.20, 43.26 and 46.03).

(60) The child protection procedures and the provisions of the Boarding Out Regulations 1955 were not used for that purpose in some cases (paras 41.56, 41.63 and 43.22 of our report).

Management

Retention and advancement of Nefyn Dodd

(61) Major causes of Gwynedd's failure to eliminate abuse in its residential homes for children were the failure to recognise Nefyn Dodd's shortcomings as Officer-in-Charge of Tŷ'r Felin and his advancement to a position of control over all the county's community homes (paras 33.11 to 33.21 and 45.03 to 45.08).

(62) As in Clwyd:

Leadership

(i) The Social Services Department failed to provide at the most senior level effective and positive leadership in the provision and monitoring of children's services (paras 44.35, 45.14, 45.15, 46.23).

Structure

(ii) The senior management structure of the Social Services Department in relation to children's services was subjected to frequent changes and was confused and defective without adequate expertise at the highest level and clear lines of responsibility and accountability (paras 44.34, 44.35).

Planning

(iii) The Social Services Department failed to establish any strategic plan for the provision of residential placements (paras 44.15, 46.01, 46.03).

Inspecting and monitoring

(iv) There were no coherent arrangements for inspecting community homes and for monitoring the performance of residential care staff for most of the period under review. The effect of this was to leave Nefyn Dodd in sole control, accountable to himself alone (paras 45.04 and 45.06 to 45.08).

Response to complaints

(v) The response by senior management to complaints, in particular to those made by Alison Taylor, was discouraging and generally inappropriate (paras 45.11 to 45.13).

Response to reports   (vi) The Social Services Department failed to respond to successive adverse reports on the community homes, most of which were of county-wide relevance in relation to the residential sector and the state of the homes (paras 46.12 to 46.14).

Information to the SSC   (vii) The information supplied to members of the Social Services Committee by officers was inadequate and, on occasions, positively misleading (paras 44.10 to 44.12 and 46.13, 46.14).

The role of councillors   (viii) Members of the Social Services Committee failed to discharge their parental responsibilities to the children in their care by informing themselves adequately about the state of children's services in the county and insisting that officers supplied appropriate information to them (paras 46.20 to 46.23).

Visits by councillors   (ix) Visits to community homes by councillors were grossly inadequate (para 46.21).

Financial allocation to children's services   (63) Inadequate financial resources were allocated by Gwynedd County Council to children's services throughout the period under review and the adequacy of the allocation was never re-appraised by reference to children's needs (paras 46.15 to 46.19).

Leadership   (64) Prior to 1991 the managerial arrangements at the most senior levels in the County Council were outdated and failed to provide an adequate oversight of the operation and performance of the Social Services Department in relation to children's services (paras 44.34, 44.35).

The Welsh Office and Central Government

Legislation   (65) Too many changes were imposed in the organisation of local government in Wales and of social services in too short a time span (paras 47.37, 47.38).

Leadership and guidance   (66) At a time of major upheaval in local government in Wales and in the organisation of social services, the Welsh Office failed to provide leadership and guidance to ensure that the provision and administration of social services were given appropriate priority and failed to inform itself adequately about what was happening in relation to those services in North Wales (paras 47.39, 47.40, 47.44).

Bryn Estyn's change of status and control   (67) The Welsh Office failed to give Clwyd County Council (or its predecessor, the then Denbighshire County Council) any guidance in relation to the management, administration, supervision and running of Bryn Estyn Community Home following its change of status from an approved school controlled by the Home Office (para 47.39).

Staffing

(68) The policy and inspectorate branches of the Welsh Office were inadequately staffed with officials of sufficient experience in children's services to support and monitor the provision of those services by local authorities in Wales effectively (paras 47.05 to 47.11, 47.43, 48.05 and 48.16 to 48.27).

Strategic planning

(69) Following the demise of regional planning in 1984, the Welsh Office failed to ensure that there were adequate strategies for the provision of residential accommodation for children in care in North Wales (including placements outside Wales) and that such strategies were implemented (para 47.40).

Private children's homes

(70) Central government failed to take any action before the Children Act 1989 to regulate private children's homes despite the provision for this in the Children's Homes Act 1982 on the initiative of a Member of Parliament (para 47.41).

Regulation and inspection of residential establishments for children

(71) The regulatory and inspectorial regimes for community homes and for private residential schools were defective and the findings of inspectors were insufficiently publicised (paras 48.19 to 48.27).

Training

(72) Insufficient priority was given to the need for appropriate training for residential care staff (including guidance on appropriate methods of physical restraint), despite a succession of reports drawing attention to the need for such training (para 47.42).

Alison Taylor's complaints

(73) Although the Welsh Office did not become aware of allegations of mistreatment of children in care in Gwynedd until September 1986 and of persistent sexual abuse in a Clwyd community home[17] until August 1990, its response to Alison Taylor's complaints was inappropriately negative and inadequate (paras 49.11 to 49.15).

The North Wales Police

Investigations generally

(74) Save for the investigations in Gwynedd from 1986 to 1988 of Alison Taylor's complaints, there was no significant omission by the North Wales Police in investigating the complaints of abuse to children in care that were reported to them prior to 1990 (paras 50.06 to 50.08). This finding includes the investigation of Gary Cooke (and Graham Stephens) in 1979 (paras 52.21 to 52.23).

(75) The evidence before the Tribunal does not justify severe strictures on the police for their response to individual alleged complaints by children in care, including absconders, but it does underline the need for vigilance and sensitivity by police officers when dealing with such complaints (para 50.31).

---

[17] Cartrefle: see Chapter 15.

(76) The investigations in Gwynedd between 1986 and 1988 of Alison Taylor's complaints were defective in many respects and may fairly be described as "sluggish and shallow". The role played by Detective Superintendent Gwynne Owen was inappropriate and the size of the investigating team inadequate. There was no liaison with the Social Services Department and relevant documents were not seized. The reports on the investigation were one-sided and regrettable in tone; and the oral report to the Director of Social Services was inadequate (paras 51.06, 51.07, 51.11 and 51.16).

1986/1988 investigations in Gwynedd

(77) The investigation of sexual abuse at Cartrefle in 1990 led by Detective Inspector Cronin was thorough and he pursued it as far as could reasonably be expected on the basis of the information before him; but the mode of access to social services files afforded to the police was unsatisfactory (paras 51.21, 51.22).

The Cartrefle investigation

(78) The major police investigation of child abuse in Clwyd from 1991 onwards was carried out thoroughly (para 51.27). It was also carried out sensitively according to most of the complainants, although a small number were critical of the method of approach to them (paras 51.28 to 51.31).

The major investigation from 1991

(79) The decision by the Chief Constable not to request that an outside police force should take over the major police investigation was justified (paras 51.34 to 51.37).

An outside force

(80) The decision of the senior investigating officer not to re-open the 1979 investigation of Gary Cooke (and Graham Stephens) was also justified (para 52.22).

Re-opening the Cooke 1979 investigation

(81) Freemasonry had no impact on any of the police investigations and was not relevant to any other issue arising from our terms of reference (paras 9.05 and 50.32 to 50.35).

Freemasonry

(82) It would be timely now to arrange a comprehensive inter-agency review of the conduct of major police investigations into the alleged abuse of looked after children (paras 51.38, 51.39).

Inter-agency review of major police investigations

(83) During the period under review there was a paedophile ring in the Wrexham and Chester areas in the sense that there were a number of male persons, many of them known to each other, who were engaged in paedophile activities and were targeting young males in their middle teens. The evidence does not establish that they were solely or mainly interested in persons in care but such youngsters were particularly vulnerable to their approaches (paras 52.32 to 52.37).

Paedophile ring

The Successor Authorities

Need for co-ordinated action

(84) The number and size of the new local authorities responsible for social services in North Wales give rise to special problems, some of which can only be solved by co-ordinated action (paras 54.08, 54.15, 54.22, 54.23).

New management structures

(85) The new management structures for social services in some counties do not all provide a single officer at senior management level who is both dedicated to and responsible for children's services and who is of sufficient seniority to influence adequately the allocation of resources to those services (para 54.06).

Financial resources

(86) There is cause for continuing concern about the adequacy of financial resources allocated to children's services. A fresh assessment of the needs of these services on an All Wales basis is highly desirable (paras 53.09, 54.04, 54.21, 54.22).

Recruitment at managerial level

(87) Difficulties are being experienced by some authorities in recruiting officers of appropriate ability and experience in child care services at senior and middle management level and there has been little cross-fertilisation of ideas and practice (paras 54.05, 54.23). Provision for appropriate management training is required (para 54.23).

Recruitment of residential care staff

(88) The recruitment of suitable residential care staff for children is a widespread problem that needs to be addressed urgently (para 54.05).

Residential care establishments

(89) The provision of residential care establishments in North Wales is inadequate and needs to be reviewed, together with the use of out of county and private establishments, with a view to co-operative action (paras 54.15, 54.16).

Fostering

(90) There is a shortage of foster parents with requisite skills and a similar review of the availability and quality of fostering services is needed (paras 54.10, 54.17, 54.18).

Inspection

(91) The present organisation of inspection units needs revision. Any National Unit should have a local base within North Wales (para 54.09). Inspection should include also the provision and quality of fostering services (paras 54.17, 54.18).

Whistleblowing

(92) There is real danger that the discouragement of "whistleblowing" may persist and positive action is required to ensure that the new procedures are implemented conscientiously and that any fear of reprisals is eliminated (paras 54.11, 54.12).

Independent visitors

(93) The need for independent visitors requires re-assessment, as do the pre-conditions for their appointment (para 54.13).

Awareness of signs of abuse

(94) Vigilance by everyone who has contact with looked after children is of great importance and this applies particularly to teachers, members of the medical profession and police officers (paras 50.31, 54.19).

Leaving care

(95) The problems for children leaving foster care may well be as severe as those facing children leaving residential care and the forms of assistance that they need may be wide ranging. The implementation of leaving care strategies will need continuous monitoring (para 54.20).

Postscript

55.11 This inquiry has revealed that many of the aspirations of policy makers in the 1960s in relation to children's services were not realised in the following two decades. Reorganisation of local government and social services led to a dissipation of specialist skills and knowledge in child care, which were not replaced. Moreover, the intention of the Children and Young Persons Act 1969 that delinquent children, whose misbehaviour was seen as a consequence of deprivation and disturbance, should receive the same programme of care and treatment as children who had suffered similarly but who had not offended was not effectively implemented.

55.12 It must also be said that, in terms of crime prevention, the care system in Clwyd and Gwynedd was notably unsuccessful. From the records available to us in respect of all but two of the 129 complainants who gave oral evidence to the Tribunal, it appears that 52 had convictions before they entered care but 85 were convicted of offences whilst they were in care and 85 are known to have been convicted after they left care; and the figures for both counties were proportionately broadly similar. It would be a mistake to attach great importance to unanalysed statistics of this kind but they do underline the gravity of the problems that local authorities face.

55.13 One of the many explanations for this sorry record may be that delinquent children saw themselves as being more severely punished than their predecessors because they were now subject to orders that could continue up to the age of 18 years instead of orders for shorter specified periods. On the other hand, some children who had not offended before were introduced to delinquency and to harsh regimes in which they were treated by some staff as "little criminals". Neither category of child received a service that could be described as remedial or therapeutic and some regimes encouraged absconsion and increased offending. It is not surprising in the circumstances that many regarded themselves as lost in care.

55.14 Despite what we have said, however, a significant number of children regarded life in care, even at Bryn Estyn, as distinctly better than life at home and did not want to return to their family of origin. They were fed and clothed regularly and preferred a more predictable life to the unstable and sometimes dangerous one that they had known. We do not subscribe, therefore, to the view that children should be kept out of care at all costs, even though radical improvements in children's services may take some years to achieve.

Recommendations (Chapter 56)

Introduction

56.01 Formulating the Tribunal's recommendations has been an especially difficult task because there have been so many relevant developments since the events that we have described occurred and even since the Tribunal was appointed. The Children Act 1989 and the regulations made under it introduced major changes in the practice of child care but they did not come into effect until two years later, close to the end of our period under review, and little of the evidence before us has provided reliable guidance as to the effectiveness of the changes in preventing child abuse and detecting it when it occurs. A separate problem has been that, since the mid-1980s, there has been a continuous flow of other initiatives in the form of reports, consultation documents, legislation and statements of government intention touching directly upon the protection of children and the quality of child care. Such initiatives continued throughout our hearings and whilst this report was being prepared.

56.02 We welcome these initiatives unreservedly but they pose for us a problem of selection when setting out our recommendations. It would, for example, be otiose for us to recommend changes that have already been embodied in legislation, even if that legislation has not yet come into effect. We received many submissions in favour of a "one stop shop" for information about persons who may become involved in the care of children and statutory status for the Department of Health's Consultancy Service Index but we make no recommendation about these matters because they have already been dealt with in the Protection of Children Act 1999. More difficult questions of selection have arisen in relation to reports already published and statements of government intention. Some of these may require legislation but many of them are matters requiring only administrative and practical action to put them into effect and there is only patchy evidence before us, at best, to indicate the extent to which this has already been carried out.

56.03 A further problem is that we have inevitably received evidence and submissions touching upon a wide range of child care issues, not all of which can be said to impinge directly upon prevention of the abuse of children in care. At the conclusion of our hearings we received helpful submissions about our recommendations from Counsel on behalf of all the parties who appeared before us and Counsel to the Tribunal, for which we express our great gratitude. As we have said earlier, we had the benefit also of hearing the views of a representative panel of experts in the course of a two day seminar, to whom we are also very grateful. In the end, however, our recommendations have to be directed to our specific terms of reference and based upon the evidence that we have received, including some helpful suggestions by witnesses themselves.

56.04 In the light of these introductory comments our recommendations are focussed upon what we regard as continuing areas of concern and the measures necessary to deal with them, whether or not a particular recommendation has already been made in an earlier report and whether or not it has been endorsed by central government. In our judgment this is the only way in which we can present a relevant body of recommendations in response to our terms of reference. In relation to such matters as recruitment and training, which have previously been considered in great detail, the form of our recommendations takes account of this.

The Tribunal's recommendations

56.05 The Tribunal make the following recommendations:

| RECOMMENDATION | Source[1] |

The detection of, and response to, abuse

Children's Commissioner
(1) An independent Children's Commissioner for Wales should be appointed.
    1 to 21
    45 to 58

(2) The duties of the Commissioner should include:

    (a) ensuring that children's rights are respected through the monitoring and oversight of the operation of complaints and whistleblowing procedures and the arrangements for children's advocacy;

    (b) examining the handling of individual cases brought to the Commissioner's attention (including making recommendations on the merits) when he considers it necessary and appropriate to do so;

    (c) publishing reports, including an annual report to the National Assembly for Wales.

Children's Complaints Officer
(3) Every social services authority should be required to appoint an appropriately qualified or experienced Children's Complaints Officer, who should not be the line manager of residential or other staff who may be the subject of children's complaints or complaints relating to children.
    18 to 21
    58(i) to (iii)

(4) Amongst the duties of the Children's Complaints Officer should be:

    (a) to act in the best interests of the child;

    (b) on receiving a complaint, to see the affected child

---

[1] Where the source is stated to be a plain number in the range of 1 to 95 it is a Conclusion set out in para 55.10 of the report. Other sources cited are paragraphs in this Summary.

RECOMMENDATION

and the complainant, if it is not the affected child;

(c) thereafter to notify and consult with appropriate line managers about the further handling of the complaint, including:

(i) any necessary interim action in relation to the affected child, the complainant and the person who is the subject of complaint, including informal resolution of the complaint, if that is appropriate;

(ii) consideration of the established procedures to be implemented, such as child protection and disciplinary procedures and including any necessary involvement of the police and/or other agencies;

(d) to ensure that recourse to an independent advocacy service is available to any complainant or affected child who wishes to have it;

(e) to keep a complete record of all complaints received and how they are dealt with, including the ultimate outcome;

(f) to report periodically to the Director of Social Services on complaints received, how they have been dealt with and the results.

Response to complaints

(5) Any decision about the future of a child who is alleged to have been abused should made in that child's best interests. In particular, the child should not be transferred to another placement unless it is in the child's best interests to be transferred.   **19, 58(ii)**

Complaints procedures

(6) Every local authority should promote vigorously awareness by children and staff of its complaints procedures for looked after children and the importance of applying them conscientiously without any threat or fear of reprisals in any form.

(7) Such complaints procedures should:

(a) be neither too prescriptive nor too restrictive in categorising what constitutes a complaint;

(b) encompass a wide variety of channels through which complaints by or relating to looked after children may be made or referred to the

RECOMMENDATION	**Source**

Children's Complaints Officer including teachers, doctors, nurses, police officers and elected members as well as residential care staff and social workers;

(c) ensure that any person who is the subject of complaint will not be involved in the handling of the complaint.

Whistleblowing (8) Every local authority should establish and implement conscientiously clear whistleblowing procedures enabling members of staff to make complaints and raise matters of concern affecting the treatment or welfare of looked after children without threats or fear of reprisals in any form. Such procedures should embody the principles indicated in recommendation (7) and the action to be taken should follow, as far as may be appropriate, that set out in recommendation (4).

20, 58(iii), 62(v)

Duty to report abuse (9) Consideration should be given to requiring failure by a member of staff to report actual or suspected physical or sexual abuse of a child by another member of staff or other person having contact with the child to be made an explicit disciplinary offence.

Field social workers (10) An appropriate[2] field social worker should be assigned to every looked after child throughout the period that the child remains in care and for an appropriate period following the child's discharge from care.

(11) Field social workers should be required by regulation to visit any looked after child for whom they are responsible not less than once every eight weeks[3]. In the case of older children, they should be required also to see the child alone and at intervals away from their residential or foster home.

30, 58(vi)

(12) Any arrangements made for the provision of residential care or fostering services should expressly safeguard the field social worker's continuing responsibilities for supervision of the placement and care planning.

59

Awareness of abuse (13) Area Child Protection Committees should arrange training in sexual abuse awareness for social services staff and for those from other departments, agencies and organisations in their area.

---

[2] "Appropriate" in this recommendation and in succeeding recommendations means a social worker with specfic training in working with looked after children.

[3] See Sir William Utting, People Like Us, 1997, The Stationery Office at para 3.46 in relation to visits to foster homes.

RECOMMENDATION

Source

(14) Steps should be taken through training and professional and other channels periodically to remind persons outside social services departments who are or may be in regular contact with looked after children, such as teachers, medical practitioners, nurses and police officers, of their potential role in identifying and reporting abuse, the importance of that role and the procedures available to them.

Police log (15) A log of all incidents, disturbances, reports, complaints and absconsions at a children's home should be kept at an appropriate nearby police station and made accessible, when required, to officers of the Social Services Department.

19, 29

Absconders (16) Police officers should be reminded periodically that an absconder from a residential care or foster home may have been motivated to abscond by abuse in the home. They should be advised that, when apprehended, an absconder should be encouraged to explain his reasons for absconding and that the absconder should not automatically be returned to the home from which he absconded without consultation with his field social worker.

75

(17) It should be a rule of practice that any absconsion should be reported as soon as possible to the absconder's field social worker and that the absconder should be seen on his return by that social worker or by another appropriate person who is independent of the home.

Strategy on investigation of complaint (18) When a complaint alleges serious misbehaviour by a member of staff, the Director of Social Services should appoint a senior officer to formulate an overall strategy for dealing with the complaint, including such matters as liaison with the police in relation to investigation and with other agencies as appropriate, the impact on the child and other residents, any links with other establishments, the handling of any disciplinary proceedings, treatment of any looked after children who are or may become abusers themselves, the management of information for children and parents, staff, elected members and the public.

Paras 15.09, 16.04 to 16.06

Liaison with police (19) Whenever a police investigation follows upon a complaint of abuse of a looked after child, the senior officer referred to in recommendation (18) or another senior officer assigned for the specific purpose should establish and maintain close liaison with the senior

76, 77

investigating officer appointed by the police for that investigation and the local authority's officer should be kept informed of the progress of the investigation.

Disciplinary proceedings (20) Any disciplinary proceedings that are necessary following a complaint of abuse to a child should be conducted with the greatest possible expedition and should not automatically await the outcome of parallel investigations by the police or the report on any other investigation. In this context it should be emphasised to personnel departments and other persons responsible for the conduct of disciplinary proceedings within local authorities that: **21, 39, 62(v)**

 (a) police or any other independent investigation does not determine disciplinary issues;

 (b) disciplinary proceedings may well involve wider issues than whether a crime has been committed;

 (c) the standard of proof in disciplinary proceedings is different from that in criminal proceedings; and

 (d) statements made to the police by potential witnesses in disciplinary proceedings, including statements by a complainant, can and should be made available to local authorities for use in such proceedings, if consent to this is given by the maker of the statement.

(21) Personnel departments and other persons responsible for disciplinary proceedings within local authorities should be reminded that:

 (a) in deciding whether or not a member of staff should be suspended following an allegation of abuse to a looked after child, first consideration should be given to the best interests of the child;

 (b) suspension is a neutral act in relation to guilt or innocence;

 (c) long periods of suspension are contrary to the public interest and should be avoided whenever practicable;

 (d) depending upon the gravity of the allegation of abuse, the employment of a member of staff in another capacity not involving contact with children or other vulnerable persons may be an appropriate decision at the time of suspending

RECOMMENDATION Source

or finally, having regard to the importance of protecting looked after children from abuse.

Review of procedures in major investigations and guidance

(22) In the light of the recent experience gained in both England and Wales in major investigations of alleged wide ranging abuse of children in care/looked after children, an inter-agency review of the procedures followed and personnel employed in those investigations should now be arranged with a view to issuing practical procedural guidance for the future. In any event guidance is required to social services departments and police forces now in relation to:

82

(a) the safeguarding and preservation of social services files;

(b) the safeguarding and preservation of police records of major investigations, including statements and the policy file;

(c) access by the police to social services files;

(d) the supply of information about alleged and suspected abusers by the police following an investigation; and

(e) the sharing of information generally for criminal investigation and child protection purposes.

The prevention of abuse

Recruitment of staff

(23) Social Services Departments should be reminded periodically that they must exercise vigilance in the recruitment and management of their staff in strict accordance with the detailed recommendations of the Warner committee[4]; and compliance with them by individual local authorities should be audited from time to time.

25 to 27

Approval of foster parents

(24) Similar vigilance should be mandatory in relation to all applications for approval as foster parents. In particular, any application to foster by a member of a local authority's child care staff should be stringently vetted by a social worker who is not known to the applicant.

27
Para 26.10

Induction training

(25) Social Services Departments should ensure that appropriate and timely induction training is provided for all newly recruited residential child care staff.

28

---

[4] Choosing with care, 1992, HMSO.

	RECOMMENDATION	Source
Training generally	(26) The Tribunal endorses all five of the most recent recommendations of Sir William Utting in "People Like Us"[5] in relation to the content and provision of training for staff in children's homes and the care units of residential special schools and recommends that they should be implemented as expeditiously as possible.	
	(27) It should be a requirement that senior staff of children's homes (including private and voluntary homes) must be qualified social workers or, if that is not practicable before appointment, that it should be a condition of their appointment that they undertake qualifying training within a specified period.	**26**
	(28) Central government should take the initiative to promote and validate training in safe methods of restraint with a view to making such training readily available for residential child care staff and foster parents.	**12, 28, 49**
	(29) Suitable specialist training in child care at post-qualifying level should be made widely available and, in particular, to the senior residential care staff of children's homes and to field social workers.	
Attracting suitable staff	(30) There should be a national review of the pay, status and career development of residential child care staff and field social workers to ensure as far as possible that there is a sufficient supply of candidates for such posts of appropriate calibre.	

The quality of care

Assessment	(31) Whenever it is possible to do so, an appropriate social worker should carry out a comprehensive assessment of a child's needs and family situation before that child is admitted to care.	**31, 58(vii)**
	(32) All emergency admissions should be provisional and should be followed, within a prescribed short period, by a comprehensive assessment of the child's needs and family situation.	**37, 62(iii)**
Care planning	(33) The comprehensive assessment referred to in recommendations (31) and (32) should form the basis for the preparation of a care plan in consultation with and for the child within a prescribed short period after the child's admission to care.	**31, 58(vii)**

---

[5] Sir William Utting, op cit, at paras 12.22, 12.28, 12.31, 12.34 and 12.37.

RECOMMENDATION	Source

(34) An appropriate social worker should be designated as the person responsible for the implementation of the care plan and supervision of the looked after child.

Foster carers

(35) Foster carers should receive continuing support and have access as necessary to specialist services. In this context we endorse the recommendations of Sir William Utting in relation to training in "People Like Us"[6].

Leaving care

(36) The daily regime in residential establishments and foster homes should encourage and provide facilities for the acquisition of skills necessary for independent living.   32, 58(viii)

(37) A leaving care plan should be prepared for each looked after child, in consultation with that child, a year in advance of the event and should be reviewed periodically thereafter until the child ceases to require or be eligible for further support.   58(viii)

(38) The duty upon local authorities under section 24(1) of the Children Act 1989 to advise, assist and befriend a child with a view to promoting his welfare when he ceases to be looked after by them should be extended so as to ensure that placing authorities provide the level of support to be expected of good parents, including (where appropriate) help to foster parents to provide continuing support[7].

Fostering breakdowns

(39) Every local authority's fostering service, whether provided directly or by another agency, should monitor breakdowns in placements with a view to analysing the causes and remedying any faults in the service and should report upon them periodically to the Director of Social Services.   Para 54.18

Compliance with safeguards

(40) Appropriate key indicators of compliance with safeguards for looked after children should be developed, covering particularly: 34, 62(i)

    (a) the allocation of a designated social worker to each looked after child;

    (b) compliance with fostering and placement regulations;

    (c) statutory review requirements; and

    (d) rota visits by elected members.

---

[6] Sir William Utting, op cit, at paras 12.23 and 12.34.
[7] Sir William Utting, op cit, at para 8.64.

RECOMMENDATION	Source

Private children's homes and residential schools

Registration of homes (41) All private children's homes should be required to register with the independent agency referred to in recommendation (47). **71**

Governing body (42) The owner of a private children's home and the owner of a private residential school approved generally for SEN children or receiving SEN children with the consent of the Secretary of State should be required, if the establishment is above a size to be determined, to appoint an appropriately constituted governing body under arrangements approved by the relevant regulatory authority, to include representation from the local social services and education authorities (as appropriate) and the local community. **71**

Accounts etc (43) The accounts and other relevant financial information relating to private children's homes and private residential schools approved generally for SEN children or receiving SEN children with the consent of the Secretary of State should be disclosed to the relevant regulatory authorities. **71**

Regulation of schools (44) There should be an urgent review of the legislation governing the regulation of private residential schools to include particularly: **71**

    (a) approvals and consents under section 347 of the Education Act 1996[8] and for provisional registration of schools,

    (b) the Notice of Complaints provisions and the procedures for the withdrawal of approvals generally, and

    (c) the interaction with the provisions for registration of private children's homes,

with a view to establishing a stricter and more readily enforceable regulatory regime.

Assessment (45) Any placement of a child by a local education department or by a social services department in a residential school should be preceded by:

    (a) consultation between the departments as to whether an assessment by an appropriate social worker of the child's needs and family situation

---

[8] Previously section 11(3) of the Education Act 1981.

RECOMMENDATION

Source

is needed as well as an educational assessment; and

(b) in the light of (a) and any subsequent assessment, a decision about the need for (and extent of) any further involvement of the social services department with the child to ensure continuity of planning for the child's long term welfare and protection of the child's rights.

Emergency admissions (46) Emergency admissions should not be made to private residential schools.

Inspection

Inspection agency (47) Without prejudice to the continuing role generally of the Social Services Inspectorate for Wales, an independent regulatory agency for children's services in Wales should be established, with a local base or local bases in North Wales, and charged with the responsibility of inspecting:

38, 62(iv), 68

(a) all local authority, voluntary and private children's homes;

(b) the welfare provision in residential schools;

(c) fostering services; and

(d) the other components of children's services.

(48) When inspections are made by the agency of homes, schools or services mentioned in recommendation (47) at least one of the inspectors should have substantial experience of child care.

Joint inspection of SEN schools (49) The agencies responsible for educational and welfare inspections of private residential schools accommodating children with SEN pursuant to section 347 of the Education Act 1996 should be required to agree joint programmes of inspection and reporting.

71

Common standards (50) A common set of standards should be applied to the local authority, voluntary and private sectors in relation to residential provision and other services for looked after children.

Reports (51) Copies of the reports of inspections of local authorities' children's homes and services should be sent to the Chief Executives as well as the Directors of Social Services.

40, 62(vi)

(52) Copies of reports of inspections of private and voluntary children's homes and of private residential schools should be sent to the Director of Social Services of any

RECOMMENDATION

Source

placing authority with a child at the school and of the authority in whose area the establishment is located.

(53) The agency referred to in recommendation (47) should present an annual report on all aspects of its work, including any constraints upon that work and any shortfall in fulfilling its obligations.

Senior management

Structure (54) There should be at least one full member of a local authority's social services department management team with child care expertise and experience.

35, 36, 62(i)(ii)

(55) The responsibility for policy and service development and for oversight of the delivery of a local authority's children's services should be assigned to one member of the social services department management team of at least Assistant Director status.

36, 62(ii)

(56) Staffing resources at intermediate management level for a local authority's children's services should be sufficient in number and quality to enable positive and close supervision and support to be given to residential establishments and the fostering service.

38, 62(iv)

Training (57) Local authorities in Wales should review their current arrangements for management training and development for senior managers, including social services managers, giving particular attention to the development of skills in strategic planning, policy implementation and performance appraisal.

34 to 38, 62(i) to (iv), 64

Elected members

Responsibilities (58) Elected members should from time to time be advised about and reminded of their responsibilities to develop policy and to oversee and monitor the discharge by the local authority of its parental obligations towards looked after children.

42, 62(viii)

Reports by Director of Social Services (59) It should be the explicit duty of the Director of Social Services to assist and support elected members in discharging those responsibilities and, in particular:

40 to 42, 62(vi) to (viii), 63

(a) to inform elected members of all matters of concern touching upon children's services, including reports upon them, whether adverse or favourable;

RECOMMENDATION

(b) to provide information on comparative spending on children's services by local authorities in Wales and an analysis of that information;

(c) to submit an annual report to the Social Services Committee on the department's performance in relation to children's services including its record of compliance with required safeguards for looked after children.

Guidance about visits

(60) The purpose and scope of visits to children's homes, whether by councillors or by senior and intermediate managers, should be clearly defined and made known to all such visitors.

Rota visits

(61) The willingness of councillors to visit children's homes should be a pre-condition of appointment to the committee responsible for the homes and the importance of fulfilling the duty to visit and to report on visits conscientiously should be emphasised to them. Elected members should be provided with appropriate guidance, including reference to the need to be vigilant in protecting the interests of the child residents as well as to be supportive of the staff.   43, 62(ix)

Strategic issues

Advisory Council

(62) An Advisory Council for Children's Services in Wales comprised of members covering a wide range of expertise in children's services, including practice, research, management and training, should be established in order to strengthen the provision of children's services in Wales and to ensure that they are accorded the priority that they deserve.   65 to 72

(63) The functions of the Advisory Council should include:

(a) advising on government policy and legislation with regard to their likely impact on children and young people;

(b) commissioning research;

(c) disseminating information and making recommendations.

Nationwide review of children's services

(64) There should be a nationwide review of the needs and costs of children's services based on local authorities' development plans and leading to a comprehensive and costed strategy for those services, including any necessary education and health elements.

35, 37, 42,
62(i)(iii)(viii),
63, 66, 69
Para 54.22

	RECOMMENDATION	Source
Local authorities plans	(65) Local authorities, in collaboration with voluntary and other relevant organisations and acting together with other local authorities where appropriate, should prepare costed development plans for children's services as a prelude to the proposed nationwide review, such plans to ensure (amongst other things) that:	37, 62(iii)

(a) there is an adequate range of residential care provision of appropriate quality, including secure provision, within reasonable reach of a child's family or other relevant roots; **Paras 54.15, 54.16**

(b) such residential provision includes safe places where children can recover when relationships break down;

(c) as in (a), there is an adequate range of fostering facilities available of similar quality and accessibility; **Para 54.17**

(d) all residential placements are designed to be developmental and therapeutic rather than merely custodial;

(e) full educational opportunities are available for looked after children, including remedial education. **24, 58(v)**

Use of residential schools	(66) Central government should examine the extent to which residential schools are being used as a substitute for social services care and support, and identify the implications for children's long term welfare.	89
Availability of placements	(67) Provision should be made for repeated monitoring at appropriate intervals of the availability and quality of residential placements and fostering services on a nationwide basis.	Para 54.17
Management training	(68) Consideration should be given at national level to the need for, and provision of, training and management development for senior managers in local authorities in Wales, including the availability of such facilities for social services managers[9].	34 to 38, 62(i) to (iv), 64
Resources at national level	(69) Adequate resources should be provided to ensure that the departments in Wales responsible at national level for children's services are sufficiently and appropriately staffed to support and monitor the provision of these services in Wales.	68

[9] See also Recommendation (57).

	RECOMMENDATION	Source

Statistics   (70) The national statistics services in Wales should be strengthened to provide a comprehensive management information system.

Supplementary matters

Law Commission   (71) The Law Commission should be invited to consider the legal issues that arose in relation to the publication of the Jillings report and the associated problems, as explained in Chapter 32 of this report.   **44**

Guidance on inquiries   (72) Subject to the preceding recommendation, guidance to local authorities on the setting up and conduct of inquiries and the dissemination of reports thereon should be up-dated and re-issued[10].   **44**

---

[10] See Ad Hoc Inquiries in Local Government (1980) published jointly by the Society of Local Authority Chief Executives and the Royal Institute of Public Administration.

Printed in the United Kingdom by The Stationery Office
02/2000   474911   19585